For
Debbie
with
best wishes
from
Gillian

17 x 98

A Feast for the Eyes

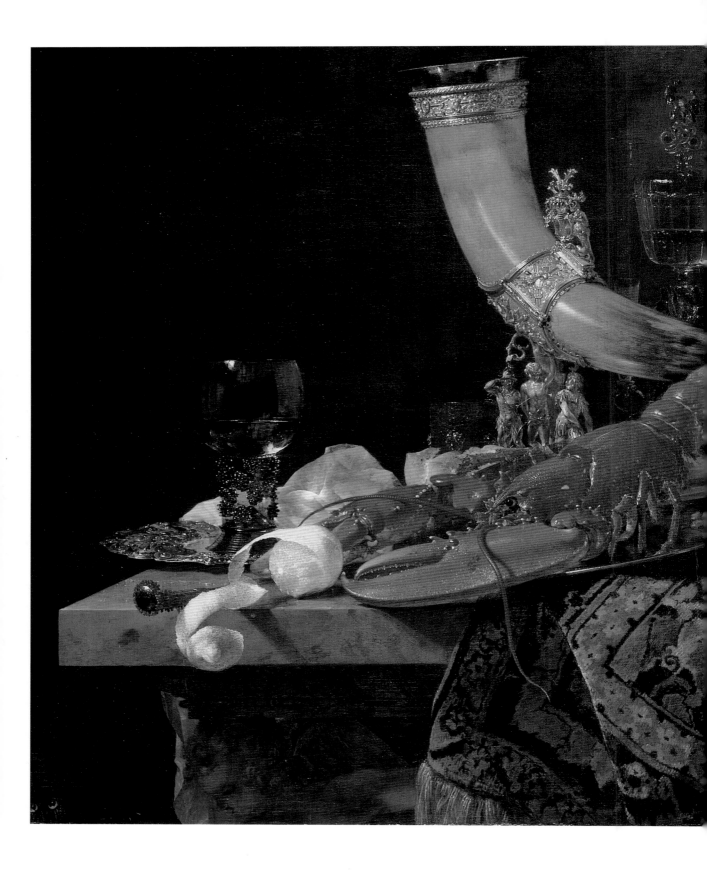

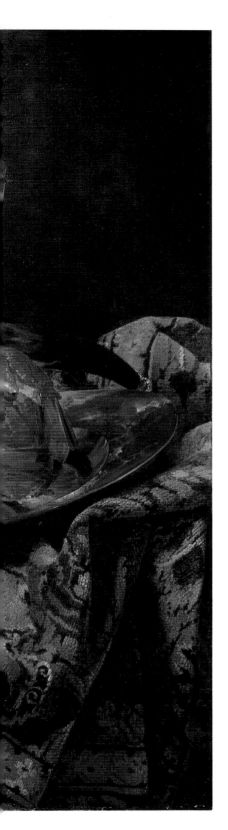

A Feast for the Eyes

GILLIAN RILEY

National Gallery Publications, London

Distributed by Yale University Press

© National Gallery Publications Limited 1997
Text © Gillian Riley 1997

First published in Great Britain in 1997 by
National Gallery Publications Limited, 5/6 Pall Mall East, London SW1Y 5BA

ISBN 1 85709 179 5

525226

British Library Cataloguing-in-Publication Data.
A catalogue record is available from the British Library.
Library of Congress Catalog Card Number: 97–67608

Editors: Felicity Luard and Isabel Moore
Art History Consultant: Erika Langmuir

Typesetting by Kitzinger, London

Printed and bound in Italy by Grafiche Milani

Frontispiece: Willem Kalf, *Still Life with the Drinking-Horn of the Saint Sebastian Archers' Guild, Lobster and Glasses,* about 1653.

Contents

Acknowledgements

Many friends contributed sustenance, inspiration and expertise, especially Ann and Trevor Beavan, Josephine Bacon, Françoise Berserik, Elizabeth Carmichael, Sebastiano Castiglioni and Jane Patterson, Alan Davidson, Gallo Nero, Bertie Goodwin, Peter Graham, Terry Hudson and family, the Lancellotti family, John and Audrey Laski, Bruno Laurioux, John McLaughlin, Janny de Moor, Jill Norman and the Estate of Elizabeth David, Elisabeth Lambert Ortiz, Alicia Ríos, June di Schino, Layinka Swinburne, Ann and Franco Taruschio.

Patricia Williams and Rosemary Davidson encouraged this book in its infancy; Erika Langmuir and Felicity Luard helped in its growth; Isabel Moore edited with cheerful precision; Tony Kitzinger, with exemplary tact and professionalism, brought the design to maturity; but my warmest thanks are to James Mosley without whose generous understanding and support this project could never have been completed.

Gillian Riley

Foreword

A glance through this book, especially if followed by a walk through the National Gallery, will go a long way to convincing you that while music may be the food of love, painting is perhaps little more than the love of food. Picture after picture, from Renaissance Italy to nineteenth-century France, shows fruit and fowl, vegetables and fish, and shows them at every stage – being bought in the market, prepared in the kitchen, and served at the final banquet. At some of the tables, it must be admitted, events rather overtake the menu: guests are turned to stone, and gods suddenly appear, unexpected and, on occasion, most unwelcome. But throughout the centuries and across Europe, there can be no denying the importance of eating.

The food itself, the experts assure us, is frequently symbolic. And there can indeed be little doubt that many of the apples that appear in the earlier part of the Collection are meant to remind us of Adam and Eve's ill-judged dalliance with unknown fruit, that the peacock which perches on the parapet in Crivelli's *Annunciation* represents eternal life, or that the lemon held by Morando's Saint John the Baptist stands for something, even if nobody seems certain exactly what.

But, as the recipes that Gillian Riley has assembled here demonstrate, such symbols – whatever they mean – can be extremely good to eat. Adding the sense of taste to that of sight, the gallery-goer can now enjoy not only the paintings of Michelangelo, Caravaggio and Van Gogh, but also the food that they relished. And this is in a sense a tradition of the National Gallery. During the Second World War, the Gallery created the first museum café in this country, allowing the public for the first time to combine the pleasures of the eye and the table. Both were at that point severely rationed: only one Old Master picture a month (because of the danger of bombs) and very limited supplies of food. Freed from both restrictions, this book, which is essentially about the link between cooking and looking, can draw on the full riches of the Collection and the culinary traditions of the whole of Europe. Together, they offer boundless opportunities for delight.

Neil MacGregor
Director

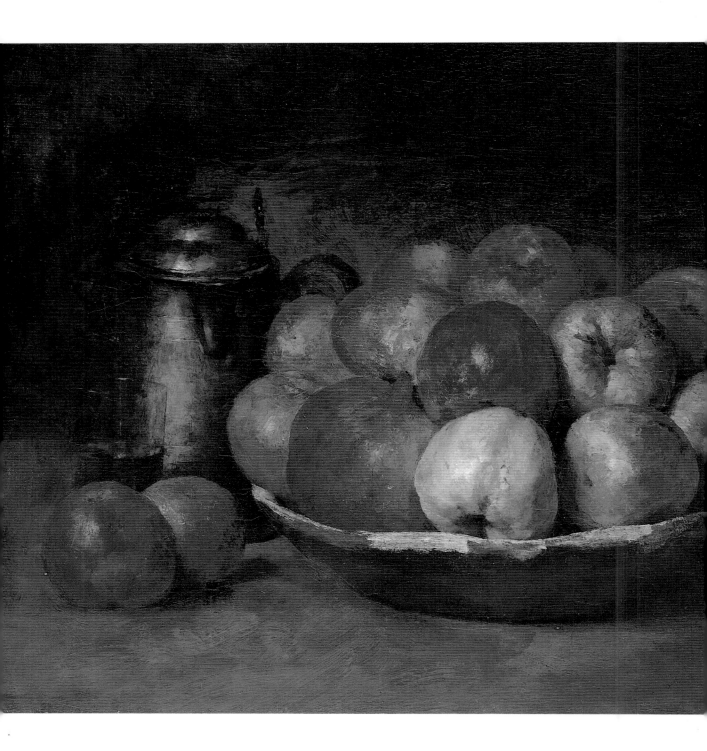

Introduction

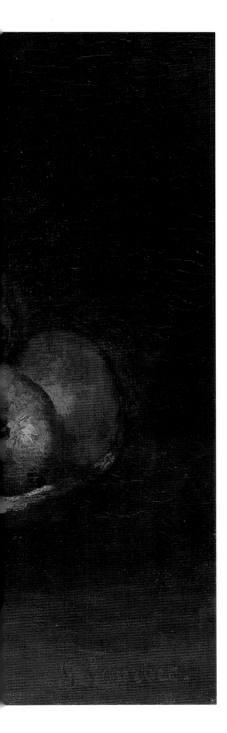

A visit to the National Gallery in London is a feast for all the senses, stimulating curiosity about the people and painters who fill the noble rooms and spaces. Wondering about what these artists had to eat is an agreeable way of getting to know them, of understanding something about personalities and motivation, perhaps even a gateway to the soul. Michelangelo might have encouraged the myths about his high-minded superiority to the more mundane pleasures of life but his letters tell a different story – his delight in consignments of Tuscan sausages, chickpeas and marzolino cheese sent to him at his Roman villa, and the loving little sketches of simple Florentine food on the back of a letter. The warmth and humanity of the artist are revealed as we ponder on his gastronomic tastes.

Paintings offer glimpses of society that illustrate the insights we find in cookery manuscripts. Earlier Florentines had less frugal tastes in food than Michelangelo. Though spiritually uplifted by ornate altarpieces they would have wallowed, knife in hand, in the earthly delights of a late medieval banquet, where Jacapo di Cione's richly patterned angels' robes were echoed in the spiced sauces and intricate music of the feast. The secular counterpart of such religious opulence – the heraldic colours of tapestries, damask hangings and the liveries of the pages – was repeated in the food – the beige mush of everyday fare, boiled pulses and roots, quite transformed by the strong, warm hues of saffron and sanders, the brilliant greens of fresh herbs staining egg and pasta and broths, the weird blues from verdigris and lapis lazuli, the warm autumnal glow of cameline sauce, the unearthly bright white of *biancomangiare* dotted with crimson pomegranate seeds, contrasted with the velvet black of the gravy covering a roast wild boar, with an edging of brilliant lemon slices round the dish, glittering like the gold leaf of a halo. Crystallized flowers kept their bright colours, and preserved roots and fruits twinkled with frosting while transparent glass dishes of jams and jellies glowed in the torchlight and pallid junkets quaked on emerald green vine leaves.

Crivelli applied this decorative tradition in the altarpieces he executed for clients in the Italian Marches, and his tangible fruit and cucumbers figure in recipes of the region.

Caravaggio's paintings provide insights into the tense atmosphere of Counter-Reformation Rome and his own obsessive realism – the perfectionism that provoked a violent row over a dish of artichokes yet gave us the perfectly cooked guinea fowl in *The Supper at Emmaus*. His contemporary Bartolomeo Scappi left us recipes for this and for the hundreds of dishes that figure in the lavish banquets he orchestrated for popes and princes.

Canaletto conveys the everyday appearance of Casanova's Venice, where we ponder on the fishy splendours of the Lagoon and the gastronomic clues to Casanova's celebrated flight from the prison of the Piombi. He dined out on the gripping account of this escapade, a two-hour narrative, with gastronomy playing a part in his adventures.

Scenes of everyday life from seventeenth-century Holland tell of pleasure in prosperity, where sumptuous food and drink grace the tables of rich merchants, and bread and cheese and beer abound in smoke-filled taverns; paintings that hold the key to an understanding of the endearing combination of guilt and self-indulgence of that doughty trading nation. Pieter de Hooch conveys the harmony and wealth to which his clients aspired: calm, sunlit interiors peopled with elegant figures sipping wine or making music. Jan Steen sends the whole thing up with hilarious scenes of domestic mayhem and profligate overindulgence, while Teniers shows how the other half lived, a boorish enjoyment of a different kind of plenty. Recipe books of the period, written for wealthy country-house kitchens, tell of an unexpectedly subtle, delicate cuisine – the products of hothouse and walled garden cooked with delicacy in butter and cream, with mild spices and fresh green herbs.

Velázquez uses a story from the Bible as a pretext for a Spanish domestic scene, where the sanctity of everyday life is revealed in the jugs and dishes of a humble kitchen, while the young Goya teases with the appurtenances of an almost elegant picnic and Meléndez reveals more about his marriage than he realizes in a superb still life, the contents of a winter store cupboard.

The grossness and elegance of British gastronomy are echoed in Hogarth and Gainsborough and its virtues acclaimed by William Cobbett in his fulsome praise of the home breadmaker.

Bread, and the pleasures and pains of its production, looms large in the background to scenes from French life from the seventeenth to the twentieth century. The contrast between the gravity of the *Grand Siècle* and the frivolity of the *Ancien Régime* is immediately comprehensible in the very different family groups by the Le Nain brothers and Lancret, where the dignified bread and wine of an independent rural society are worlds away from the fashionable hot chocolate poured ceremoniously from a silver pot for a charming family ensconced in an artificial and insecure Arcadia.

When Van Gogh says he painted sunflowers with 'the enthusiasm of a Marseillais devouring his bouillabaisse', he delights us with flavours as well as with vibrant warm colours, shedding a mellow light on the last few months of his tormented life. Cézanne, too, loved the food of Provence; its complex, aromatic daubes resemble his canvases in the time required to achieve their ultimate perfection, the long, slow intensifying of flavour, the resonances of texture and colour – the ingredients of both being the earth and air and dazzling sensations of the south. It is enjoyable to imagine Cézanne at one of Monet's lunches, timed tyrannically early so that the old boy could catch the afternoon light on his lily ponds, lifting the soup plate to his beard to catch the last fragrant drops, and devouring lamb chops from the point of his knife in a gesture that would have been recognized by the participants in that medieval Florentine banquet.

Collecting the recipes has been a voyage of discovery, learning to listen to the voices of painters and cooks and the people who enjoyed their labours – eloquent, reticent, grumpy, cheerful, inspired, prosaic, long-winded and sometimes impenetrable. The search for a personality and a tone of voice among aromas and ingredients, as one looks for temperament and character in brush strokes and chalk marks, instigated journeys into the past that illuminate the present, joining painters and cooks in a harmony of sensations and memories, bringing the tastebuds into line with the eyeballs, creating aromas evocative of the images on the walls, and presenting something of a challenge to the compiler. In selecting the recipes I have tried to bring uniformity without pedantry, coherence without tedium and retain echoes of these strong-minded, assertive personalities.

If the gastronomy of the past teaches us anything it is to avoid a rigid dogmatism, to remember that very few recipes demand an absolute precision, that an intelligent, imaginative understanding of what is going on is more helpful than blind obedience to a set of rules. The cook of a prosperous Tuscan merchant would have shared his master's skills in 'gauging' amounts and values, as indeed the painter hired to decorate the walls of his palace deployed the same cast of mind, using complex systems of spatial geometry with the ease with which the cook would assess the weight and succulence of a joint, marry that to the heat of a fire, the speed of the spit and the amount of spices to suit his master's state of mind that morning, to produce a harmonious and satisfying composition. So indeed do most of us cook, following coherent instructions sensibly but modifying a recipe to suit the tastes of family and friends, and the good things discovered in the market that morning.

The enjoyment of food, like the pleasure we take in looking at paintings, is personal and idiosyncratic; this selection of images and recipes for your entertainment and delight welcomes the treasures of the National Gallery to the nerve centre of the home – the kitchen.

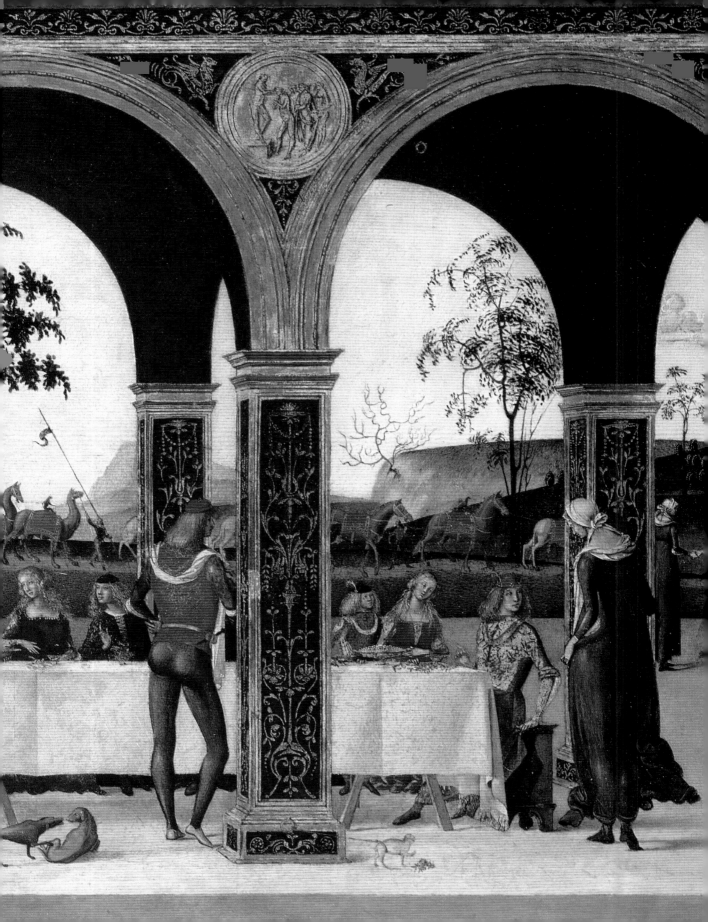

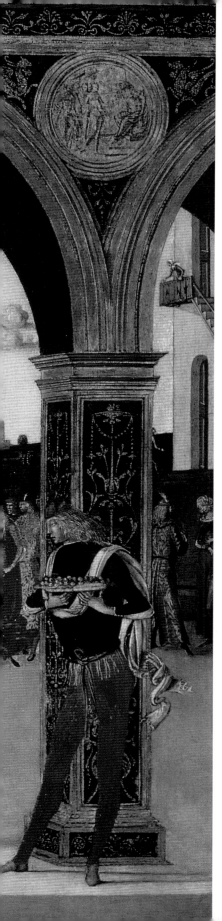

The Profligate Splendours
OF THE RENAISSANCE BANQUET

The depressing story in Boccaccio's *Decameron* of Patient Griselda, perfect wife, mother and doormat, was strangely popular throughout Renaissance Europe. It was the ideal subject to decorate marriage chests and bridal chambers, a role model for young wives, although the virtuous long-suffering heroine may have seemed an ironic contrast to the strong-willed termagants who in the real world ran the households of prosperous Tuscan families.

This three-panel painting from Siena illustrates the story of Griselda as a moral tale in the here and now, about the year 1500, with fashionable people going about their everyday lives. The story unfolds like a strip cartoon, telling how Count Gualtieri of Saluzzo chose Griselda, a young woman of humble birth and great beauty, to be his wife. Paranoia or political expediency drove this unpleasant character to inflict cruel humiliations on Griselda as a test of her fidelity. She survived the apparent loss of her children, divorce and the arrival of a new bride for the harsh Gualtieri. The newcomer turned out to be her own daughter, radiant in red velvet. The wedding banquet unrolls across the final panel, following the various stages of this distressing charade – first Griselda in a drab grey dress sweeping the floor, then humbly offering her rival the seat of honour at the start of the meal, and eventually triumphing as heroine at the end, with puzzled pages proffering exquisite fruit tarts and dishes of spiced comfits to the equally confused guests.

A post-feminist view of the story might appreciate Griselda's intelligence and subversive charm. She probably rumbled her husband quite early on in the marriage, knowing that her children, as was the custom, were getting a good upbringing in some other noble household, and set about consolidating her power base with consummate skill. No-one but Griselda was remotely capable of organizing the three-day wedding feast for the new bride. She was called back from her father's modest farm to mastermind this combination of feasting, music, dancing and sport. Griselda's submissive speech, welcoming her replacement, entirely demolished her hapless husband. She suggested with quiet venom that he treat the fragile little thirteen-year-old with less harshness than she had had to put up with. Overcome with remorse, Gualtieri crumpled in tears, acknowledged his daughter, gave Griselda a new gown and ordered the banquet to proceed.

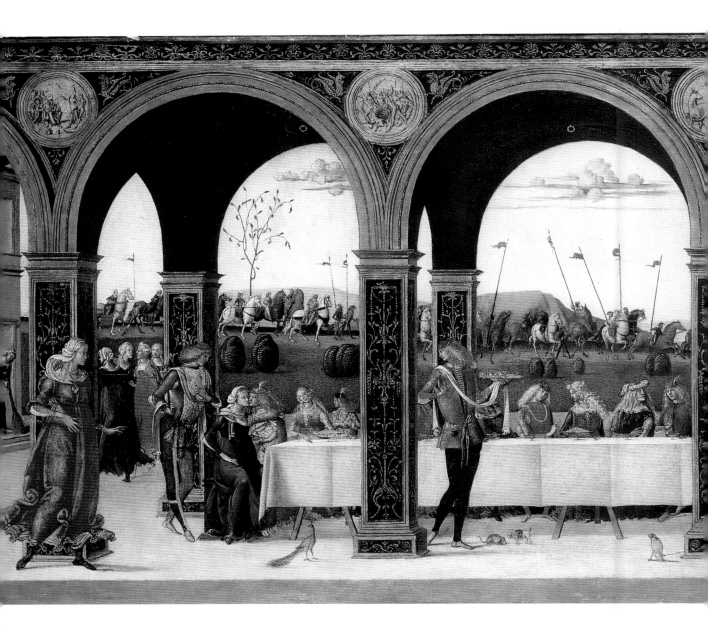

Previous page: Master of the Story of
Griselda, detail from *The Story of
Patient Griselda, Part III.*

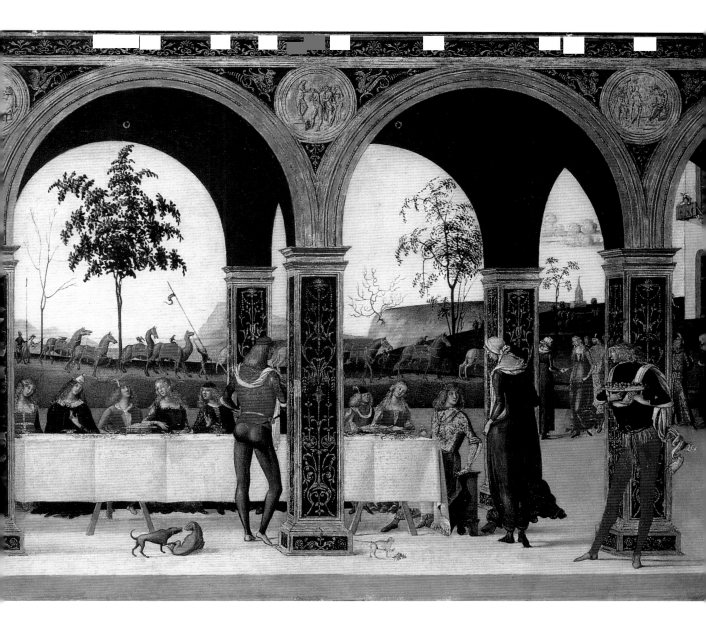

Master of the Story of
Griselda, *The Story of
Patient Griselda, Part III* ,
probably about 1493–1500.
The wedding feast is spread
out on trestle tables in the
shade of an elegant modern
loggia, with the bridal
procession winding through
the Tuscan countryside in
the background.

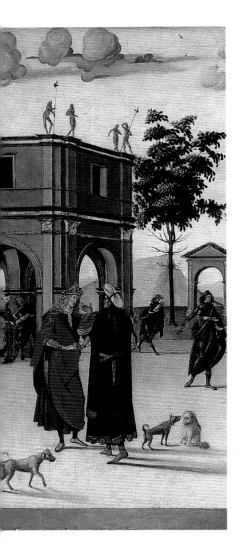

The painting was probably commissioned to commemorate the double wedding in Siena in 1493 of the brothers Antonio and Giulio Spannocchi. Rich bankers with lucrative connections to Rome through the Sienese Piccolomini family (Pius II, one of the most celebrated humanist popes, was a member), they vied with other powerful Sienese nobles in building and adorning palaces and staging magnificent banquets to show off their wealth.

The background to Griselda's banquet in the painting recalls the triumphal arch built in Siena to celebrate the Spannocchi wedding and the procession bringing the bride from her distant home. The detail on page 17 is the humble farm from which Griselda had come, and to which she was subsequently banished. The banquet is set in the airy loggia of a fine modern palace.

As well as the confections of sugared pine nuts, crystallized flowers and fruit preserved in syrup which delighted guests at a typical Renaissance banquet, there would have been vast amounts of meat and poultry, like those presented to the Emperor Charles V when he stayed in one of the Petrucci palaces on a visit to Siena in 1536: forty calves, ninety sheep, a hundred kids, two hundred and fifty pairs of chickens, hens, pigeons and much wild game, two hundred loaves of best white bread, the same quantity of marzipan, comfits and sweetmeats, a hundred barrels of the finest wine and perhaps the greatest luxury of all – six moses-baskets of artichokes, the first green vegetables of spring.

The renowned *panforte* of Siena might well have been one of the sweet and spicy confections which were served as appetizers at the start of such a feast. At that time, though, *panforte* was not a Sienese speciality but was made everywhere, part of the tradition of dishes using dried fruit, spices and nuts of which mince pies, stollen and Christmas cakes are a survival. This version is adapted from a manuscript collection of medical recipes from Bologna and a sixteenth-century nun's cookery notebook from Perugia. The modern use of vanilla is unauthentic, but not to be discouraged.

Panforte MAKES ONE 18 CM (7 IN) CAKE

100 g (²/₃ cup) almonds, shelled but not skinned
50 g (¹/₃ cup) pine nuts
50 g plain flour (¹/₂ cup all-purpose flour)
50 g (¹/₂ cup) fine breadcrumbs
50 g (¹/₃ cup) mixed dried fruit
50 g (¹/₃ cup) candied peel

¹/₂ tsp each of cloves, cinnamon, cardamoms, anise seeds, black peppercorns, nutmeg, all ground together with a 3 cm (1¹/₄ in) length of vanilla pod (bean) in a mortar or processor
A pinch of salt
3 tbsps runny honey

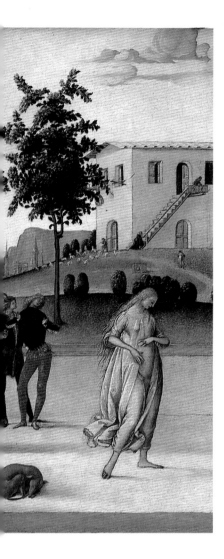

Details from *The Story of Patient Griselda, Part II.*

Crush half the nuts coarsely, leaving the rest whole. Mix well with the dry ingredients in a bowl. Boil up the honey, turn off the heat and add the mixture from the bowl, mixing well. Spoon into an oiled 18 cm (7 in) pan lined with a double layer of waxed paper. Cook in a low to moderate oven until done, about 30 to 40 minutes. The cake is done when a skewer inserted into the centre comes out clean.

The renaissance banquet was a pageant of power and luxury, where music, dance, theatre, sumptuous dress and magnificent decor were the background to surging waves of dish upon dish of delicious, decorative and expensive food. The guests, seated at trestle tables spread with brilliant white linen cloths, strewn with flowers and laid with gold and silver plates and goblets, chose with prudent restraint from the lavish succession of dishes presented by the well-drilled hierarchy of carvers and pages. Carving was a performance art – executed standing up in front of the guests, the meat or fowl impaled on a stout fork while, with ritual gestures, virtuosi flourished deadly sharp knives in elegant arabesques to yield bite-sized portions, to be dipped in sauces and eaten elegantly with the tips of the fingers or from the point of a knife. Forks were hardly necessary, but came in handy for sticky fruit in syrup. Perfumed water and fresh towels were presented throughout the meal, and the tablecloths deftly changed between courses.

When Pope Leo X ('God has given us the papacy, let us enjoy it') made his nephew Giuliano de' Medici a Roman citizen, he won the populace over to his blatantly political manoeuvring with a magnificent feast in a specially constructed theatre on the Campidoglio on 13 September 1513. A somewhat bemused Marcantonio Altieri left a detailed description of the festivities. Twenty-five courses, starting and ending with sweetmeats, included the rather old-fashioned way of serving a cooked creature – peacock, young calf or rabbit – stitched up in its original plumage or fur in a simulated grove or forest made from jasmine blossom or branches of bay. Pies, ornate pastries, roast and boiled meat and fowl with colourful, aromatic sauces and relishes, were handed round on gold and silver dishes from the *credenza*, a sort of vast, outdoor dresser and sideboard built to display the splendour of plate and prepared dishes which were presented between the cooked courses. Giuliano and the Roman nobility ate very little of this profusion of rich food. The rest was distributed among the spectators, ranged in tiers, and what was left was tossed to the crowds waiting outside. Pies, stuffed rabbits and joints of meat flew through the air – conspicuous consumption, spectacle, a placatory gesture – on that hot September evening. The guests were cooled by great ice sculptures and refreshed with perfumed water gushing from a mobile fountain while incense and scented flowers bedecked the tables.

Spices were never, contrary to popular belief, used to mask the taste of tainted meat. Far too expensive and seductive to be used for such a doubtful purpose, they were prized because they were delicious. Spicy food was costly but above all it tasted sensational. The lavish use of spices was both a hedonistic experience and a display of wealth, a political statement.

This festive recipe adapted from an early manuscript, deploys a gentle mixture of cheese, herbs and spices inserted under the skin of the breast and as much as you can reach of the chicken. It is best to use one medium or two small birds; in the time taken to cook a large one the cheese mixture might dry out.

Chicken in a Spiced Cheese Overcoat SERVES 4

1 medium or 2 small free range chickens
100 g (½ cup) ricotta
100 g (½ cup) cream cheese
50 g (½ cup) freshly grated Parmesan
50 g (⅓ cup) fresh white breadcrumbs
50 g (½ cup) ground almonds, soaked in about 125 ml (½ cup) milk for 5 to 10 minutes
1 egg, beaten

2 tbsps each of chopped fresh parsley and mint
1 tbsp chopped fresh marjoram or basil
2 tsps or more of this spice mixture, freshly ground in a processor or with pestle and mortar: 8 cloves, 5 cm (2 in) stick of cinnamon, 5 cardamoms, 12 black peppercorns, ½ tsp anise seeds, 1 tsp coriander seeds
Softened butter

Mix together the cheeses, breadcrumbs, soaked ground almond mixture, egg, herbs and spices to get a soft but firm mixture for the stuffing. Gently pry the skin of the chicken away from the flesh of breast and legs without tearing. Spread the mixture between skin and flesh to a depth of about 1.5 cm (½ in), and put any remaining inside the cavity of the bird. If necessary sew up the chicken skin and cavity, or close with a skewer, to prevent the stuffing oozing out. Carefully butter the chicken and protect the breast with a double layer of foil, removing it 10 minutes before the end to brown the skin. Bake in a moderate oven until done, about 1 hour for two small birds, 1½ hours for a larger one. Test for doneness after an hour; the juices should run clear when a skewer is inserted into the thigh.

Opposite: Carlo Crivelli, detail from *The Vision of the Blessed Gabriele*, probably about 1489.

This dish is a meal in itself; a light first course could be a salad of rocket and sliced oranges with hazelnut oil. A dessert of ricotta beaten with mascarpone, marsala, chopped candied peel and cherries in brandy might follow.

Wild Duck & Prunes SERVES 4

4 thick slices of unsmoked bacon
or pancetta, chopped
12 pickling or other small onions,
peeled
20 pitted prunes
6 cloves
1 cm (½ in) stick of cinnamon
½ tsp freshly grated nutmeg
4 cm (1½ in) knob of fresh
ginger, chopped

1 thumbnail blade of mace
3 garlic cloves, chopped
4 bay leaves
2 wine glasses of red wine
(enough to cover the birds)
1 tbsp wine vinegar
Salt & pepper
2 large oven-ready wild ducks
4 slices of toasted, preferably
home-made, bread

Cook the bacon in a flameproof casserole for a few minutes. Stir in the onions and fry until they are transparent. Add all the remaining ingredients except the ducks and toasted bread and bring to the boil. Lay the ducks, breast down, on top of them, cover and cook in a low to moderate oven until done, about 1 to 1½ hours. Test for doneness after an hour, for much depends on the age of the ducks; the juices should run clear when a skewer is inserted into the thigh.

Remove the birds from the casserole and carve the breasts from the carcasses. Keep the breasts warm (you can use the rest of the birds for another recipe). Strain the cooking liquid into a pan, reserving the prunes and onions. Skim the fat from the top of the liquid and boil fast to reduce to a strong, aromatic sauce. Put a slice of the toasted bread in each of four dishes. Arrange a portion of duck breast on each one and surround with prunes and onions. Strain over some of the juices and serve the rest separately.

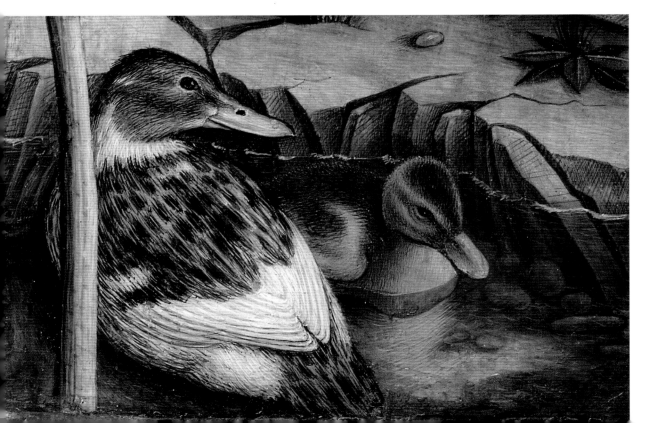

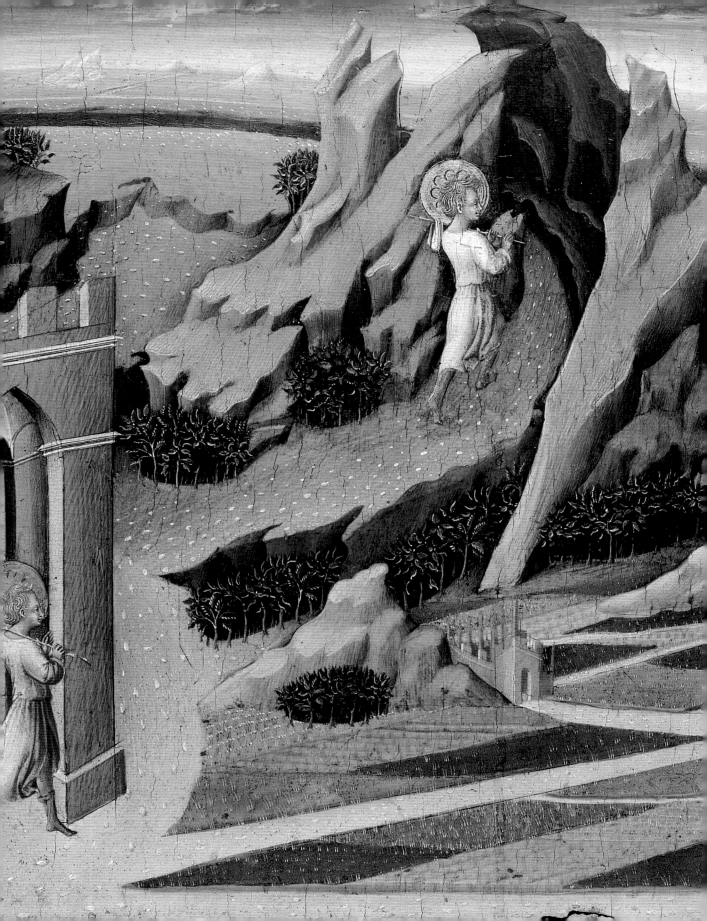

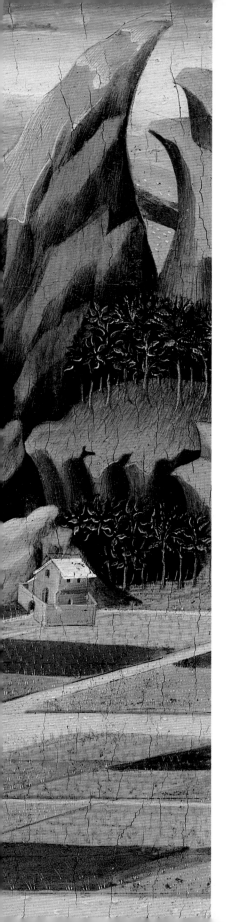

Landscapes & Larders

PARSIMONY & PLENTY
IN RENAISSANCE TUSCANY

Happy in his choice of wilderness the young Saint John could gaze down from the rugged heights upon the smiling cultivated slopes of Giovanni di Paolo's native Tuscany. This mid-fifteenth-century landscape embodies the essentials of Tuscan gastronomy. The austerity of the beautiful rocky hillsides and the frugal neatness of the trim, prosperous farms with their orderly little plots of vegetables and pulses evoke Florentine food at its best – peasant food raised to a point of high art, superb quality meat and vegetables cooked and seasoned with careful harmony.

The gastronomy of Renaissance Tuscany displays a simplicity very different from the richly spiced banqueting stuff served up at international gatherings of princes, popes and emperors. The same could be said for much of Florentine art, prizing as it did classical purity and restraint above the ornate, decorative work of other styles.

The Florentine humanist Poggio Bracciolini had the best of both worlds. He worked as a papal secretary in Rome, had a stint in England (weather, food and girls all dreary), wined and dined with the rich and famous while keeping up warm friendships with impoverished intellectuals like his fellow citizen Niccolò Niccoli, who in spite of his grumpiness was a much loved authority on classical literature and art. An erudite Latinist and collector of lost classical manuscripts, deftly liberating them from the obscurity of unappreciative monastic libraries, Poggio was a gourmet, womanizer and author of a somewhat smutty book of jokes in Latin. He married astonishingly late in life and settled down to a happy home life with Vaggia, thirty years younger than himself and blessed with charm, an equable temperament and a decent dowry. It was during this period, when Poggio was back in Florence with the honourable post of Chancellor of the city, that a modest meal in his house made a lasting impression on the young Bartolomeo Platina, who later moved to Rome to become Vatican Librarian and author of a bestselling book on food, *De Honesta Voluptate et Valetudine* (*On Honest Pleasure and Good Health*). He enjoyed Poggio's chicken cooked in *agresto* (a sauce made from sour or unripe grapes), simple, wholesome family fare, and included it in his book.

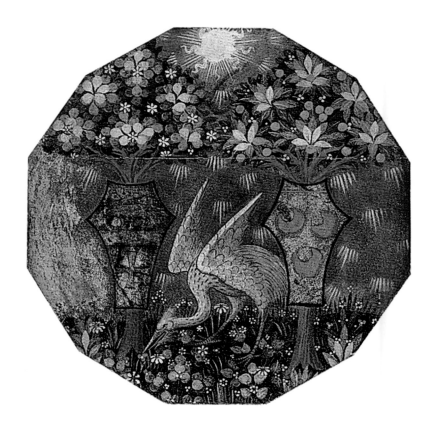

Master of the Cassoni, reverse side of a *desco da parto*, probably 1440–60. This was a ceremonial platter on which comforting food, perhaps a dish of *biancomangiare*, was brought to sustain a woman after giving birth. Here oranges and lemons and possibly wild strawberries provide nourishment for a young egret.

Chicken with Sour Grapes SERVES 4

1 medium free range chicken, cut into pieces
4 slices of unsmoked fatty bacon or pancetta, chopped
Garlic if wished
Olive oil
250 ml (1 cup) fruity dry white wine, or the freshly squeezed juice of
   sharp grapes
A pinch of saffron
Salt & black pepper
1 tbsp each of chopped fresh parsley, marjoram, mint and basil

Fry the chicken pieces, bacon and garlic in the oil until golden.
Add the wine or grape juice, saffron and salt and pepper. Simmer,
uncovered, until the chicken is done, about 30 to 40 minutes. Stir in
the herbs just before serving. Simple, refreshing and healthy, as
Platina emphasized.

Platina borrowed recipes from the culinary notebooks of his friend
the cook Martino, drinking companion in the Roman taverns that
then as now resounded to the passionate discussion of seasonings
and sauces, with a generous acknowledgment of his friend's genius
and enthusiasm. By the time of his death from the plague in Rome in
1481 at the age of sixty, Platina was famous as scholar and author of

Previous page: Giovanni di Paolo, detail from *Saint John the Baptist retiring to the Desert*, probably about 1453.

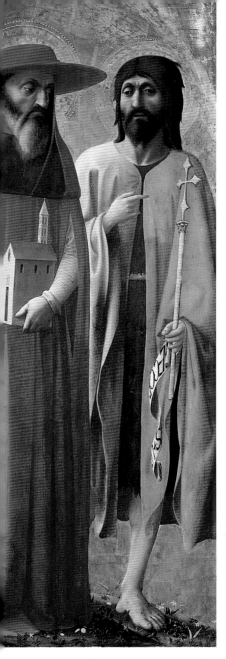

Attributed to Masaccio and Masolino, detail from *Saints Jerome and John the Baptist*, probably between 1423 and 1428. Part of a work which may have been painted by the two artists for the basilica of S. Maria Maggiore in Rome.

an erudite life of the popes, with a reputation for wild living and out-rageously anti-establishment outbursts. His simple taste in food was partly the effect of early poverty, but was also a deliberate return to the austere lifestyle of the heroic founders of the Roman Republic, farmers who turned ploughshares into swords in the defence of civic liberties, living as simply as the Tuscan peasants whose beans, lentils and sausages were delighting Poggio and his colleagues.

Masaccio and Alberti were two of the many Florentine artists and scholars who braved the dangers and discomforts of the long journey to ramble enthusiastically among the ruins of Rome, sketching details of broken arches and inscriptions. The great marble letters across the façade of Santa Maria Novella in Florence were designed by Alberti to remind us of the plain, unadorned letters on Republican tombs in Rome. We can see them on the scroll held by Saint John the Baptist in this panel by Masaccio and Masolino, where the flowers and plants under the feet of the saint remind us of simple herb sauces, modest alternatives to the spiced concoctions of the old-style gothic cuisine. One such herb sauce is in Platina's recipe for *spigola*, the fish that he used to catch in the Tiber between the Ponte Milvio and the present Ponte Sant'Angelo.

Sea Bass with Herb Sauce   SERVES 4

4 medium sea bass or other firm-fleshed white fish, cleaned,
    scaled and wiped dry
Olive oil, salt & pepper
FOR THE SAUCE:
A handful each of chopped fresh parsley, young spinach leaves,
    thyme, marjoram, fennel or whatever fresh herbs are to hand
    (about 4 handfuls)
Garlic if desired
Salt & pepper
150 ml (5/8 cup) olive oil
Lemon juice or vinegar to taste

To make the sauce, blend everything together in a food processor or blender, but go easy with the lemon juice or vinegar. Alternatively this sauce can be made with a pestle and mortar, to get a different, rougher texture. Rub the prepared fish with a little olive oil, season and cook quickly under a grill (broiler) or in a hot oven for about 5 to 10 minutes on each side. Serve warm or cold, with the sauce.

Pietro Aretino, malicious and unreliable letter-writer and polem-icist, nevertheless rings true when he writes about food. He tells of the men who gather fresh herbs and greenery and pound them up with oil and garlic to make a *salsa verde* which they sell in the streets of Arezzo, his native city. Bachelors, he said, eat best – no hassle with

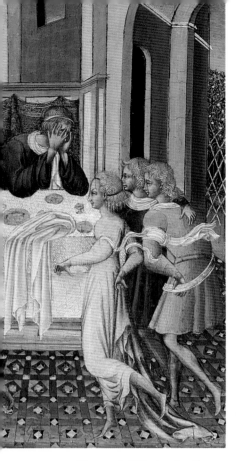

Giovanni di Paolo, detail from *The Feast of Herod*, probably about 1453.

noisy and incompetent women, the freedom to wander out for a little walk and come home with a nice melon, a basket of early strawberries, a bunch of radishes and a handkerchief full of salad leaves.

Florentines had a reputation as vegetable eaters and even the relatively wealthy enjoyed the roots, pulses and fresh greenery from their estates without the addition of meat.

The evocative name of the next recipe, *strozzapreti*, has been applied to various pasta dishes, particularly those chewy concoctions made with flour and water and twisted into strangulatory shapes which might well have achieved their aim, pleasure balancing pain in equal measure. The version of spinach 'ravioli' is a Florentine speciality.

Spinach Priest-Stranglers   SERVES 4

1 kg (generous 2 lbs) spinach, washed, picked over and drained	75 g (¾ cup) freshly grated Parmesan
2 medium eggs	Freshly grated nutmeg
150 g (scant ⅔ cup) rich firm ricotta; the watery kind is not suitable	Salt & pepper
	Flour
	Melted butter and more Parmesan for serving

Sweat the spinach in its own juices until soft, this may take anything from 5 to 10 minutes depending on the spinach, and drain well. Chop finely and mix with the eggs, ricotta, Parmesan and seasonings. Form into lumps the size of corks and roll them in flour. Bring a large pan of water to the boil and drop them in, a few at a time. Simmer gently until they come bobbing up to the surface – this will not take long, about 2 to 3 minutes. Remove at once and put into a warm dish, anointing each layer with generous amounts of melted butter and Parmesan.

When in 1475 Niccolosa Serragli, known as Monna Choxa (the shortened form of her name Madonna Niccolosa, with guttural Florentine pronunciation), oversaw the work on the memorial chapel to her deceased husband Matteo Palmieri in the church of San Pier Maggiore in Florence, she made sure that the painter Francesco Botticini followed the detailed brief he was given. A vast panel above the altar – which today greets visitors to the National Gallery in London as they ascend the great granite stairs of the Sainsbury Wing – shows the Assumption of the Virgin, wafted from her coffin, bedecked with lilies, up into concentric rings of angels, saints and holy people, to be received by Christ in Majesty in a decorative mix of mortals and divinities. Nothing quite so visionary about the bottom line, though: portraits of Niccolosa and Matteo against the background of their Tuscan properties. Land, prestige and wealth, spelled out for all to see. An inheritance writ large. (They were childless – all

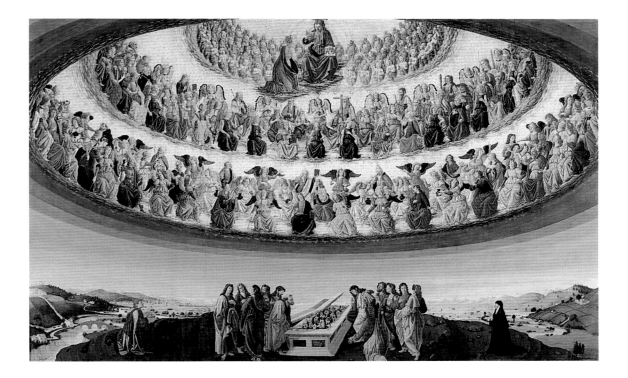

Francesco Botticini, *The Assumption of the Virgin*, probably about 1475–6.

the more reason to set the record straight for their heirs, Matteo's nephews.) This immense painting seems to sum up the polarities of the Florentine temperament – an austere religious faith and a tight-lipped, beady-eyed devotion to the commercial realities of life, the two united by a passionate patriotism. Land and wealth below and the soul's salvation above. With Florence and Fiesole glimmering in the distance, we can pick out in the bottom left-hand corner the clear outlines of the Villa Luna and the farm La Schifanoia, 'Begone Dull Care', both Matteo's property. On the right are farms in the Val d'Elsa that Niccolosa brought as her dowry when she married Matteo in 1433 – a smallholding near Castellina in Chianti, seen up on the hill among trees with a little church nearby, and 'The White House', a larger farmhouse between Tavernella and Certaldo.

Matteo, originally an apothecary, became a successful adminis-trator and diplomat in the Florentine Republic. He published treatises on politics and public life, his idealism tempered by the wary pragmatism of a shrewd businessman. A wise citizen, he wrote, should invest in land and houses, and above all, like a typical Tuscan, in a stake in the countryside. This he should cherish, not as princely refuge from the cares of the city, like the villas of the Medicis, but as a source of provisions and as a return to the roots from which so many of the Florentine artisan and merchant class had come. Matteo's tax returns list his properties and the revenue

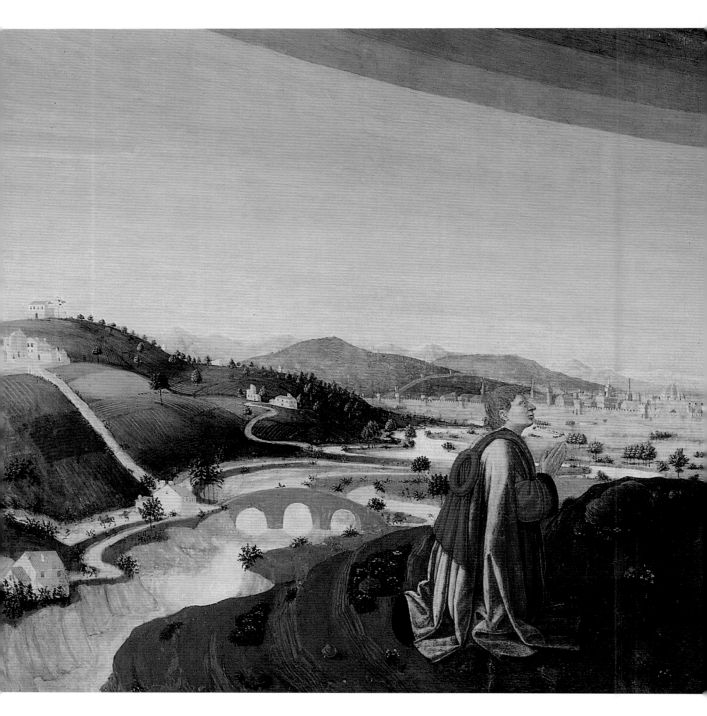

Francesco Botticini, details from
The Assumption of the Virgin
showing Matteo Palmieri
and his wife Niccolosa, with
their Tuscan properties in
the background.

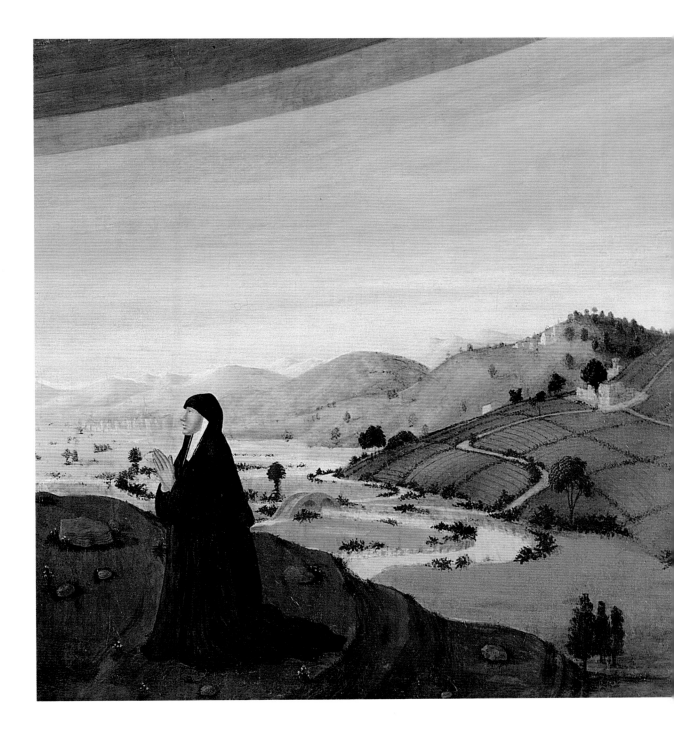

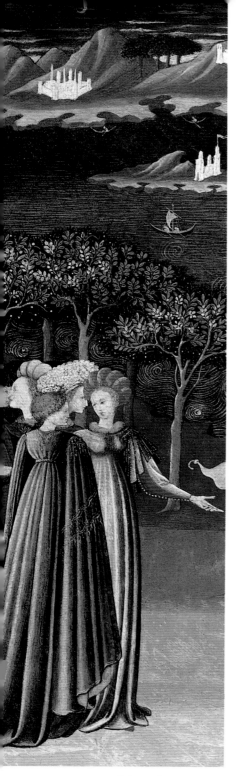

they produced. To wheat, oil and wine, the glorious trinity of Mediterranean staples, were added beans, lentils and chickpeas; chickens, aromatic hams and salami; eggs; and game from the woods.

As an apothecary Matteo would have enjoyed the costly spices that were used in gastronomy and medicine, including the rare and expensive luxury, sugar, which, used in frugal amounts, acted more as a catalyst to other flavours than as a sweetener. His farms yielded the herbs and pungent roots that were a much cheaper way of adding flavour to pulses and vegetable soups, and the wine vinegar and olive oil that gave bite and unctuousness. Wheat, ground by his own mill, became the superb, crusty, unsalted bread that is still the staple and chief glory of Tuscan cuisine.

In this version of an apparently basic but very sumptuous dish, more of a meal than a soup, the qualities of fresh vegetables, oil and good white bread are critical. Use only the best.

Ribollita   SERVES 6

100 g (²⁄₃ cup) dried cannellini
   beans, washed but not soaked
2 or 3 thick slices of unsmoked
   fatty bacon or pancetta, diced
2 garlic cloves, chopped
1 large onion, chopped
1 green cabbage, chopped
1 large carrot, diced
1 medium parsnip, diced
2 celery stalks, stringed and
   chopped

1 litre (2 quarts) good meat or
   chicken stock
Rosemary, sage and bay leaves
6 slices of good white bread
   (preferably home-made),
   stale or toasted
Salt & pepper
1 tbsp chopped fresh parsley
1 tbsp chopped spring onions
   (scallions)
Extra virgin olive oil to taste

Cook the washed beans in unsalted water for an hour or so until almost tender. (If they are the newly dried beans of the previous summer, they will not need soaking for an autumn or winter dish. Soaking does not help the flavour and can make pulses mushy.) Retain the cooking liquid.

Cook the bacon in a large pan for a few minutes. Add the garlic and onion and brown together quickly. Add the other vegetables, the beans and their liquid, half the stock and the herbs. Bring to the boil, add the slices of bread and simmer gently until the vegetables are cooked, about 15 to 20 minutes. As the bread swells add more stock, but keep the soup thick. Taste and season with salt and pepper. Serve with the chopped parsley and spring onions (scallions) and a good libation of the olive oil added by each person at the table. The heat releases the aroma of the oil, which perfumes the whole dish.

An excellent vegetarian version can be made using fresh or canned tomatoes and vegetable stock, omitting the bacon and meat stock.

This is even better reheated the next day, hence the name *ribollita* – 'twice cooked'.

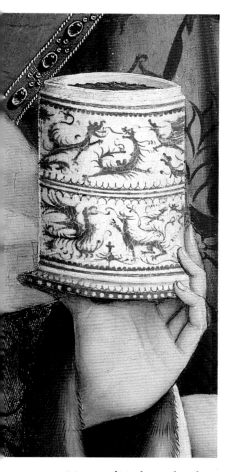

Master of Liesborn, detail from *Saints Cosmas and Damian and the Virgin*, probably 1470–80.

Matteo kept the family business, the pharmacy, going, even though its location in a narrow street round the back of Santa Maria Novella was not very profitable. He would not recognize it today. To a cold and weary tourist on a late winter afternoon, before the first swallows swoop over the Canto alle Rondini, it seems a haven of perfumed delights. Extravagantly restored in 1848 this Albert Memorial of a pharmacy glows with stained glass and gothic fixtures and fittings. Grand Florentine ladies with the high cheekbones and cold eyes of Monna Choxa come here to buy floral perfumes, and old women from the blocks of apartments around the station stop by for packs of 'nerve pills' and mint pastilles. Healing and exotic spice concoctions still flourish in the pharmacy; the aromatics that once flavoured Florentine food are no longer popular, however, and hardly appear in the cuisine of today, though the fennel seeds in *salame finocchiona* remind us of their use in the past: part preservative, part digestive.

Cavallucci di Siena, a traditional walnut sweetmeat, is a survivor of the strongly flavoured medieval luxuries sold by apothecaries. Nobody now knows why they are called 'little horses'.

Cavallucci di Siena MAKES ABOUT 12–15

150 g (1¼ cups) flour
100 g (⅔ cup) shelled walnuts, coarsely chopped
50 g (4 tbsps) butter
50 g (½ cup) ground almonds
25 g (2 tbsps) candied orange peel
½ tsp anise seed
½ tsp ground mixed spices: cloves, cinnamon, nutmeg and cardamom
A syrup made from 150 g (⅝ cup) sugar and 2 tbsps water, simmered
    until thick

Add all the other ingredients to the syrup and mix well. Pour out on to a floured surface and make into little oval shapes with a cookie cutter, dusting with flour to stop them from sticking. Bake on an oiled baking sheet in a low to moderate oven until pale and firm, about 20 minutes.

Even the most hard-headed Tuscans had a deep love of the countryside and its products. During a period of political eclipse Macchiavelli enjoyed the enforced retreat to his farm, pottering about the terraces, getting under the feet of his labourers and drinking his fresh young wine in the shade of the pergola.

Another landowner, the vain and self-regarding Lodovico Buonarroti, was shocked by his wayward son's choice of career – painting and sculpture. As a mere artisan he would bring disgrace and dishonour to the family. But Lodovico need not have worried.

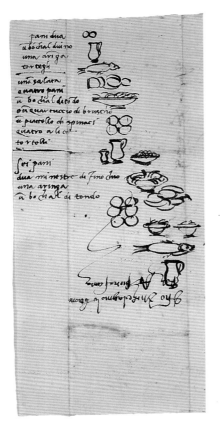

Michelangelo's menus,
after 1517. Florence, Casa
Buonarroti.

Opposite: Pontormo, detail
from *Joseph with Jacob in
Egypt,* probably 1518.
The small boy sitting on
the bottom step, pensively
clutching a shopping bag,
is a portrait of the artist's
pupil and friend, Bronzino,
linking this complex
rendering of the life of
Joseph with everyday
Florence.

His son Michelangelo turned out to be a chip off the old block who
invested his not inconsiderable earnings in real estate, town houses
and productive holdings in the Tuscan countryside. He managed
them with tight-fisted tenacity, toiling to restore the land after the
civil unrest and devastation of 1527, and keeping a beady eye on
everything, even when living as far away as he could get from his
tiresome family in the city he really preferred, Rome.

Consignments of Trebbiano wine, marzolino cheese, salami and
sausages and the usual sacks of chickpeas, beans and chestnuts
trundled the long and often perilous journey from Florence to
Rome. Sometimes mishap or malevolence caused repercussions that
exploded on the head of Michelangelo's long-suffering nephew
Lionardo, managing the estates in Florence. A consignment of wine
that was either off or tampered with, given as a present to the Pope,
was never forgiven: 'Lionardo, I am beside myself with rage! Never
let this happen again!'

Menus sketched on the back of a letter by Michelangelo when he
was living near Carrara selecting marble for the tomb of his great
patron, tormentor and friend, Pope Julius II, give some idea of his
tastes. One little meal consists of bread rolls, a dish of fennel stewed
in oil, a salt herring and a jug of wine, sketched with a relish for the
sensuous shapes of bowl, jug and platter and the earthy flavours
of basic country food. Another less frugal meal offers a salad, some
bread rolls, a dish of spinach, four salted anchovies draped over the
generous rim of a noble bowl, some *tortelli* and two kinds of wine.

Stewed Fennel   SERVES 4

4 bulbs of fennel	Salt & pepper
Olive oil	2 tbsps freshly grated Parmesan

Trim off any green fronds from the fennel bulbs and reserve. Slice the
fennel lengthways and put them with 1 tablespoon of olive oil in a pan
large enough to take them in one layer. Cook gently, covered, until
the oil and fennel juices become absorbed into the fragrant mass,
about 30 minutes. Stir in the Parmesan and decorate with the reserved
green fronds. Eat hot. This makes a meal in itself, but also goes well
with a plain roast, or as *contorno* or side salad to a plate of salami and
prosciutto crudo.

By 1536 Michelangelo, as a member of the papal household, was
granted dining rights in the Vatican. It is agreeable to imagine him
in his old age sharing some of the sumptuous banquets prepared by
the great cook Bartolomeo Scappi for his patron Cardinal Lorenzo
Campeggi and remember how the polarities of Italian gastronomy –
rugged simplicity and voluptuous complexity – that rub shoulders

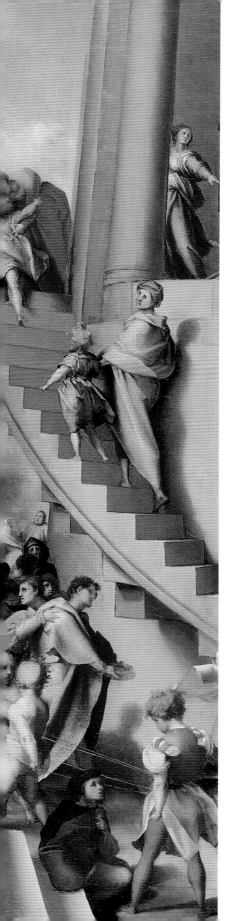

in Scappi's elaborate menus are echoed in Michelangelo's art: the glowing *colori cangianti*, shimmering layers of contrasting colour, of the Sistine Chapel, and the 'slaves' intended for Julius II's tomb, emerging with titanic effort from the obdurate block of marble that contains them, like hunks of rough Tuscan bread.

But there was a depressing side to Florentine austerity: the hysterical puritanism of the Dominican friar Savonarola, whose strident preaching disturbed even Michelangelo, with its prohibition of wine shops and eating houses and a total ban on any kind of fun, created, inevitably, a reaction, and by the sixteenth century the somewhat effete hedonism of the later Medici rulers was beautifully caught in Bronzino's portraits and paintings. Bronzino expressed his gastronomic enthusiasms in verse, including some charming lines in praise of onions which include this simple salad. Purslane, once a common vegetable, can sometimes be found in Greek or Turkish delicatessens; its slightly bitter tasting fleshy leaves and stems are good eaten raw in salads, or cooked and dressed with butter or olive oil. If it is unobtainable, lamb's lettuce could be used instead.

Purslane & Onion Salad SERVES 4

1 bunch of spring onions (scallions), chopped
1 bunch of purslane, washed and trimmed of the coarse stems
½ cucumber, peeled and diced
A few leaves of rocket and basil, torn, not chopped
Extra virgin olive oil
Salt & pepper

Dress the salad ingredients with the oil and salt and pepper, and serve at once.

Bronzino had been a pupil of Pontormo, a reclusive personality whose foibles seem familiar to us today. A preoccupation with his digestive tract and a sense that his moods and creativity were linked to diet and sleep, created a compulsion to record in detail his simple but very agreeable meals in a diary which, with its little thumbnail sketches of the figures in his frescoes in the church of San Lorenzo, is fascinating to both food and art historians. Pontormo writes with remorse of a lavish Sunday lunch with Bronzino – wonderful fish from the Arno, a chicken and far too much of a tart filled with spiced ricotta – and the penitent, dyspeptic bread and watered wine for supper. A solitary meal in his solitary studio apartment (reached by a wooden ladder that he hauled up on a pulley to exclude unwelcome guests) from which, like Saint John, he could contemplate in seclusion the goings on of his fellow Florentines below and the tranquil Tuscan hills beyond.

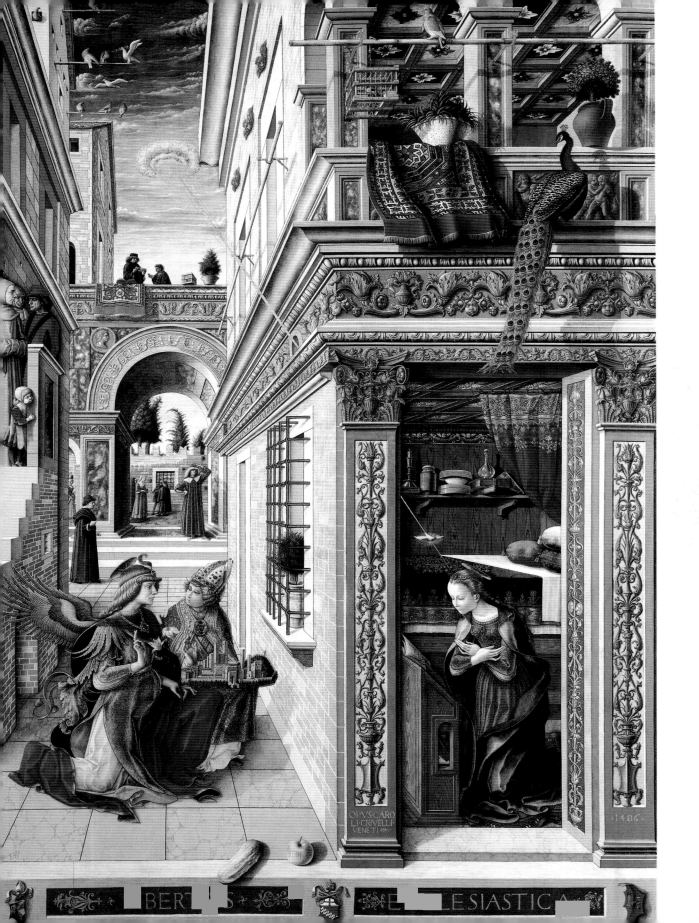

Peacocks & Preserves

THE HIDDEN CUISINE
OF THE ITALIAN MARCHES

Carlo Crivelli,
Saint Catherine from the
predella of *La Madonna della
Rondine* (*The Madonna of
the Swallow*), about 1490–2.

If any Italian hill-top towns could be said to have a low profile they would have to be the secretive, self-contained, elegant little cities of the Italian Marches – dotted over the gentle, rolling countryside tucked away between the Adriatic and the Apennines, glad not to be part of the turbulent mainstream of history, getting on with life in this verdant pocket of calm prosperity. Linked politically and gastronomically with Umbria and Romagna in the north and Abruzzo in the south, but with their own special identities, these towns provided the ideal clients and patrons for the Venetian painter Carlo Crivelli.

Crivelli spent the most productive years of his life in the Marches, busy, respected, and possibly even happy, though his paintings do not exude contentment. In fact the little documentary evidence we have of his private life hints at tragedy – the love affair that went disastrously wrong during his early years in Venice and the death of his only son in Ascoli in 1488.

Crivelli was prosecuted for abducting Tarsia, the wife of a sailor, in 1457, fined two hundred *libras* and imprisoned for six months. That is all we know. But the women in his paintings are not the calm, gentle beauties of Bellini and Mantegna – the straight nose, hooded lids over smouldering brown eyes and the lascivious mouth of Saint Catherine from the altarpiece *The Madonna of the Swallow* suggest a less than cosy view of femininity. Perhaps, settled at last in the Marches, Crivelli took to heart the local proverb – *El pan d'un giorn; el vin d'un ann; e 'na sposa d'quindic ann* – the day's bread; the year's wine; and a fifteen-year-old bride. His wife Iuranda survived him by twenty-four years.

The Virgin Mary, the young bride in Crivelli's *The Annunciation, with Saint Emidius* commissioned by the town of Ascoli Piceno in 1482, is surrounded by all the comforts of a well-to-do, modern town house. Her bedroom displays the rich coverlet and neatly turned down embroidered linen sheet of the traditional dowry. In the countryside the dowry would have been brought to the bride's new home in an ox-cart piled high with her worldly goods, covered with the embroidered sheets, secured with the pins (*squilli*) that would later be given to the village girls who helped unload and display it.

Carlo Crivelli,
*The Annunciation, with
Saint Emidius*, 1486.

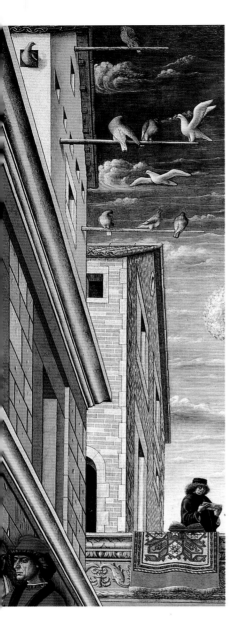

A charming part of the wedding feast was the gift to the bride of a pair of doves, symbols of fidelity and fecundity, which flutter at the top left of the painting with their companions in the domestic dovecote. Not to be confused with the carrier pigeon, seen on the parapet below, which had the honour of bearing ahead of mere human messengers the news of the political independence conferred on Ascoli Piceno in 1482 by Pope Sixtus IV.

The heavenly dove zooms in on its mission as a beam of supernatural light penetrates the quiet room, linking the divine with the everyday, irradiating the calm domestic scene where the Virgin presides sedately over her snug and prosperous domain.

The traditional cuisine of the Marches has some delicious recipes for tame pigeons or squabs. Woodpigeons in no way resemble these tender birds – their dry, gamey flesh needs long cooking – so if you cannot find any squabs use poussin or quail for a similar effect, adjusting cooking times accordingly.

Pigeons Stuffed with Chestnuts   SERVES 4

2 garlic cloves, chopped
6 slices of unsmoked fatty bacon
   or pancetta, 2 diced, 4 left whole
A little butter
4 or 5 sage leaves
200 g (1 cup) chestnuts, cooked,
   peeled and chopped (vacuum-
   packed chestnuts or

unsweetened chestnut purée
   would be fine)
Salt & pepper
Freshly ground cinnamon
4 pigeons
Garlic if wished
4 bay leaves
1 wine glass of dry white wine

Cook the garlic and diced bacon in the butter until almost golden. Add the sage leaves and chestnuts and mix together. Season with salt, pepper and cinnamon and stuff each bird with some of the mixture. Sprinkle with more seasoning, and garlic if you are using it, put a bay leaf on each bird and wrap in a bacon slice, securing it with a cocktail stick. Put the birds in a roasting pan and pour in the wine. Cook in a hot oven until done, about 45 to 60 minutes. Serve hot, with the pan juices.

Any tasty small bird, like a hen pheasant, would be good cooked this way.

The shelf above the Virgin's bed is well equipped with comforts, boxes of *cotognata*, or quince paste, a jar of preserves and a flask of pure water or refreshing cordial. Like all good housewives of the time she would have put down the rich harvest of fruits and nuts in jams, pastes and preserves, using expensive, exotic sugar or the cheaper honey or grape must. The *mostarda di frutta* eaten today as a

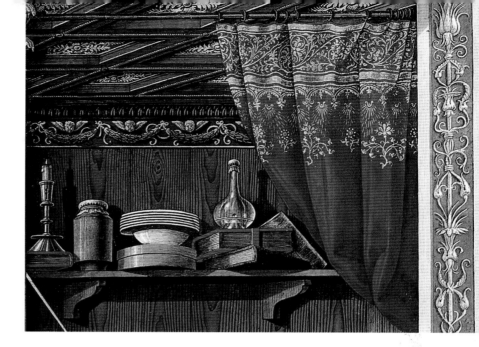

condiment to plain boiled meat or chicken, is a survival of these spiced preserves, with fruit in a syrup flavoured with mustard and other spices. In fact our word 'mustard' derives from the grape must used for the syrup, which eventually gave its name to the predominant spice.

This fourteenth-century recipe produces a concentrated fruit paste which can be cut into disks like coins or draughts, or diamond shapes, and layered with bay leaves and spices.

Apple Paste

2 tart and 2 sweet apples, peeled and cored
Honey
Whole spices to taste: cloves, a stick of cinnamon, allspice berries
Several dozen dried bay leaves
Icing (confectioner's) sugar

Grate the apples and weigh them. Add their weight in honey (calculate this from the weight of the honey in the jar, not by getting it all over your scales or measuring cup) and simmer together for as long as it takes to make a dense, thick paste, about 40 minutes. Add the spices towards the end of cooking and keep tasting to get the desired effect. When the paste is stiff let it cool and turn out onto an oiled surface, removing the spices. Pat out to 1 cm (½ in) thick and cut into lozenge shapes, or into circles with a small glass. Dust with the sugar and spread out to dry on waxed paper. A very low oven or an airing cupboard is a good place to do this. Store in an airtight box, layered with bay leaves and fine or icing (confectioner's) sugar. It should keep for months.

Carlo Crivelli, details from *The Annunciation, with Saint Emidius.*

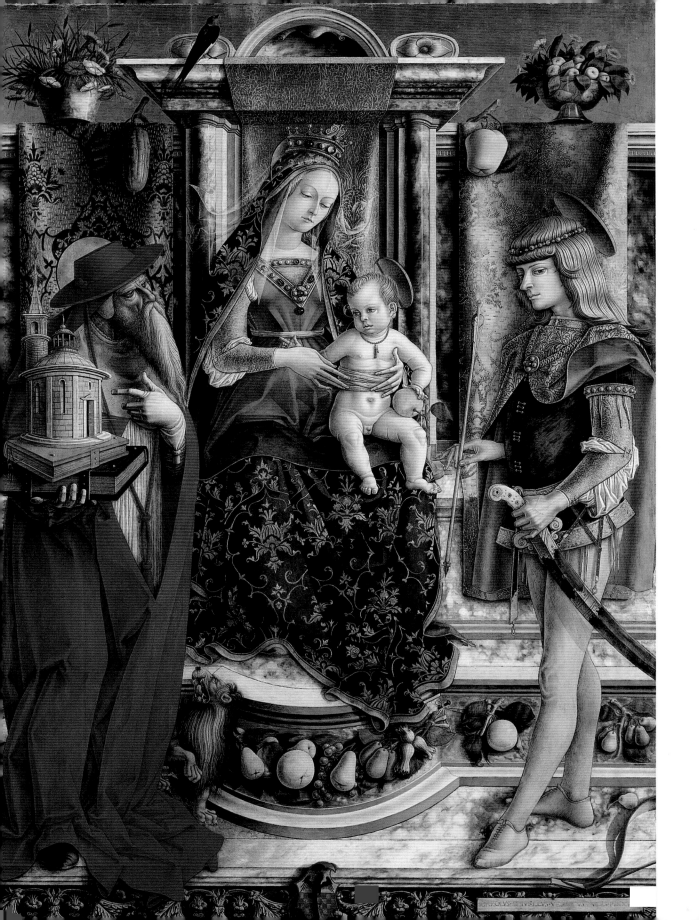

Swags of voluptuous fruit decorate many of the paintings by Crivelli and his contemporaries, Mantegna and Squarcione. The symbolism of apple and gourd must have been intelligible to all (the gourd the immortality of Christ, the apple the fruitfulness and purity of His Mother), the trompe l'œil rendering of these mundane objects makes them seem both tangible and magical, characteristic of the way Crivelli combined the very up-to-date realism of Italian Renaissance painting with the decorative, richly patterned textiles and furnishings of more old-fashioned styles.

William Morris loved Crivelli for his craftsmanship and realism, the little touches of everyday life that creep into even his most rigidly conventional paintings, where saints and the Virgin and Child appear to the exact specifications of ecclesiastical clients, but pots of flowers, tame birds and oriental carpets seem to have an independent life of their own.

Crivelli's knobbly cucumbers ask to be picked up and eaten, but for cooking it is perhaps best to stay with tasty little courgettes (zucchini). This recipe is a version of the Italian *sformato*, a less ethereal way than a soufflé of combining eggs and vegetables.

Baked Courgette Mould SERVES 4

4 medium courgettes (zucchini)	3 medium eggs, separated
2 tsps salt	Salt & pepper
1 tbsp butter	Grated nutmeg
2 tbsps flour	4 tbsps freshly grated Parmesan
150 ml (⅝ cup) milk	

Grate the courgettes (zucchini) coarsely and put in a strainer over a bowl. Add the salt and toss together, leaving to drain for 45 minutes. Butter an 18 cm (7 in) soufflé dish or mould and have a baking pan quarter filled with hot water waiting in a preheated moderate to hot oven. Meanwhile make a stiff béchamel sauce with the butter, flour and milk. Keep it warm. Beat the egg whites until stiff. (You could omit this and just use the whole eggs, beaten.) Squeeze the grated courgettes (zucchini) gently to extract as much liquid as possible. Stir this into the sauce, keeping it stiff rather than runny. Then mix in the courgettes, add the egg yolks (or whole eggs) and season with pepper and nutmeg and more salt if it needs it, remembering that the Parmesan will add yet more. If using beaten egg whites fold them in now, and last of all the Parmesan, aiming to get an unequal distribution of flavour rather than a totally homogenous blend. Pour the mixture into the prepared dish or mould, place in the pan of hot water and bake until risen and golden on top, about 30 to 45 minutes.

This dish has a pleasantly firm texture, not puffed up like a soufflé, and is good hot or tepid.

Carlo Crivelli,
La Madonna della Rondine
(*The Madonna of the
Swallow*), about 1490–2.

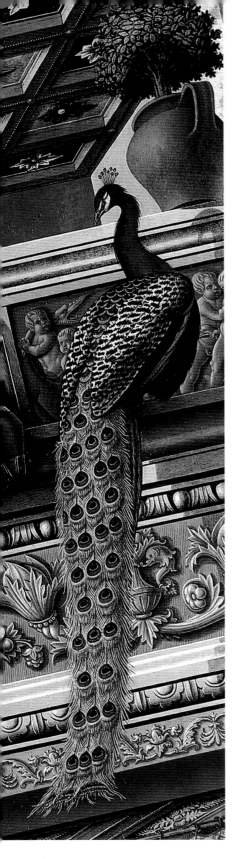

Crivelli's capacity for taking pains, his richly detailed decorative effects, must have appealed to patrons who enjoyed the complex cooking of the Marches, which was in marked contrast to the fine simplicities of other regions. The ingenuity which still goes into the painstaking fabrication of intricately crafted pockets and swirls of almost transparent hand-made pasta, like *ravioli*, *pincinelle*, *recchiatelle* and *panzarotti*, is more than craftsmanship – it is the magic of women making a special festive dish, deft hands and busy tongues manipulating the stuff of village life, the chatter and humour that bind a community together; just as Crivelli's *Annunciation* is intricately wrought from the comings and goings and self-awareness of a busy little modern town.

The area around Ascoli is famous for its huge green *gentili* olives, brought to a pitch of soft, delicious succulence in a marinade flavoured with wild fennel. Not content with eating them as they are, as a prized luxury, the Ascolani give them the Crivelli treatment: make a rich stuffing of raw ham, cooked chicken, Parmesan, cinnamon, nutmeg, salt, pepper, a rasping of lemon zest, breadcrumbs and egg; insert this into the pitted olives, coat them in flour, egg and breadcrumbs and deep-fry them. Then eat them hot. Delicious.

Crivelli's peacock would have been recognized as a symbol of immortality but also as the star turn of a celebratory banquet, when the proud bird would be cooked in spices, stitched back into its feathers and presented in majesty to the sound of trumpets, a rare old gastronomic cliché. Simpler to cook a *faraona*, guinea fowl (guinea hen), still reared in semi-wild conditions around the Marches today.

Stuffed Guinea Fowl   SERVES 4

300 ml (1¼ cups) chicken stock
175 ml (⅔ cup) white wine
3 cm (1¼ in) stick of cinnamon
Small knob of fresh ginger, peeled and chopped
½ tsp grated nutmeg
Pinch of saffron
1 large guinea fowl (guinea hen) or medium chicken
FOR THE STUFFING:
3 tbsps ground almonds

1 tbsp freshly grated Parmesan
1 tbsp good breadcrumbs
1 tbsp dried fruit soaked in a little sherry vinegar
4 slices of fatty bacon, chopped
1 tsp each of ground cinnamon and freshly ground black pepper
1 egg
1 tsp sugar
Salt

Put the stock, wine, cinnamon, ginger, nutmeg and saffron into a large pan and boil for 10 minutes to combine the flavours. Mix all the stuffing ingredients together and put inside the cavity of the bird. Secure with skewers, making sure the bird is well trussed and won't lose its shape when cooking. Put into the stock in the pan and simmer until tender, about 1 hour. Serve hot with a sauce made by reducing some of the cooking liquid and thickening it with ground almonds.

The glittering decorative detail of Crivelli's paintings is echoed in the richness and variety of the landscape of the Marches where mountains, meadows and a gentle coastline offer contrasting visual and gastronomic pleasures. Chestnuts, mushrooms, truffles, nuts and game from the woodlands join the fragrant herbs and vegetables of the meadows and are linked by a variety of pasta dishes to the renowned olives of the plains and the profusion of fish from the coast. Polenta in many forms came later, but the pasta is a reminder of how the basic staple, wheat flour, can be used to provide inexpensive everyday nourishment or transformed into elaborate festive concoctions. The most luxurious (*vincisgrassi* is a good example) are probably best eaten once a year as a treat for the very special occasions for which they were devised. Rather than attempt to recreate such a dish at home, easier to try the simple but delicious 'little ears' pasta dish below, which does not even call for the skills needed to roll out paper-thin sheets of pasta.

Recchiatelle SERVES 4

FOR THE PASTA:
500 g strong white flour (5 cups all-purpose or bread flour)
1 medium egg
1 tsp olive oil

FOR THE DRESSING:
2 tbsps butter
4 tbsps freshly grated Parmesan
3 tbsps concentrated juices from a meat or chicken roast
Freshly ground black pepper
Freshly grated nutmeg

Knead the pasta ingredients together until smooth and springy. Leave to rest, covered, for 30 minutes. Take a small lump of the mixture and roll into a little ball the size of a hazelnut. Place the ball in the palm of your hand and, with a floured thumb, press into a vaguely concave shape. Carry on in this way until the mixture is used up, sprinkling these 'little ears' with flour as you lay them on paper towels or a shallow plate. Cook in batches in a large pan of boiling salted water until done but still firm, about 2 to 3 minutes. Lift them out with a slotted spoon and put in layers in a warmed dish, dressing each layer with some of the butter, cheese and meat juices. Season with pepper and nutmeg, and serve hot.

Carlo Crivelli, detail from *The Annunciation, with Saint Emidius.*

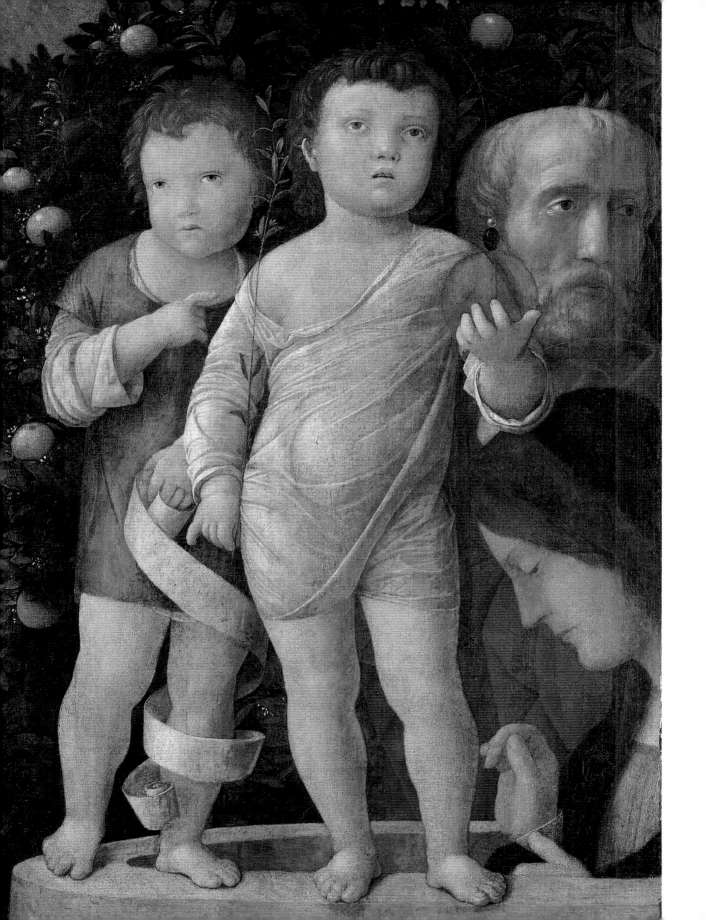

'Golden Lamps in a Green Night'
CITRUS FRUITS & THEIR USES

When the mythical Aegle and her sisters, daughters of Hesperus, landed on the shores of Italy, wafted by friendly breezes and helpful tritons, the legend says they brought with them their treasured 'golden apples'. Oranges, in fact, exotic fruit cultivated by the Medes and the Persians, cherished by Alexander the Great and recorded by his botanist Theophrastus. Aegle planted hers around Lake Garda, where they have flourished ever since.

When Andrea Mantegna, not usually seen as a cheerful hedonist, set off on his day trip to Lake Garda on 23 September 1464, he revelled in the clear, bright air, the company of his friends, the intoxicating association of legend, serious archaeology and the thrill of the chase. Mantegna's search for classical inscriptions on the ruined temples and fallen columns in the orange groves, some incorporated into the fabric of Christian churches, became a self-consciously pagan revel. His disreputable companion, the calligrapher and antiquary Felice Feliciano, left a euphoric account of the discovery of twenty-seven superb inscriptions as they caroused through the groves of oranges and lemons, perfumed with blossom and melodious with birdsong. Bedecked with garlands of ivy and myrtle, the party took a boat to Sirmione, reclining on oriental carpets and refreshed with every comfort.

This happy day seems to have made a lasting impression on Mantegna. The beauty of the exquisitely drawn Roman letters which often embellish his paintings is matched by the radiant glow of oranges and lemons suspended among their glossy dark green leaves in the background of many of them. The numinous Christ Child opposite seems to be a serene infant, and the bright fruit add to the tranquillity of the scene.

Mantegna and his companions may have enjoyed a simple meal of fish from the lake as they paused for refreshment during their outing. Here is a version of a traditional dish evolved to brighten the somewhat insipid whitefish of the *Coregonidae* family, supposed to be unique to Lake Bracciano, near Rome, but in fact a freshwater fish found all over Europe.

This traditional recipe, from Anguillara Sabazia on the shores of Lake Bracciano, works well with an oily fish like farmed trout or

Andrea Mantegna, *The Holy Family with Saint John*, about 1500.

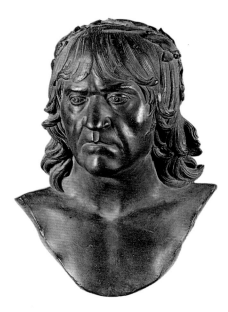

Detail of a nineteenth-century cast from a bronze portrait bust of Mantegna in his memorial chapel in S. Andrea in Mantua.

mackerel and looks most elegant made with a wild sea trout. The pink flesh, parsley and lemon create a decorative dish without any straining after effect. A plain green salad, some crusty bread and a white wine resilient enough to stand up to the lemon, are all you need for a light lunch.

Trout with Lemon Stuffing SERVES 4

4 medium trout or 1 wild sea trout, about 1–1.5 kg (2–3¼ lbs), cleaned but not boned
2 lemons, preferably organic and unwaxed, scrubbed, sliced, and small seeds discarded
2 or 3 garlic cloves, finely chopped
2 tbsps chopped flat-leaf parsley
Salt & freshly ground black pepper
A little sugar to balance the acidity

Wipe clean and dry the fish with paper towels. Mix the lemons, garlic and parsley in a bowl and season with salt, pepper and sugar. Stuff the fish with the mixture and leave it in an ovenproof dish for an hour or so to absorb the flavours. Cover the fish loosely with foil and bake in a preheated hot oven for 10 to 15 minutes for small fish, up to 30 minutes for a larger one, testing from time to time to avoid overcooking.

Classical associations, Christian symbolism and the local agri-business must all have come into the brief when Mantegna painted his magnificent triptych in the church of San Zeno in Verona, with its vast voluptuous swags of fruit, including an impressive variety of lemons, citrons, limes and oranges shining out from their dark green leaves and fragrant flowers. Mantegna knew well enough that the Virgilian groves of Benaco (Lake Garda's name in classical times) were in fact financed by the rich businessmen of Verona, who provided the capital for the sophisticated irrigation and protective covering that these sensitive trees required, and controlled the flourishing export trade in the fruit.

Later generations of Veronese painters seem to have shared Mantegna's enthusiasm for citrus fruits. Gerolamo dai Libri graces his *The Virgin and Child with Saint Anne* with a beautiful citron tree. The calm tranquillity of this painting gives no hint of the turmoil which engulfed Verona in the early sixteenth century. A contemporary chronicle recounts the misery and confusion that ensued when Verona abandoned her centuries-long alliance with Venice and became a prey to hordes of armies – Spaniards, Germans, Papal troops, Venetians and Swiss (the only well-behaved ones). Bad weather, crop failures and two years of recurrent outbreaks of the plague added to her woes. Lemons or citrons may be celebrated in this

Opposite: Gerolamo dai Libri, detail from *The Virgin and Child with Saint Anne*, 1510–18.

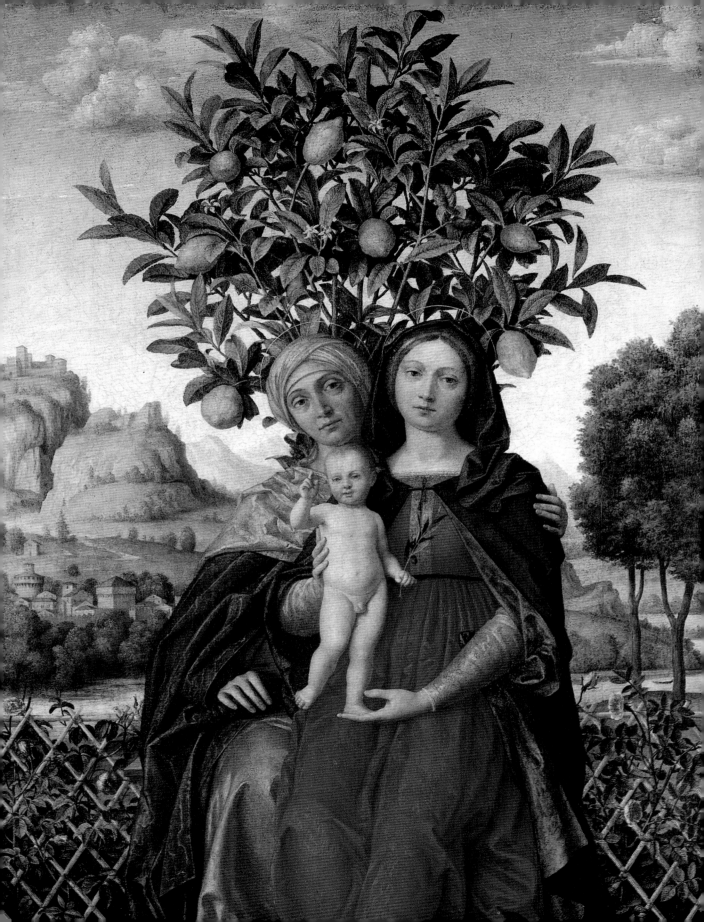

painting as an antidote to the plague, or in the belief that prayers to Saint Anne and a good slug of lemon juice eased the pains of women in childbirth, or simply as one of Verona's commercial achievements. The protective trellis enclosing the group is characteristic of the skilled techniques of citrus culture. Citrons, and indeed all citrus fruit, are often found in paintings of Christ and his mother, the marvel of perfumed flowers and fruit flourishing at the same time symbolizing Mary's role as both virgin and mother – layer upon layer of meaning and association, alongside the immediate, uncomplicated appeal of a beautiful, fragrant and fruitful tree.

Citrons, familiar to us as 'candied peel', were prized for their dense, aromatic perfume. It is hardly surprising that they share the same name in Italian, *cedro*, as the cedars of Lebanon, whose musky scent they resemble. Somewhere around 136 BC the cones of the cedar were replaced by equally potent perfumed citrons, the 'fruit of a goodly tree' in the Jewish Feast of Tabernacles. In this ceremony, originally a festival for the wine, oil and fruit harvests, the participants each hold a fragrant *etrog*, or citron, and aromatic fronds of palm, myrtle and willow. The scent and strangely potent shape of the citron, suggesting both nipple and phallus, remind us of ancient fertility rites. To this day orthodox Jews say that biting off and eating the flower end of the *etrog* will aid an infertile woman to conceive and can also ease the pains of childbirth.

A sumptuous dessert which includes citron and myrtle leaves links the Jewish community of Victorian London with these ancient beliefs. Lady Judith Montefiore in *The Jewish Manual* of 1864 describes a *Bol d'amor*, in which strands of beaten egg yolk are cooked in a sugar syrup, dried slowly, piled up in a ceremonial pyramid and adorned with gold leaf, spices, candied citron and myrtle leaves.

We shall never know precisely what Paolo Morando, a friend and colleague of Gerolamo dai Libri, meant by his use of a lemon or citron ceremoniously held in the right hand of the angel, in his painting of *The Virgin and Child, Saint John the Baptist and an Angel*. It could have been a reference to the Song of Songs or a symbol of the fruitfulness of the Virgin, like the more usual apple or pomegranate, or the bitter-sweet foreknowledge by the Virgin of the eventual death of her son, or it could even have been another reminder of the respite from the plague. Indeed long before citrus fruit were known to prevent scurvy they had a multitude of medicinal uses – as a cure for fevers and plagues, remedy for the bites of scorpions (held responsible for almost any insect bite or skin infection) and as an antidote to poison. Hence the prelates and princes who savoured a citron salad at the start of a banquet would have found it a reassuring item on the menu as well as a refreshing indulgence.

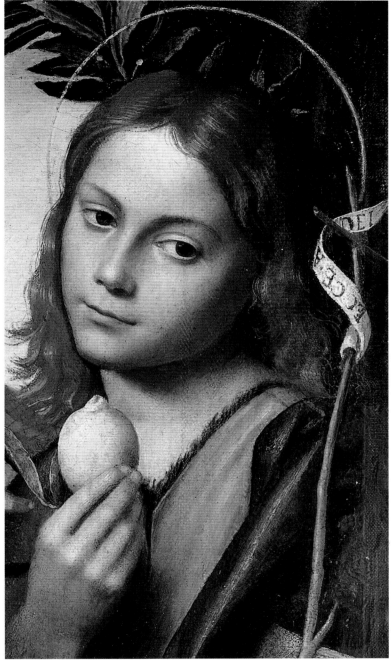

Paolo Morando, detail from
*The Virgin and Child,
Saint John the Baptist and
an Angel*, probably about
1514–18.

Overleaf: Paolo Uccello,
detail from *The Battle of
San Romano*, probably
about 1450–60.

We do know that cooks of the period used the peel and juice of all citrus fruits with the care accorded to a precious commodity. They seem to have the same role in Renaissance art as they have in gastronomy; to add grace notes of cheerfulness and sparkle to the rich complexities of a composition, be it banquet or altarpiece. Vinegar and verjuice would have given sourness and acidity to food,

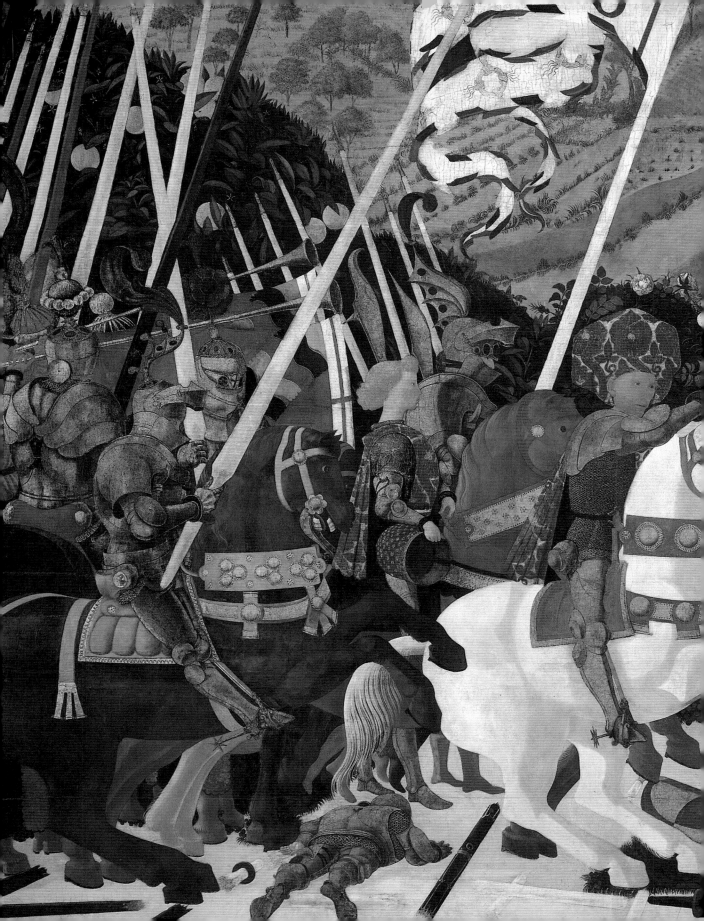

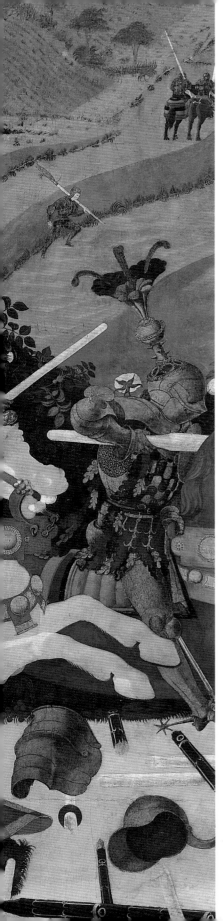

but no visual appeal; oranges and lemons preserved in syrup or sliced raw as decoration and relish for rich roasts, or as tart salads or pickles, added colour and pattern to the carefully orchestrated sequence of dishes. The great cook Bartolomeo Scappi usually included a salad of thinly sliced citrons, seasoned with salt, sugar and rosewater, in the first course of his banquets. Glowing on their dish among the silver and gold of the table setting, the snowy white linen and the sprigs of flowers, the citrons would have sweetened the room with their aroma, stimulating the palate, vibrating like the clear, shrill notes of the flute above the plangent lute of the musicians.

Bartolomeo Scappi's Pickled Lemons

This has the characteristic ambivalence of so many Renaissance dishes, sweet and savoury combined, and makes a refreshingly benign pickle which is good with fish, beans or lentils, and any spicy Middle Eastern or Indian meal. Cut 6 well-washed lemons or limes into wedges and pack them into jars, topped up with any juice from the chopping up and dry white wine, 1 tablespoon of salt and 4 tablespoons of sugar. Keep in a cool, dark place for a week or so before using.

Sharp Citrus Salad

A salad of sharp grapefruit or orange, peel, pith and all but without seeds, washed, finely sliced and seasoned with a generous pinch of salt, freshly ground pepper, a teaspoon of sugar and a tiny trickle of extra virgin olive oil makes a good accompaniment to a rich roast or fatty duck. This can be embellished with pitted black olives or a little sliced sweet red onion.

The 'Golden Apples of the Hesperides' have had many interpretations and so have the five red orbs on the escutcheon of the Medicis. Disdaining the prosaic or even derogatory suggestion that they may have been pawnbroker's balls or apothecary's pills, Florentines recognized the palle as oranges – the word *medici* could mean 'oranges' as well as 'physicians'. Sheltered orange groves graced the villas the Medicis built themselves as country retreats, and some claim to recognize in the figure of Mercury in Botticelli's *Spring* a portrait of Giuliano de' Medici enjoying himself knocking down oranges with his staff. So the oranges glowing among the shattered lances and prone corpses of Uccello's *The Battle of San Romano* are agreeably appropriate in a painting gracing a room in the Medici family palace. Here mortal combat sanitized as an exercise in perspective and a display of pageantry reminds us of the mock battle celebrated at Ivrea to this day, when the protagonists pelt one another with oranges.

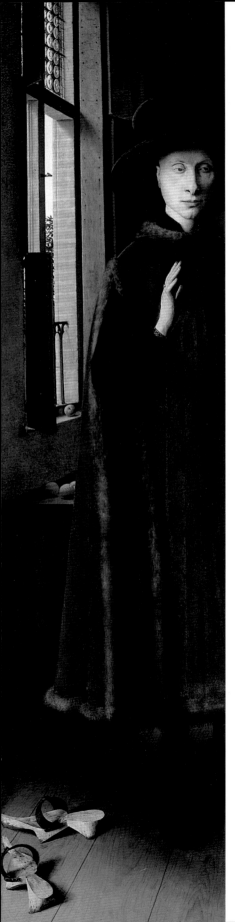

Carefully hoarded, quinces will last until the first Seville oranges arrive just after Christmas, and make a wonderful sharp, aromatic sauce to eat with cold duck or goose, or roast pork.

Quince & Seville Orange Sauce

1 large quince	4 cloves
1 Seville orange	60 g (5 tbsps) sugar
3 cm (1¼ in) stick of cinnamon	

Cut the unpeeled quince into quarters and cut away the core. Simmer in a little water until soft. Process the pulp or crush in a mortar with a pestle and put back in the pan. Season with the juice of the orange, some slivers of zest, the cinnamon stick and cloves. Taste and add sugar to achieve a sauce of the sweetness required. Cook for a little longer, but take care not to boil away the evanescent aromas of the fruit. Remove the cinnamon and cloves when they have contributed as much flavour as needed.

Alternatively increase the quantity of sugar and boil until the mixture becomes a fine red jam.

Slices of bitter or other varieties of orange provided the finishing touches to this rich chicken dish derived from medieval Arab gastronomy. Florentine banquets at the time of the Medici flaunted such ostentatious displays of expensive ingredients.

Medieval Chicken   SERVES 4

1.5 kg (about 3¼ lbs) free range chicken, cut off the carcass into serving pieces	4 cm (1½ in) stick of cinnamon
	6 cloves
6 bay leaves	Thumbnail blade of mace
1 Seville or sharp orange	1 tsp chopped fresh ginger root
1 wine glass each of white wine and water	2 garlic cloves, chopped
	2 heaped tbsps ground almonds
12 pitted prunes	Salt & pepper
12 pitted dried dates	A sprinkling of rosewater

First make some stock by simmering the chicken carcass, 2 bay leaves, a strip of orange zest, white wine and water in a large pan for 30 minutes. Soak the prunes and dates in a little of it while the chicken is cooking. Put the chicken pieces into a large pan with the rest of the stock, add the whole spices, garlic and remaining bay leaves, cover, and simmer for about 45 minutes. When almost done, stir the ground almonds into the cooking liquid and simmer until thick. Add the prunes and dates and warm through for 5 minutes. Check the seasonings and sharpen the sauce with orange juice if necessary. Decorate with thin slices of orange, skin and all. Sprinkle with rosewater just before serving.

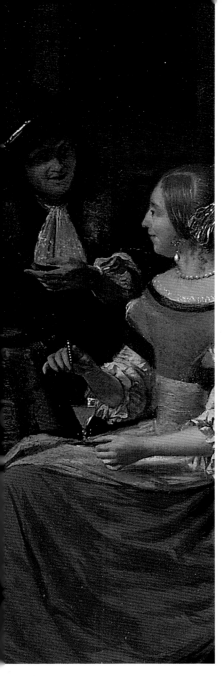

Pieter de Hooch, detail from *A Musical Party in a Courtyard*, 1677.

Opposite: Jan van Eyck, detail from *The Portrait of Giovanni (?) Arnolfini and his Wife*, 1434.

Renaissance Chicken

By contrast a simple domestic meal described by Bartolomeo Platina, the humanist scholar who was at one time a protégé of the Medicis, uses oranges in the new 'modern' manner, as a modest seasoning to enhance portions of roast chicken. Carve a chicken roasted to your taste and just before serving sprinkle with Renaissance Stardust, Seville orange juice and rosewater.

Renaissance Stardust

Pulverize 1 teaspoon of salt, 2 tablespoons of sugar and a finger length of cinnamon in a coffee grinder and store in an airtight jar ready for use.

Oranges and lemons were even more precious in the Netherlands, as expensive imports or the pampered produce of luxurious local hothouses. The rich tradition of Belgian food today is an opulent reminder of the gastronomic splendours of the medieval Burgundian kingdom, which embraced large chunks of the Low Countries as well as the region of Burgundy in France. Conquest by Spain in the sixteenth century brought Spanish fashions in dress and food to enrich the cultural brew enjoyed by those rich Italian expats, the merchant Giovanni Arnolfini and his wife, who displayed oranges as ornaments in their well-appointed home in Bruges.

Orange & Pistachio Tart   SERVES 4

FOR THE PASTRY:
225 g plain flour (2 cups all-
  purpose flour)
125 g (9 tbsps) butter
50 g (½ cup) ground almonds
1 tbsp sugar
1 tsp grated orange zest
A pinch of salt
1 egg, beaten (the size of the egg
  is not critical!)

FOR THE FILLING:
3 sweet oranges or 4 clementines,
  peeled and finely sliced
50 g (scant ¼ cup) sugar
1 amaretto biscuit (cookie),
  crumbled
1 tsp freshly ground cinnamon
15 g (1 tbsp) unsalted butter
55 g (½ cup) shelled pistachios,
  skinned & coarsely ground

First make the pastry by processing or rubbing together all the ingredients to make a stiff dough. Chill in the refrigerator for an hour. Roll out the pastry on a floured surface and use to line a 23 cm (9 in) pie pan. Line with foil, weigh down with dried beans and bake 'blind' in a preheated moderate oven for 30 minutes. Remove the foil and beans and arrange the orange slices in the pastry case in a decorative overlapping pattern. Strew with sugar, amaretto crumbs and a little cinnamon, and dot with butter. Bake in a moderate oven for about 30 minutes. Five minutes before the end of the cooking time, sprinkle on the nuts.

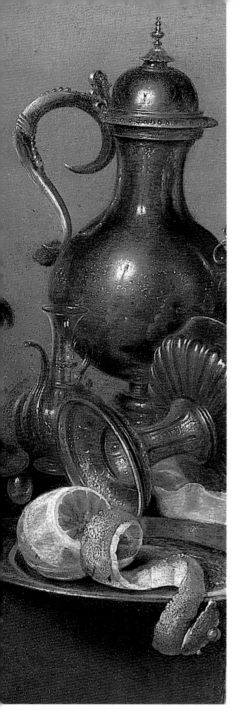

Lemon or Orange Relish

Lemons or Seville oranges diced as finely as possible with a sharp knife, the seeds removed, and dressed with salt and sugar make a lovely relish with fish, cold meats or lentils. Do not be tempted to chop in a processor, which makes a mush. Rosewater or lemon blossom water can be added if their perfume is appropriate to the meal. Contrary to belief, the white pith is pleasant and need not be discarded.

In this still life attributed to David Davidsz. de Heem we can enjoy an improbable assortment of spring fruit and flowers, cherries and convolvulus, summer wheat, autumnal nuts and the oranges of winter composed around a dish of oysters and a delicate goblet. The bitter juice of the orange makes a fragrant dressing for the oysters while the aromatic oils of the freshly peeled fruit convey a pungent flavouring to the glass of wine or spirits. The detail on page 49 from Pieter de Hooch's *A Musical Party in a Courtyard* shows an elegant young woman languidly flavouring her drink by stirring it with a knife redolent with the perfume of an orange.

A contemporary Dutch recipe book, *De Verstandige Kock* of 1667 has recipes for sweet and savoury dishes using lemon zest and juice. Obviously nothing was wasted. The freshly cut and peeled fruit, a luxury item, would be used in every possible way to take advantage of its sharp juice and fragrant skin.

In this dessert lemons add an exotic touch to the butter, cream and apples of the Low Countries.

Apple & Lemon Bake   SERVES 4–6

3 tart apples, peeled and cored
The grated zest of 2 lemons
200 g (scant 1 cup) sugar
2 egg yolks
200 ml double cream (scant 1 cup heavy cream)
230 g (1½ cups) soft white breadcrumbs
1 tsp freshly ground cinnamon
Unsalted butter to taste, the more the better

Slice the apples and put them in a buttered ovenproof dish. Strew the lemon zest over them and add half the sugar. Beat the egg yolks and cream together and pour over the apples. Mix the breadcrumbs with half the remaining sugar and the cinnamon. Spread the crumbs over the apple mixture and dot with generous amounts of butter. Finish with the rest of the sugar. Bake in a preheated moderate oven until the apples are soft and the crumbs golden, about 30 to 40 minutes.

Willem Claesz. Heda, detail from *Still Life: Pewter and Silver Vessels and a Crab*, probably about 1633–7.

Opposite: Attributed to David Davidsz. de Heem, *Still Life*, probably late 1660s.

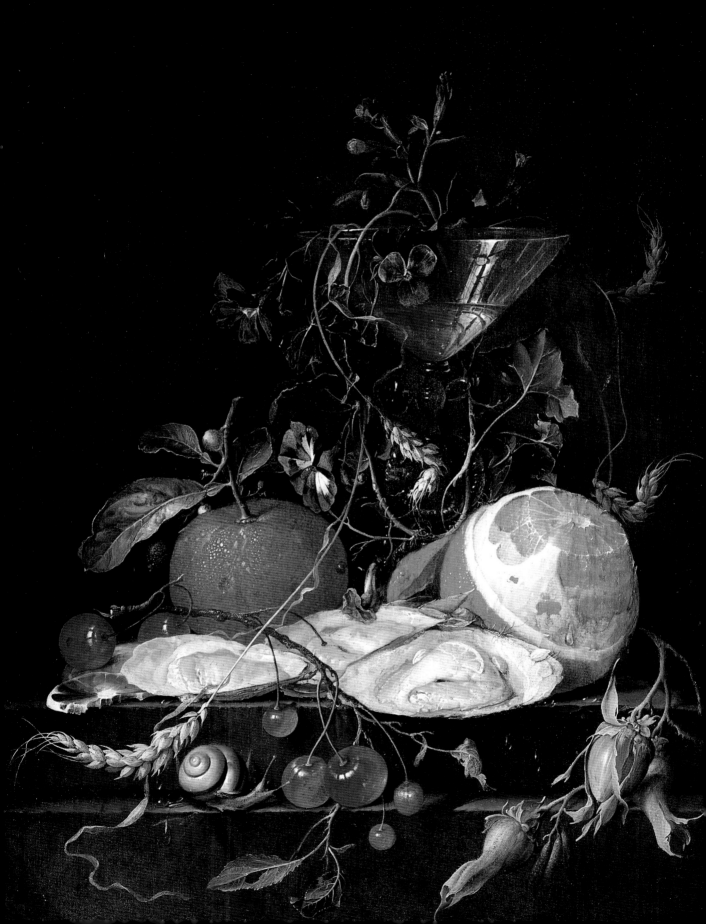

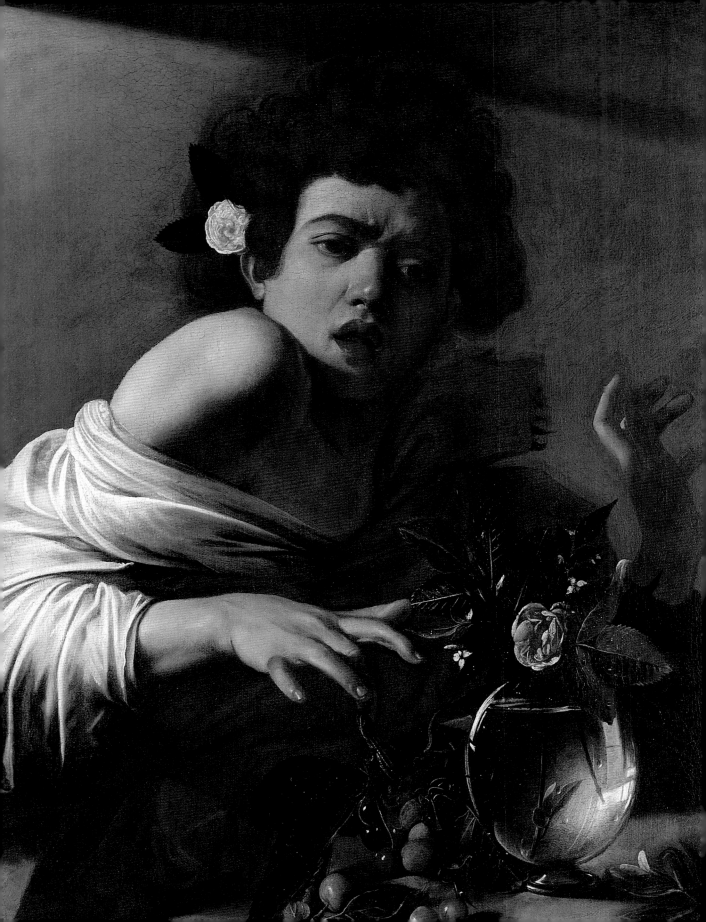

Mayhem & Gastronomy
IN BAROQUE ROME

On a sultry night in May 1598, Michelangelo Merisi da Caravaggio was arrested by the Roman police in the Piazza Navona for possession of unlawful weapons. With explosive anger the painter claimed his right as a member of Cardinal Del Monte's household to carry a sword at all times, but the pair of compasses, gleaming wickedly in the moonlight, were too much for the apprehending officer, who threw him in jail.

Of all the incidents in Caravaggio's tempestuous brushes with the law this one seems to summarize his whole career. The sword, the arrogance, the street-rage, with the compasses epitomizing the keen, passionate professionalism of his art. Mirrors, globes, lenses, rulers, compasses, were all means to an end – intense and accurate observations of the natural world, the way everyday things looked and the way real people felt and behaved.

His patron, Cardinal Francesco Maria Del Monte, a suave, cultivated man of the world, had a secret room, decorated with murals by Caravaggio, part kitchen, part laboratory, in his villa among the vines outside the Porta Pinciana on the outskirts of Rome. There among his pestles and mortars, stills, retorts, vials and carafes of purest crystal he experimented with optics and a camera obscura, alchemy and medicine, concocting strange potions and possibly more down to earth ones, for a knowledge of poisons and their antidotes would have had their uses in the convoluted intrigues of papal Rome.

Caravaggio's *Boy bitten by a Lizard* might well be pulsating with double meanings, symbolizing the sense of touch or the pangs of love, but the fruit and flowers are limpid still life ingredients, and the play of light and shadow on the clear water in the vase remind us of Caravaggio's revolutionary assertion that making a still life was every bit as demanding as a figure painting.

His early years in Rome, poor and as yet unknown, but with finely honed skills and considerable pride, produced a number of still lifes and scenes from everyday life. This particular painting sold for not much more than the price of a meal, and we hear of a portrait of an innkeeper that Caravaggio did to clear his slate. Many of his models were friends from the rough and tumble of the raucous streets that he roamed in search of mayhem. Everyone recognized the beautiful courtesan Fillide Melandroni as the model for Saint Catherine of

Michelangelo Merisi da Caravaggio, *Boy bitten by a Lizard*, 1595–1600.

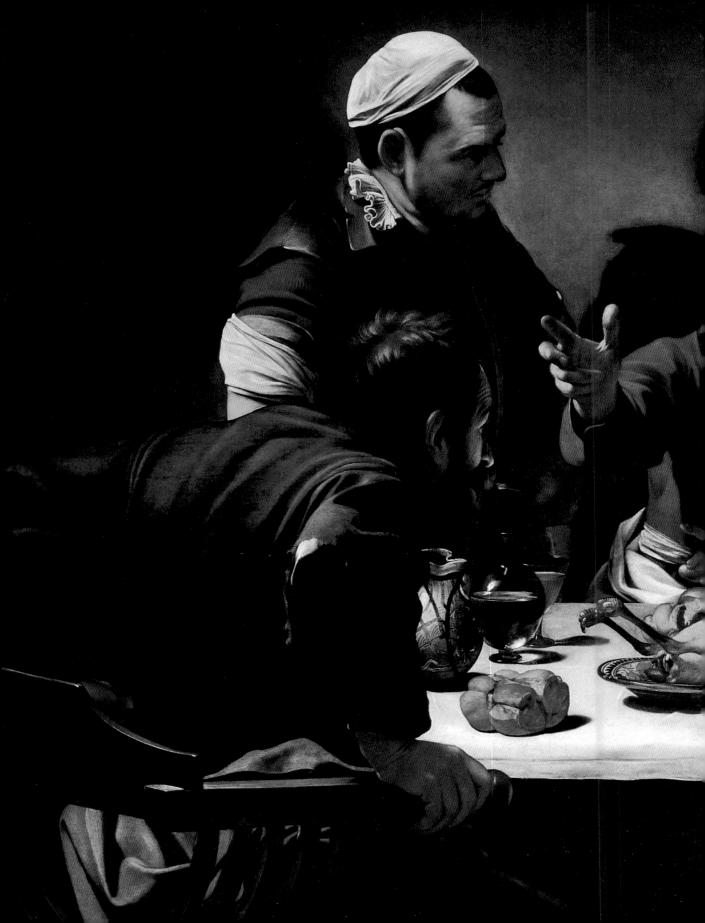

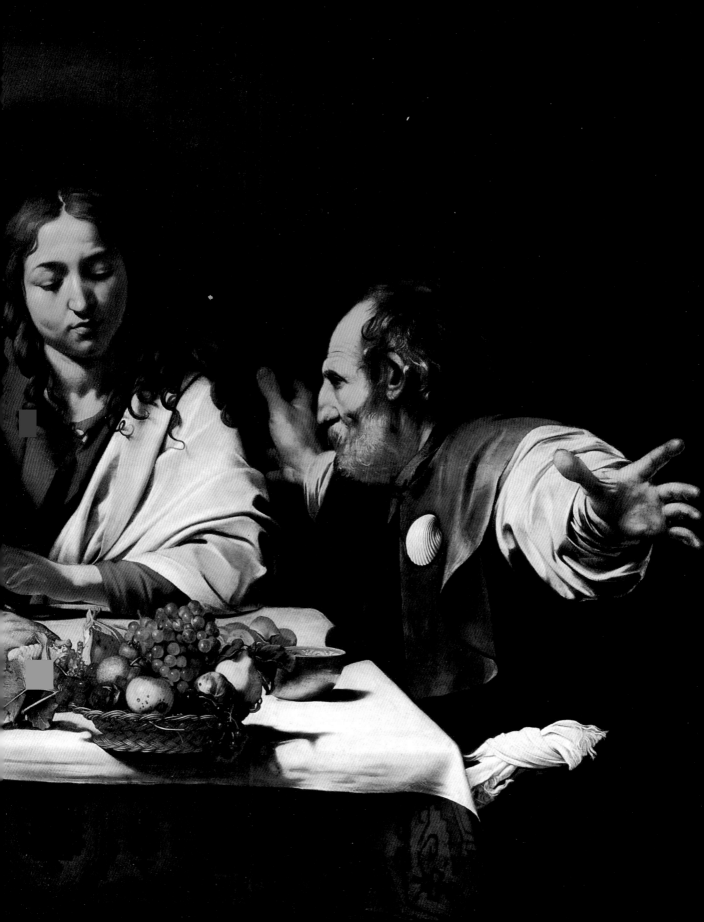

Alexandria (Thyssen Bornemisza Museum, Madrid), but when Caravaggio used his girlfriend, the prostitute Lena, as model for *The Madonna of the Pilgrims*, (Church of S. Agostino, Rome) some felt that he was taking realism too far, and the shockingly bloated, dishevelled corpse in *The Death of the Virgin*, now in the Louvre, caused such a scandal that the painting never hung in the church for which it was intended.

The innkeeper in *The Supper at Emmaus*, however, is a serious, decent host, attentive to his guests, a charismatic young man and two pilgrims – a familiar scene to the artist and his patron, the nobleman Ciriaco Mattei. But in this circle the implications of Caravaggio's realism were doctrinal as well as aesthetic. The reformed Catholic church needed to make a more direct appeal to the faithful to counteract the threat of Protestantism. Caravaggio's interpretation of the events of the Gospels – ordinary people experiencing immediate and often painful emotions – sometimes went beyond conventional limits. Here the miraculous supper at Emmaus becomes everyday life when the travellers are confronted with real food and the sudden, blinding revelation that their companion is the resurrected Jesus, young and clean-shaven as he had charmed them so many years ago and not the bearded corpse from the tomb at Gethsemane. No idealized sentimentality here but the complicated faith of a sophisticated ecclesiastical court interpreted by a harsh realist.

Nothing harsh about the meal though. A guinea fowl (hen), rolls, wine and a basket of fruit, served on a crisp linen tablecloth spread over an oriental carpet. A recipe from Bartolomeo Scappi's book of 1570 might have been followed in the preparation of this bird.

Pot Roast Guinea Fowl   SERVES 4

1 plump free range guinea fowl (guinea hen)	Sprigs of rosemary, sage, wild fennel and bay leaves
Olive oil	2 garlic cloves
12 juniper berries	Salt & pepper

Wash and wipe the bird dry with kitchen paper towels. Anoint inside and out with oil and stuff with the juniper berries and herbs, saving a few to tuck around it in the pan. Scatter with chopped garlic, salt and pepper. Cover and bake in a moderate oven until done, about 1½ hours. Test for doneness after about 1¼ hours; the juices should run clear when a skewer is inserted into the thigh.

One of Cardinal Del Monte's parties in the gardens of the Villa Medici got somewhat out of hand on 9 August 1601. A dash outside the city walls for a breath of fresh air after nightfall (prohibited because of the curfew) resulted in the arrest of Menicuccia the

Previous page: Michelangelo Merisi da Caravaggio, *The Supper at Emmaus*, 1601.

celebrated courtesan, then on the brink of a brilliant career, who insisted on being taken to prison in a coach and furthermore cajoled the impressionable policemen into arresting with her the silver dish of shrimps she had no intention of leaving behind.

Romans have always loved fresh fish. Among the ruins of Ostia Antica, once the city's flourishing port, there are the remains of food stalls where fried food and condiments were sold. A welcome modern restaurant under a pergola restores today's weary visitors, some of whom seem to have come more for the fish than the antiquities, with the menu offering fish soup and fritto misto as well as this robust mixture of spaghetti, mussels and clams, one of the simplest ways of enjoying shellfish.

Spaghetti with Shellfish   SERVES 4

500 g (generous 1 lb) spaghetti
3 tbsps olive oil
6 garlic cloves, smashed
2 or 3 dried red chiles (optional)
500 g (generous 1 lb) mussels, well-scrubbed

500 g (generous 1 lb) clams, cleaned
250 ml (1 cup) dry white wine
2 tbsps chopped fresh parsley
Freshly ground black pepper

Cook the pasta in plenty of boiling salted water. Meanwhile heat the olive oil in a capacious pan and cook the garlic until golden, with the chiles if you want the characteristic Roman flavour. Toss in the mussels and clams and turn around in the oil. Pour in the wine, cover, and cook fast until the shellfish open; this will take only a few minutes. Season with the parsley and pepper. Drain the cooked spaghetti. Strain the cooking liquor from the shellfish through cheesecloth to get rid of any lingering grains of sand and add this and the shellfish, still in their shells, to the pasta. Discard any unopened shellfish.

Caravaggio's gastronomic life in Rome veered between the coarse, cheap street food of his disreputable friends and the elegant austerities and indulgences of cardinals and princes. He must have enjoyed rough food with the rough trade, like the robust tripe dishes still around today, as well as those much more refined dinners – quails in delicate pastry cases, truffles stewed in olive oil with bitter orange juice and pepper, little tarts of plums and marzipan – with his sophisticated patrons.

Cheap food was plentiful in a city catering for a vast floating population of soldiers, beggars, pilgrims, priests and adventurers. Fried food has moved indoors now, but Caravaggio, between brawls, could have bought tasty morsels of artichokes, sweetbreads, cardoons, zucchini and mushrooms dipped in batter and fried by street vendors, as he roamed the streets.

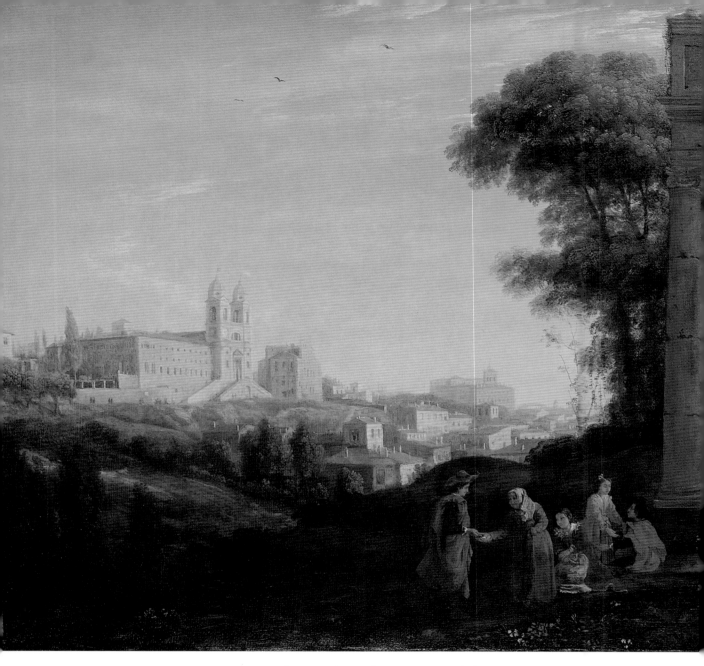

Claude Lorrain, *A View in Rome*, 1632. This painting combines a real view of Sta Trinità de' Monti in the left background, with idealized ruins in the right foreground. It was probably painted from the roof of Claude's house in the (modern) via Babuina.

Pilgrims, the package tourists of their time, enjoyed a range of robust food which can still be eaten in Roman trattorias today. Eliminate tomatoes and chile peppers, which did not arrive until much later, and there is still a fine choice of pasta dishes: a sauce of bacon, eggs and pecorino cheese or aubergines (eggplants) and ricotta; or home-made fettucine dressed with chicken livers, white wine, butter, garlic and herbs. Stews made from cheap cuts of beef, oxtail or tripe, simmered slowly in wine and aromatics; lamb from the fragrant hillsides of the Abruzzi roasted or grilled with sage or rosemary; unsurpassable mozzarella and ricotta from rich buffalo milk.

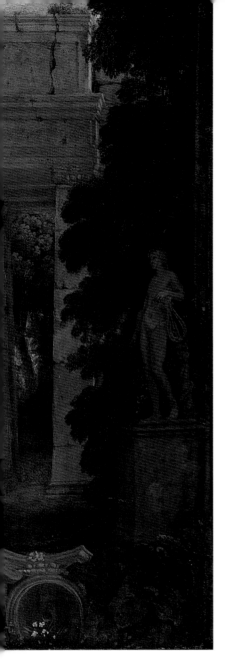

The amazing banquets described by Bartolomeo Scappi, cook to popes and princes, always had dishes of refined simplicity alongside rich and elaborate fare, for Romans, then as now, appreciated the pleasures of the first young broad or fava beans eaten raw, or a plate of tender young artichokes, like the one Caravaggio threw at the head of a waiter on 24 April 1604.

Long-simmering personal animosity perhaps, or simply the last straw on a day of tensions and frustration, but to Caravaggio – perfectionist over details – the question of oil or butter in the preparation of artichokes was paramount. When an insolent waiter served four cooked in butter and four cooked in oil on the same dish, with the suggestion that Caravaggio, if he needed to know which were which, might sniff them and see, the explosion of violence was inevitable.

Here is a characteristic recipe:

Carciofi alla Romana   SERVES 4

8 very young artichokes, outer
   leaves removed, but keeping
   2 cm (¾ in) stalks
4 garlic cloves, chopped
1 tbsp chopped pennyroyal

(*mentuccia*, mint is a possible
   substitute)
Salt & pepper
2 tbsps olive oil
1 tbsp water

The chokes of these infant artichokes are nonexistent or harmless so they do not need to be removed. Mix the garlic and pennyroyal together, season with salt and pepper and stuff some between each leaf. Put the artichokes, stalks up, in a flameproof dish with the olive oil and water. Cook, covered, in the oven or on top of the stove until tender, about 30 to 40 minutes or less depending on the size and age of the artichokes. Add a little more water if necessary. Serve at room temperature

Another brawl figuring in Caravaggio's police record was over some *biancomangiare* in a pastrycook's. This ancient dish has the enigmatic ambiguity of much medieval and Renaissance food, where no distinction was made between sweet and savoury. *Biancomangiare*, the ancestor of stodgy blancmange, was made from chicken breasts, ground almonds and cooked rice simmered in chicken stock, pounded up with sugar and spices and decorated with pomegranate seeds. Served in little pastry cases it would make an intriguing appetizer.

At the time of his tragically early death at thirty-seven, stranded, stricken with fever on the beach at Porto Ercole, Caravaggio was on his way back to the city he loved best. Four years earlier he had murdered the equally disreputable and anarchic Ranuccio

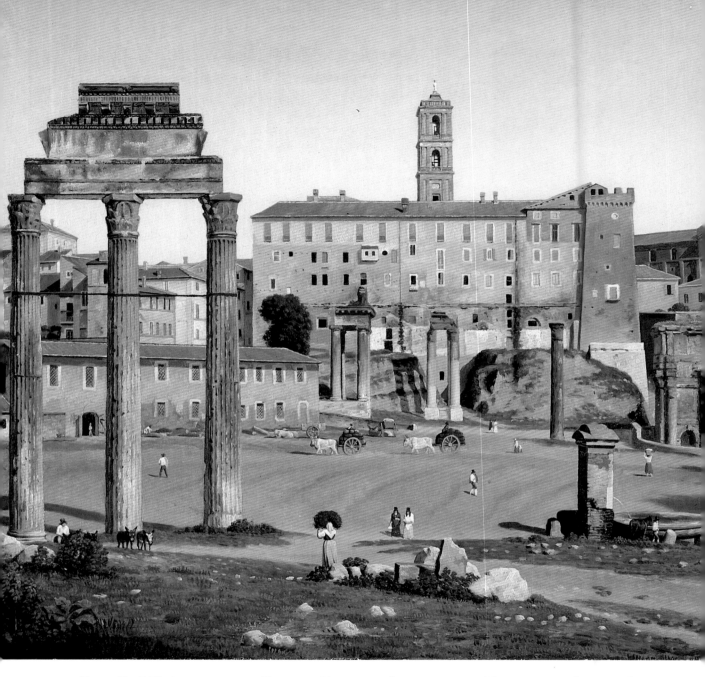

Christoffer Wilhelm Eckersberg, *View of the Forum in Rome*, 1814.

Tomassoni in a quarrel over a gaming debt, at a time when even his kindest supporters were despairing of this *'stravagante e scavezzacollo'* (extravagant and headstrong) personality, and he had fled precipitately from Rome. Caravaggio's fame would by then have guaranteed a home and patrons wherever he chose to settle, but after outstaying his welcome in Naples, Sicily and Malta, he was hastening home to a papal pardon and the realization of his dearest wish, to fill every church in Rome with his paintings.

The parallel has been made by novelists and film-makers, perhaps

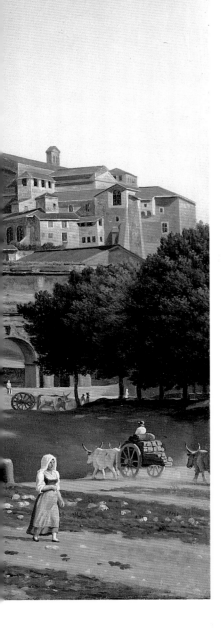

exaggerating the decadence of the painter's friends and protectors, between the Rome of Caravaggio, with orchards, vineyards and melancholy acres of picturesque ruins disappearing as the baroque urban vistas advanced, and the sleaze and *speculazione edilizia*, the illicit housing boom of the modern post-war years. A neater comparison might be with the Rome of Gioachino Belli, a morose, introverted civil servant whose scurrilous, funny and often rumbustiously obscene verse in Roman dialect immortalizes the street life of the city in the 1830s and 40s. The alleyways and piazzas where Caravaggio strutted, sword in hand, were very much the same then, before the dread hand of the northern Piedmontese destroyed so much of the old town by turning this warm, generous-hearted baroque city into the capital of a newly united Italy. Cows still grazed in the Forum, the Campo Vaccino, vineyards and orchards nestled between ceremonial pilgrim ways and grand palaces, and the wild herbs that flourished on ruins and patches of vacant ground perfumed salads and stews. The noisy, raunchy, good-tempered knockabout humour of this proud but in some ways provincial Rome might well have been more congenial to Caravaggio than the alienated urban sprawl evoked by Pasolini and Moravia in the 1940s and 50s.

A dish that would never make today's gastro-tourist menus is *pajata*, typical of the way popular Roman cooking makes imaginative use of morsels discarded further up the social scale. The intestines of young animals are cleaned, leaving the milky residue within intact, twisted into pretzel shapes, cooked slowly in an aromatic sauce, and served with hefty ribbed *rigatoni* and characteristic insolence by hosts who would have been all too familiar to Platina and Belli.

These coarse, tasty morsels devoured by cardinals and street urchins in Belli's sonnets were tamed but not emasculated a century later by an enterprising young Roman housewife. By the time she was twelve the entrancing Ada Boni had already set her mind on her life's partner and her chosen career. Her passion for cooking progressed from preparing exquisite treats for her family to journalism, broadcasting and a cooking school in Rome where genteel young ladies recreated the robust dishes of trattorias and family kitchens, not such a far cry from the rowdy Roman taverns of four hundred years earlier, which Platina claimed were the 'grammar schools of gastronomy'. A big hug from Queen Margherita at the opera launched Ada into high society, to remind Romans of their fast disappearing culinary heritage.

A version of this recipe for beef olives figures in Platina's book of 1465 and Boni's *Il Talismano della Felicità* (*The Talisman of Happiness*) of 1932 and her classic work on the cooking of Rome.

Beef or Veal Olives   SERVES 4

8 thin slices of rump steak or
   fillet of veal, about 500 g
   (generous 1 lb)
Olive oil
FOR THE STUFFING:
50 g (2 oz) Parma ham, diced

100 g (1 cup) freshly grated
   Parmesan
1 tbsp chopped fresh marjoram
1 tsp fennel seeds
Salt & pepper
A little chopped garlic if desired

Flatten the beef or veal slices and spread some of the stuffing over
each one. Roll up and secure with strong thread or string. Grill
(broil) or fry in olive oil until browned outside and done within,
about 15 minutes.

Roast Lamb

The fragrant lamb from the Abruzzi hills is roasted or grilled, flavoured
with the pungent local herbs, rosemary, sage or marjoram. There is no
substitute, but something comparable can be achieved using well hung
milk lamb, cooked unfashionably long and slow. Take a whole shoul-
der, trim off surplus fat and pierce with the tip of a sharp knife at points
to admit slivers of peeled garlic and rosemary leaves. Rub all over with
salt and roast on a rack in a baking pan with a glass each of dry white
wine and water in the bottom to catch the drippings. Cook for 2 to 3
hours in a low to moderate oven. The meat should carve easily, best
done before serving, with some of the pan juices (skimmed of their fat)
poured over.

It has been said that much of the popular public food of Rome used
the leftover offal and extremities from papal and noble tables, but in
fact nothing was ever wasted even in the grandest kitchens, where a
delicate brawn from pigs' ears and snouts would figure alongside a
tender loin of veal or spit-roast chicken. 'Apostolic Broth', a delicate
herb soup made from a rich meat stock using up scraps of offal and
meat, comes from Scappi's recipe book.

Lovage has a powerful flavour resembling celery leaves, which
are a possible substitute; a little more lemon zest could replace the
lemon balm if this is unavailable.

Apostolic Broth   SERVES 6

500 g (generous 1 lb) spinach
4 dark green cos (romaine)
   lettuce leaves
A few leaves each of sage, rosemary, marjoram and thyme
1 bunch each of all or any of these
   fresh herbs: parsley, lovage,

mint and lemon balm
2 litres (4 quarts) good home-
   made meat or chicken stock
2 egg yolks
3 tbsps single (light) cream
Salt & pepper
Lemon juice and zest

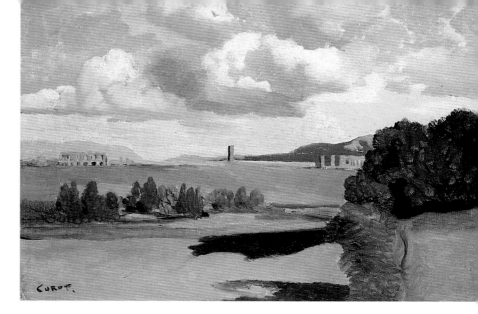

Jean-Baptiste-Camille Corot, *The Roman Campagna, with the Claudian Aqueduct*, probably 1826.

Wash, shake dry and chop the spinach, lettuce leaves and herbs or process them in some of the stock. Add to the rest of the stock in a pan. Simmer gently for a very short time, then stir in the egg yolks mixed with the cream to thicken slightly. Overcooked the fresh green colour will be lost and the eggs could curdle. . . Season before serving with salt, pepper, a drop or two of lemon juice and a rasping of zest.

Think of cows grazing on the Forum and gentle buffaloes chewing away in the silent spaces of the Campagna and try to imagine the superb quality ricotta and mozzarella that go into so many simple Roman dishes. Tasteless imports from far-away Nordic lands are no substitute for these rich dairy products. The delicate purity of a fine, creamy ricotta is pleasant on its own, spread on bread and sprinkled with sugar for breakfast or supper.

Coffee, that infidel drink, had been baptized by the prudent Pope Clement VIII, but it took another century for it to filter down from Venice and so would have been unknown to Caravaggio, who would have been even more impossible with the ubiquitous espresso augmenting the adrenaline already generated by his confrontational social life.

Creamed Ricotta with Coffee SERVES 6

500 g (generous 1 lb) fresh Italian ricotta
2 tsps freshly ground coffee, as fine as possible
250 g (generous 1 cup) vanilla sugar
1 wine glass of rum
1 tsp cinnamon sugar (Renaissance Stardust, page 49)

Beat or process the ricotta until smooth. Add the other ingredients and mix some more. Serve chilled, sprinkled with some Renaissance Stardust.

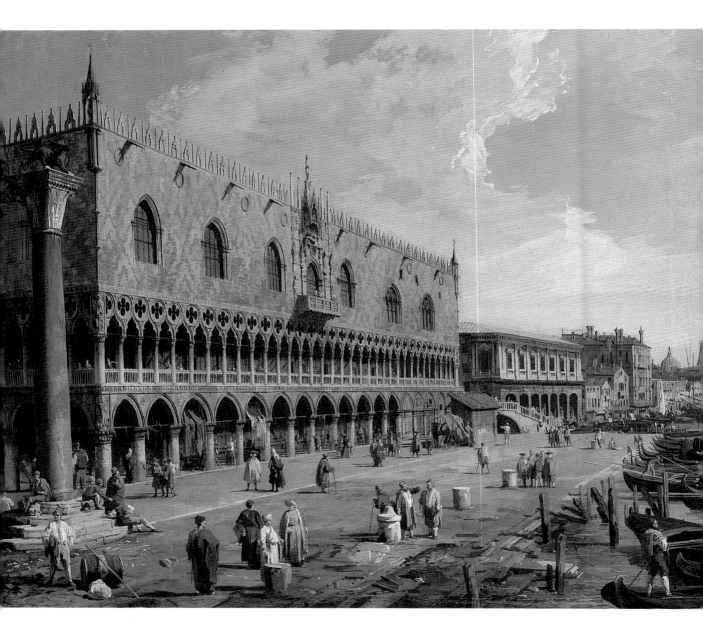

The Pleasures & Perils
OF CASANOVA'S VENICE

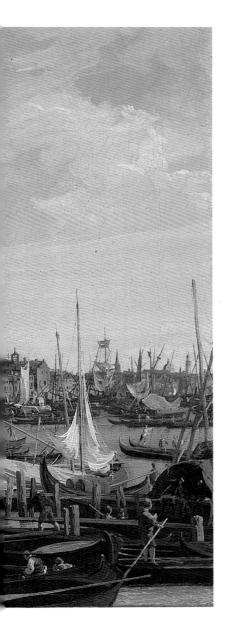

Canaletto, *Venice: The Doge's Palace and the Riva degli Schiavoni*, late 1730s.

On All Saints' Day 1756 Giacomo Casanova clambered over the roof-tops of the Piombi, the notorious Venetian State Prison where he was immured on a trumped up charge, and escaped through a hole hacked out of the ceiling of the Council Chamber. With his characteristic blend of cool and bravado, he strode briskly, no signs of panic, down the steps of the Ducal palace to the waterfront shown here by Canaletto and called loudly for a two-man gondola to take him to Fusina, thereby putting his pursuers off the scent as he made his way in the opposite direction to Mestre and safety.

Not the least of the privations and miseries endured during Casanova's eighteen months of captivity had been the renunciation of salads – he had insisted on a supply of the finest olive oil from Lucca, but had used it to fuel an illicit lamp instead. *'Addio insalata!'* It would have been unthinkable to a fastidious Italian to eat the greenery without the most important ingredient of all, olive oil, so Casanova did without both and secretly engineered his escape – holes in walls and ceilings, setbacks, betrayal and gastronomic hardship ensued, recalled years later as a gripping after-dinner narrative.

Leaving Casanova to enjoy his freedom, we return to the waterfront. Centuries before his escapade Venice had emerged from primeval slime, an improbable settlement of fishermen and traders secure on banks of shifting ooze from the elements and marauding pirates, to evolve eventually into a successful maritime nation and a sort of self-governing, self-regulating, prickly, as often as not corrupt, political entity, with tentacles stretching all over the Adriatic and beyond. With the Lion of Saint Mark a fitting symbol of her supremacy, the Republic grew and prospered; her appointed ruler, the Doge, enacted on Saint Mark's Day, 25 June, a solemn marriage ceremony between Venice and the sea, her master, sometimes destroyer and often benefactor.

Canaletto's tourist-postcard paintings were faithful to the astonishing beauty and serenity of this great city, familiar views for native sons like Casanova, grateful refugees like Giacomo Castelvetro a century earlier, and visitors from far and wide. Perhaps the most eloquent record of the supremacy of Venice in the early years of her prime was by the painter Vittore Carpaccio, whose canvases depict a self-contained world of prosperous people going inscrutably

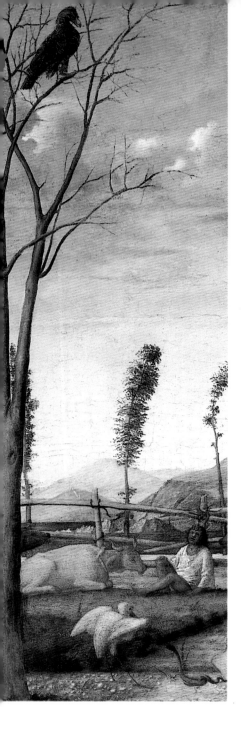

Giovanni Bellini, details
from *The Madonna of the
Meadow*, about 1500.

about their daily lives, getting vast riches and spending them with decorum, rendering due respect to God and Mammon. Carpaccio's long career, from the 1480s to 1525, much of it as one of the official painters of the Republic, spanned a period when Venice was shifting its power base from the Orient to the Italian mainland, gathering territorial possessions and enjoying the butter, cheeses and meat they supplied. His contemporary Giovanni Bellini gives enchanting glimpses of Venice's links with the land; in the background to his *The Madonna of the Meadow* are cows, tended by caring humans, in their pastures and byres. As well as the rich goodness of their milk and meat these cherished creatures were the warm, sustaining heart of every peasant home during the bleak winter months. Each evening after the household chores were done and the meagre fire had died down, the family would abandon the chilly farmhouse and crowd together for the *filò* in the byre, when, by the mellow light of lamp and candles, they sat comfortably on bales of hay, knitting and sewing, gossiping and telling tales of recent family events and ancient legends, with neighbours dropping in, spruced-up lads come to court the girls and elderly relatives round for a sip of grappa, in the fragrant fug of human and animal warmth.

A cherished creature with so many beneficent contributions to the fabric of rural life would often be quite mature by the time it came to be cooked. Here is a traditional Venetian recipe using a cheap cut of meat, which needs long slow braising.

Marinated Braised Beef   SERVES 6

1.5 kg shin of beef (about 3¼ lbs blade of beef), all in one piece
2 medium onions, chopped
4 garlic cloves, chopped
6 bay and 12 sage leaves

200 ml (¾ cup) good quality mild red wine vinegar
Olive oil
Salt & pepper
Meat stock as required

Marinate the beef, onions, garlic and herbs in the vinegar for 24 hours, turning from time to time. Take the meat from the marinade, wipe it dry and brown it on all sides in the olive oil. Tip in the marinade ingredients, season and cook gently, uncovered, until the liquid is absorbed. Top up with a little stock, cover, and cook slowly in a low oven for 2 or 3 hours, adding more stock if need be. The meat should become very tender, bathed in a small amount of rich, unctuous juice.

This is very good with polenta which did not arrive until much later, but which has now become a staple accompaniment to many northern dishes, either served soft and runny from the pot, or cooled, sliced and grilled or fried. The labour of stirring the boiling pot for forty minutes or more is well worth the result (not achieved by using the 'instant' variety), a fragrant, soothing yellow mush which makes a nice change from potatoes.

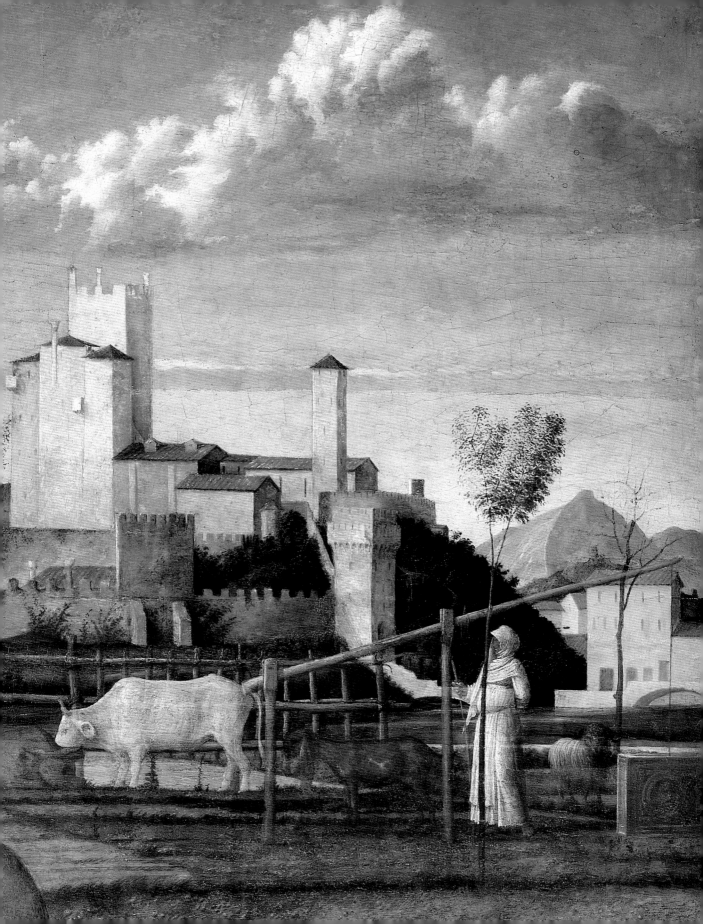

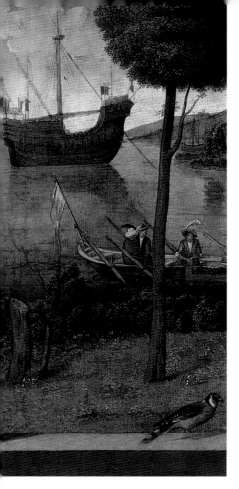

Vittore Carpaccio, detail from *Saint Ursula taking Leave of her Father (?)*, probably about 1500.

Carpaccio's sympathies lay with the old guard, or 'Lunghi', who preferred heroic battles with wind and wave and the cut and thrust of commerce rather than the murky adventures of territorial expansion of the modernizing faction, the 'Curti'. The old-fashioned gastronomy of the Republic was redolent of spices and expensive products shipped from far and wide, their rich complexity echoed in Carpaccio's series of official paintings of the legends and lives of the saints, spread like *bandes dessinées* around the walls of churches and schools.

Spices were used with restraint to produce a subtle, complex cuisine. Arab gastronomy was at one time the most luxurious in the known world, and its sophisticated use of spices entranced the uncouth Europeans emerging from the Dark Ages. The beguiling aromas of cinnamon, cloves, musk and rosewater had wafted up through Italy from the south, where Arab, Viking and Byzantine tastes cohabited with hedonistic pragmatism. Venetian merchants in the north supplied shiploads of this high-risk but greatly rewarding commodity. Later on Crusaders came reeling home from the Holy Land besotted with the culture they had failed to destroy, and demanded *paklava* instead of mother's apple pie, *bstilla*, tender pigeon with almonds in a sugar and cinnamon-encrusted pastry, rather than the greasy boiled meats of home. The Italian genius for commerce and fine living rose to the occasion, and spices became status symbols and instruments of pleasure and prestige, generating vast wealth for the hard-headed merchants who procured them.

Chicken in a Spicy Sauce   SERVES 6

1 free range chicken, cut into pieces
500 ml (2¾ cups) chicken stock
1 tbsp sugar
2 cm (¾ in) stick of cinnamon
5 cloves
100 g (⅔ cup) ground almonds
1 tbsp grated fresh ginger
2 tbsps sour grape, bitter orange or lemon juice
Rosewater

Cook the chicken pieces in the stock until almost done, about 30 minutes. Remove them and keep warm. Pulverize the sugar, cinnamon and cloves and stir some of this and the ground almonds into the liquid. Simmer until it thickens. Add the ginger and the grape or lemon juice, return the chicken pieces to the sauce and cook for 10 more minutes. Perfume with rosewater just before serving. It is as well to taste as you go along, adding the sweet and sour elements to achieve an agreeable balance.

Opposite: Attributed to Vittore Carpaccio, detail from *The Adoration of the Kings*, probably about 1490.

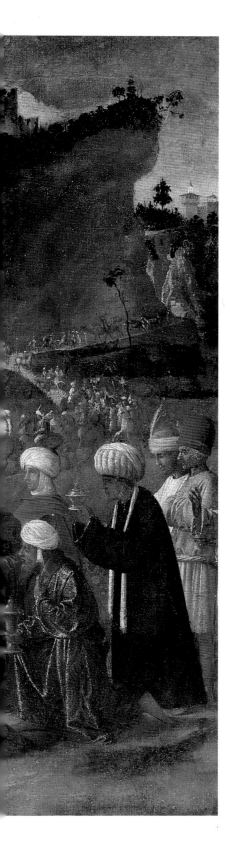

This thick sauce, like many medieval and Renaissance relishes, goes well with chicken or fish and plain boiled rice or risotto.

Spiced Prawn (Shrimp) Sauce   SERVES 4

500 g (generous 1 lb) shell-on prawns (shrimp)
1 garlic clove, chopped
125 ml (½ cup) dry white wine
Freshly ground spices:
   ½ tsp fennel seeds, 2 cloves, 2 cardamom pods, 6 black peppercorns, 1 blade of mace,
1 cm (½ in) stick of cinnamon
2 bay leaves
125 g (1 cup) ground almonds
1 egg yolk
2 tbsps chopped fresh herbs such as parsley, thyme and basil
Olive oil

Shell the prawns (shrimp) and marinate them in the garlic, half the wine and some of the spices. Cook the shells and debris in the rest of the wine with a little water and the bay leaves to get about 150 ml (⅔ cup) of concentrated stock. Strain into a saucepan, add the ground almonds and simmer until it starts to thicken. Add the egg yolk, prawns (shrimp) and their marinade, herbs and more spices to taste and a dash of olive oil. Stir and warm through without boiling. Serve hot or tepid as a sauce to plain baked fillets of sea bass or red snapper.

One of the consolations of murky, damp winters days is the pleasure with which rich Venetians, unable to flaunt an expensive car, dress themselves and their wives in ankle-length mink coats, in the sartorial tradition of the time of Carpaccio. Another is the arrival of the first harbingers of spring, long before swallows and violets: tiny baby artichokes, no bigger than walnuts, which are enjoyed raw, *al pinzimonio*, dipped in a puddle of olive oil with salt and pepper.

Venetian artichokes were described with enthusiasm by Giacomo Castelvetro, a native of Modena who had worked for over twelve years in the book trade in Venice. He, like Casanova, had had a bad time in the Piombi and dined out often on the experience. In 1609 Castelvetro fell into the grip of the Inquisition. Hardly a surprise, for his outspoken Protestantism and possible connection with the scheme of Sir Henry Wotton, the British ambassador, to convert the whole of the Venetian Republic to the reformed religion, made him a marked man. After some high level diplomatic activity (Castelvetro had once been Italian tutor to James I of England), he was freed and departed for exile in England. There, homesick, he set out to wean the English from their gross consumption of meat and sweet things by writing beguilingly of the fruit and vegetables of his native Italy, with simple ways of preparing them. Castelvetro described the advantages, later in the season, of buying ready-trimmed artichoke 'bottoms' (Venetian dialect has even earthier

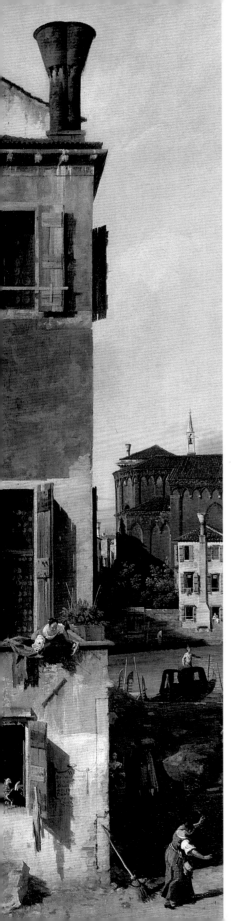

names for them) from the market women who, with a sharp knife and a deft twist of the wrist, would cut away all the leaves and choke, rub them with a cut lemon, and send the purchaser on her way, all the hard work done, to simmer them in olive oil, a little water, garlic, salt, pepper and fresh mint, to be eaten cold or tepid, or used with other things in pies and tarts. These 'bottoms' have always made a cheap and plentiful vegetable with an earthy taste and texture, a sort of potato *avant la lettre*.

The very first young artichokes are prepared by cutting away the outer leaves and retaining the stem and heart, whose inedible hairy choke has not yet developed. Ways of cooking them aroused violent emotions, as we observed in Baroque Rome.

Passionate about salads, Castelvetro explained how to make a good *mischianza*: a selection of fresh young herbs and salad leaves was washed carefully, well dried and seasoned with a little salt, not much vinegar and plenty of oil. The perfect version might be perfumed with a few drops of genuine traditional balsamic vinegar from Modena, a product with no resemblance at all to some faked-up commercial versions.

Italian style Vegetables

Hardly a recipe, more a way of life. The freshest vegetables can be cooked in little water, or none at all if, like spinach, they create their own liquid, thus avoiding the barbaric practice of throwing away flavour and vitamins with the cooking water. When nicely done, not *al dente* (a term applied to pasta not vegetables, and a cruel way to treat something that should be served up tender, not crunchy), the vegetables may be served tepid or at room temperature with a dressing of good olive oil, Seville orange or lemon juice and salt and pepper.

Castelvetro's Garlic Broccoli

Two or three chopped cloves of garlic cooked with each serving of broccoli in just a little water somehow disposes of the rank cooking smells which can inhibit our use of the brassica vegetables. By the time the water has evaporated the broccoli will be just tender, to serve hot or at room temperature with good olive oil, Seville orange juice and plenty of pepper.

Fresh herbs and salad plants lose their aromas rapidly after cutting, so many Venetian housewives grew pots of them for instant use. Castelvetro enjoyed the way they ogled passers-by from behind screens of French beans planted in window boxes, and Canaletto, over a century later, painted similar homely details in the *Campo San Vidal*.

The prickly and waspish Pietro Aretino was another polemical writer who, like Castelvetro, took refuge in the tolerant climate of Venice. In 1525 he left Rome under a cloud and settled down to the congenial vocation of publishing witty, eloquent and often scurrilous letters about his famous contemporaries, who were only too glad to reward him handsomely for his praise of their virtues or bribe him heavily to keep silent about the rest. Once, pausing to point out his friend Titian's studio to some visitors, he smelled the enticing aroma of spit-roast birds, abandoned his companions on the doorstep and invited himself to lunch.

Quails in Vine Leaves SERVES 4

4 ready prepared quails
Salt & pepper
1 garlic clove, chopped
4 very thin slices of Parma ham
Lemon zest

12 fresh vine leaves
1 small wine glass of dry white wine
A knob of butter

Season the birds inside and outside with the salt, pepper and garlic. Fold a slice of Parma ham around each one, scrape on a little lemon zest then wrap the quail up in vine leaves, tying each little parcel up with fine string. Lay them in an ovenproof dish, pour over the wine and roast in a hot oven for 30 minutes, topping up the wine if necessary. When done put the birds on a serving dish, removing any scorched vine leaves. Swirl a knob of butter into the cooking juices and pour over before serving.

Aretino rejected the convention of writing serious prose in Latin – he penned his pungent, witty letters in the Italian vernacular, just as his friend Titian portrayed the subjects of religious paintings in modern dress rather than in the classical garments of the past.

Venetian painters sometimes worked topographical details and even portraits of contemporaries into the fabric of their paintings, from the vast cavernous kitchen in Tintoretto's *Christ washing the Disciples' Feet* to *The Family of Darius before Alexander* of Veronese, whose protagonists, dressed in the height of fashion, are grouped in a grandiose palace courtyard.

Veronese's worldly portrayal of religious subjects got him into trouble with the Inquisition but he wriggled his way out, re-naming the opulent modern banquet in his Last Supper, with its richly dressed women and effeminate courtiers, *Supper in the House of Levi*. Details of food in these elaborate meals were implied rather than rendered with the clarity of a still life, but the voluptuous tones of flesh and brocade have all the sensuousness of food. Pink prawns

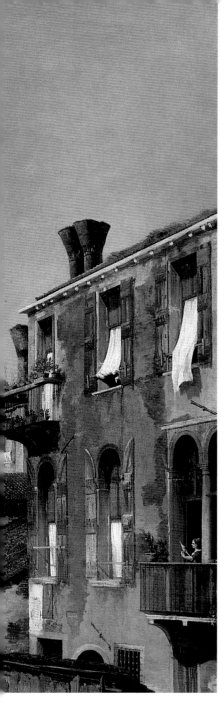

Canaletto, details from
Venice: Campo S. Vidal and Santa Maria della Carità ('The Stonemason's Yard'), 1726–30.

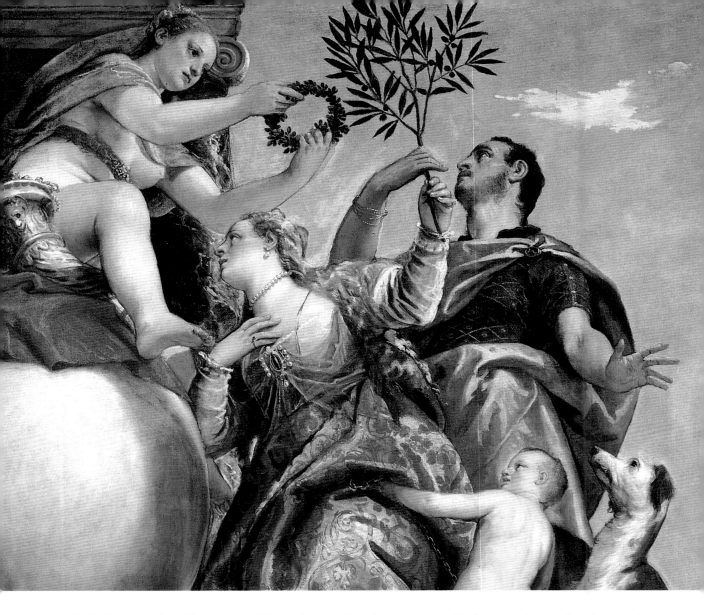

Paolo Veronese, detail from *Allegory of Love, IV ('Happy Union')*, probably 1570s.

(shrimp) stirred into buttery scrambled eggs and served with a swirl of cream on leaves of red Treviso radicchio glow like the lush protagonists of Veronese's *Allegory of Love*.

Fresh vegetables and salads were brought by boat to the markets of Venice from the mainland and the fertile islands on the Lagoon. The tiny early peas were especially prized, and were eaten ceremoniously by the Doge every year on Saint Mark's Day in *Risi e Bisi*, a simple dish of rice and peas which is much greater than the sum of its parts. If the peas are very tender they will take less time to cook than the rice; if they are big and getting a bit floury they will take more. The tiny little peas of Saint Mark's Day need to be added to the rice after ten minutes cooking. Thus the amount of stock required will vary somewhat.

Risi & Bisi   SERVES 4

1 medium onion, chopped
1 tbsp each of butter and olive oil
400 g (scant 3 cups) Italian rice
   such as *Vialone Nano,*
   Carnaroli or *Arborio*
400 ml (1⅔ cups) good chicken
   stock, more or less

1 kg (generous 2 lbs) fresh young
   peas (weight before shelling),
   shelled
1 slice of Parma ham, cut up small
Salt & pepper
Freshly grated Parmesan to serve
   separately

Soften the onion in the butter and oil. Stir in the rice. Pour in the
stock and bring to the boil. Reduce the heat and simmer, covered, for
10 minutes. Add the peas and Parma ham, bring to the boil again, and
simmer until done, adding more stock if it seems to be getting dry.
Season with salt and pepper if necessary. Take off the lid and let some
of the liquid evaporate if it seems too runny. Dot with a little butter
just before serving with the Parmesan.

Squid & Peas

The combination of squid and peas is irresistible. Simmer some
prepared sliced squid in water and dry white wine for 2 to 2½ hours
together with a seasoning of chopped onion, garlic and bay leaves.
Add the peas towards the end of cooking, timing depends on age, and
simmer until done. This rich, aromatic dish is good with plain bread
and a robust wine, red or white.

Fish, fresh from the Lagoon or the Adriatic, grilled or fried and
served with a little olive oil and a squeeze of lemon, needs no recipe.
Some Venetian ways of cooking fish are surprising, though, in their
ingenuity.

Sea Bass with Sage & Grappa   SERVES 4

12 fresh sage leaves
1 sprig of parsley
1 garlic clove
4 black peppercorns
1 tsp rock salt
1 tbsp or more of butter

2 medium sea bass, cleaned, with
   heads and tails removed
1 small wine glass of dry white
   wine
Grappa or brandy

Mash the sage, parsley, garlic, peppercorns, salt and butter in a mortar
or food processor. Spread this into the fish cavities, keeping 2 teaspoons over. Put the fish in an ovenproof dish and pour over the wine.
Dot with the rest of the aromatic butter. Bake in a hot oven for 15 to
20 minutes. When only just done take out of the oven and pour over a
good slug of grappa. Set the lot alight. If you do this at table have a
lid the size of the dish to hand to douse excessive combustion.

Other recipes are equally surprising in their simplicity. If red mullet isn't obtainable, red snapper fillets make an excellent substitute in this delicious dish.

Baked Red Mullet SERVES 4

Olive oil

4 medium-sized red mullet (or snapper), filleted and scaled (8 fillets in all)

4 slices of Parma ham

8 sage leaves

Salt & pepper

A little dry white wine

Oil an ovenproof dish big enough to hold the fish assembled as explained below. Lay a slice of ham on each of four of the fillets and put two sage leaves and a grating of pepper on top of each one. Cover each fillet with another fillet and press together. Brush the tops of the fillets with a little oil and arrange in the prepared dish. Bake in a hot oven until done, about 10 to 15 minutes depending on the thickness of the fillets. Remove the fish to a serving dish and boil down any cooking juices with a little wine to get a concentrated sauce, taste and add salt if necessary.

Looking back in 1787, Casanova never could understand why he had been imprisoned, for his behaviour was neither better nor worse than that of the countless pleasure-seeking, frivolous, and not so frivolous, libertines who flocked to Venice in the ultimate stages of her decline. He would certainly have appreciated Cleopatra's banquet sketched by Tiepolo in a setting of opulent Venetian splendour, with a richly laid table in a baroque courtyard, gold and silver plate on the vast *credenza*, and an obsequious page proffering the goblet of wine in which Cleopatra, with characteristic extravagance and bloody-mindedness, is about to dissolve a million-dollar pearl. Maybe a reflection on how Venice itself, the Pearl of the Adriatic, cut off from the mainstream of political and diplomatic Europe, was dissolving in a whirl of mindless decadence.

Casanova would have made a brilliant food writer – apart from his own incorrigible hedonism, the first requisite, he had a keen memory for detail, particularly for measurements. Sceptics who checked his meticulous accounts of the various prison cells and his tortuous escape route were confounded by the accuracy of his observations. Unfortunately for us he was too much of an artist to interrupt the carefully crafted flow of his narrative to digress into gastronomic details; nothing at all about the lavish meal and fine wines ordered by a temporary cell-mate, the rich Count Tommaso Fenaroli, but devoured by our hero. One of the dishes could have been this recipe from a northern Italian cookery manuscript of about the same period.

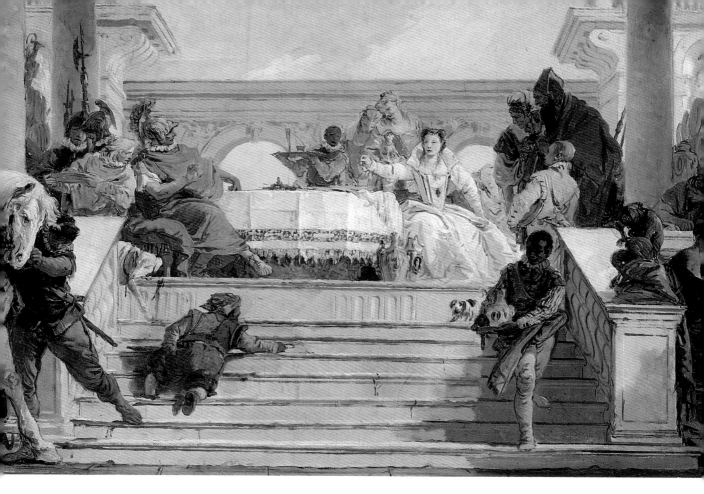

Giovanni Battista Tiepolo, detail from *The Banquet of Cleopatra*, 1740s.

Casserole of Turkey Escalopes   SERVES 4

600 g (1½ lbs) turkey breast fillet, skinned and thinly sliced (about 8–10 slices)
6 finely chopped shallots, softened in butter, lightly salted
225 g (½ lb) mushrooms, sliced, cooked briskly in butter, lightly salted
50 g (½ cup) good breadcrumbs
50 g (½ cup) chopped fresh parsley
50 g (½ cup) whole basil leaves
Freshly ground black pepper
Olive oil
125 g (4 oz) pancetta or dry-cured unsmoked bacon, sliced
1 wine glass dry white wine
Salt

Put a layer of turkey slices in an ovenproof casserole, strew with shallots, mushrooms, breadcrumbs and the herbs, pepper and a little oil; continue with layers of turkey and aromatics and finish with the bacon slices, overlapping to make a nice cover. Pour over the wine and cook in a moderate oven until the turkey is done, about 50 minutes. The bacon may have provided enough salt, so taste and adjust before serving. Sharpen the sauce with lemon juice if necessary, but taste first, as many a fine dish can be ruined by an ill-judged addition of lemon.

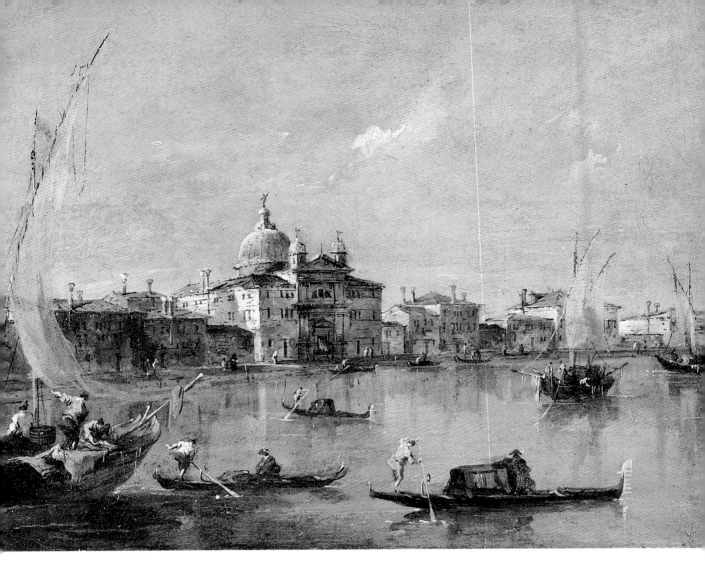

Francesco Guardi, *Venice:
The Giudecca with the Zitelle*,
1780s.

Throwaway lines about how in his dejection Casanova had nothing but soup for supper, or how the intense heat took away his appetite for a meal of rice, make frustrating reading. Once a luxury ingredient, but by the eighteenth century a staple crop in Italy, rice was probably one of the more interesting items of food prisoners could send out for with their not ungenerous subsistence allowance.

Risotto is the most versatile and satisfying medium for enjoying the wonderful varieties of rice. Simply cooked with no preliminary frying, in a light chicken stock coloured and flavoured with saffron and enriched at the end of cooking with a lump of butter and a generous amount of Parmesan, a plain risotto is unbeatable. Vegetarian versions can be made with asparagus cooking water or the liquid in which dried mushrooms have been soaked. The marriage of good quality rice such as *Arborio*, *Vialone Nano* or *Carnaroli* with good local seafood remains one of the glories of Venetian cuisine.

Seafood Risotto SERVES 6

Fish stock made from the bones and trimmings of the fish, the prawn (shrimp) shells, ½ tsp saffron, 1 large tomato, 2 bay leaves, 2 garlic cloves, 250 ml (1 cup) dry white wine and 1 litre (2 quarts) water
450 lb (1 lb) *Arborio* or other good Italian risotto rice
2 garlic cloves, chopped
Salt & pepper
500 g (generous 1 lb) firm-fleshed fish such as halibut, monkfish, swordfish, skinned, filleted and cut into small cubes
500 g (generous 1 lb) cooked shell-on prawns (shrimp)
500 g (generous 1 lb) mussels, scrubbed and cooked briefly in a wine-glass of dry white wine, the liquid strained and added to the stock

Start off by bringing about half the stock to the boil in a wide, shallow pan (presenting the maximum surface for the rapid evaporation of the liquid), put in the rice and garlic, bring back to the boil and cook for 15 minutes, stirring frequently and adding more stock as needed. At this point taste to check the saltiness, add some if necessary. Just before the rice is done add more stock and the prepared fish and cook gently, shaking the pan to avoid breaking it up. At the last minute season with freshly ground black pepper and add the prawns (shrimp) and mussels to warm through, stir carefully and serve at once.

Purists might prefer white pepper, but the black is more aromatic and the dark specks are quite acceptable in this dish. Freshly grated Parmesan is an optional additional seasoning.

A very simple risotto can be made with plain water or stock from *bollito misto* (boiled mixed meats); a handful of chopped bronze fennel stirred in with a little freshly grated Parmesan at the end makes a fine summer first course; or try cooking the rice with plenty of bay leaves and some diced pumpkin, and serve with a flourish in the hollowed out pumpkin shell as a comforting winter's dish.

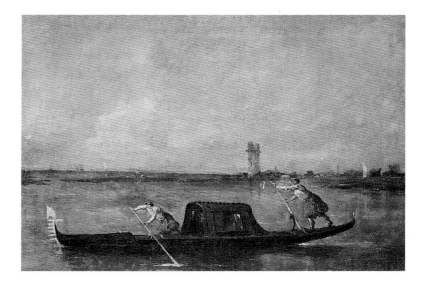

Francesco Guardi,
A Gondola on the Lagoon near Mestre, after 1780.

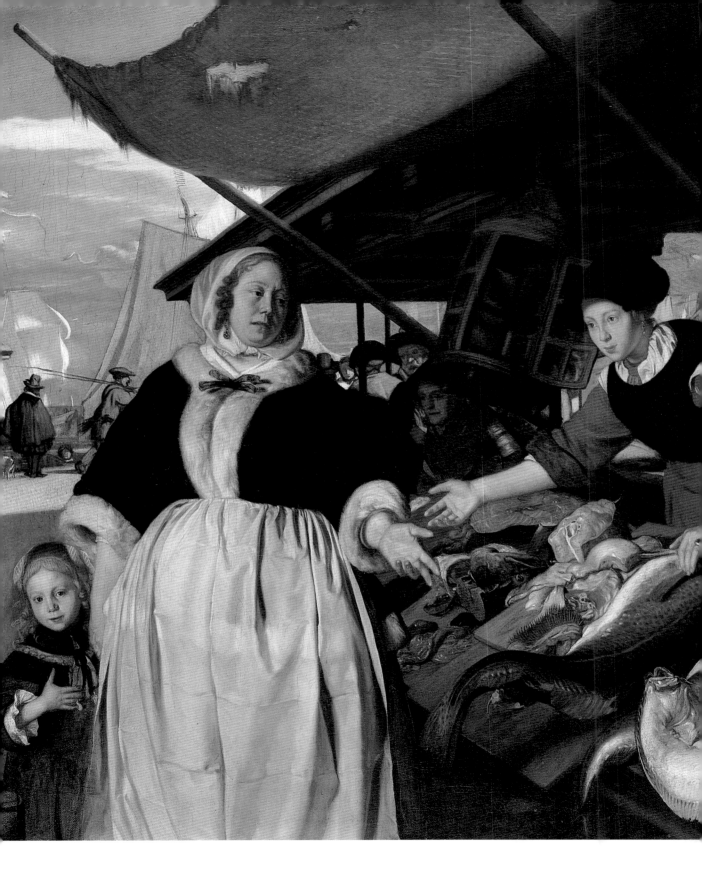

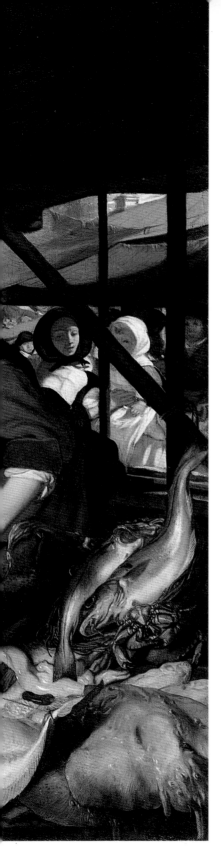

Squalls & Squabbles
IN AMSTERDAM FISHMARKET

Nothing but the best for Adriana van Heusden and her little daughter. The freshest of fresh fish, unloaded that minute from the quayside at the Haarlem Lock, straight on to the stalls of the New Fishmarket in Amsterdam. A quick dash between showers, braving the bitter east wind, with a harsh early spring sunshine striking low on the red flannel overblouse and raw hands of the marketwoman and the child's rosy cheeks. Adriana bargains with robust dignity for the turbot, haddock and monkfish on offer, her ample form padded out in a smart, fur-lined jacket and protected by a beautifully laundered, full-length cotton apron. Her husband, Joris de Wijs, must have been proud to have this image of Adriana in her prime painted in 1662 by the artist Emanuel de Witte, at that time their lodger. It is sad to record that the painting subsequently set them all at loggerheads, with bitter recriminations and lawsuits about payment and price – quite lacking the decorum of Adriana's marketing. De Witte muddied the waters by producing several versions of the original from which he refused to be parted, and the dispute rumbled on for decades, with Adriana's second husband embroiled in the fray. We shall never know who won the battle for ownership. There is mystery, too, attached to de Witte's death; he disappeared during the winter of 1692, and his body only came to light when the canals defrosted in the early spring.

Contemporary Dutch recipe books included some agreeable sauces for fish using the characteristic flavourings of the mid-seventeenth century such as nutmeg, mace, cloves and cinnamon – a strangely restricted range, considering that Holland dominated the world's spice trade, with every exotic condiment known to man perfuming the holds of her powerful merchant vessels.

Fish with Butter and Spices

Season a fish such as sea bass or trout with a mixture of nutmeg, mace and pepper mixed with butter, the roe of the fish if you can get it and chopped hard-boiled (hard-cooked) eggs. After baking in plenty of butter, remove the fish and mash two or three anchovies in the cooking juices until they dissolve, add a squeeze of lemon, check the seasoning and pour over the fish. One recipe of the time suggests decorating the rim of the serving dish with a sprinkling of oregano.

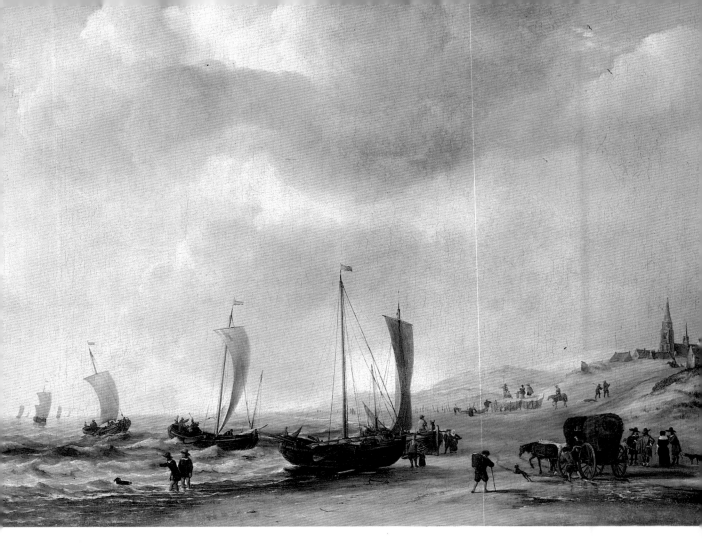

Willem van de Velde the
Younger, *The Shore at
Scheveningen*, about 1660.

Opposite: Peter Paul Rubens,
*Portrait of Ludovicus
Nonnius*, about 1627.

Previous page: Emanuel de Witte,
*Adriana van Heusden and her
Daughter at the New Fishmarket in
Amsterdam*, about 1662.

Another way to get fresh fish was to dash down to the beach as the
boats came in and trudge home across the dunes with the pick of the
catch. Here a party of smart folk dismount from a carriage as fishing
boats arrive on the beach at Scheveningen. One can do the same today, though the dunes look much less romantic now, flattened out
and reinforced against the buffeting of the tides with lorryloads of
sand and grit brought in to replace the erosion of wind and wave. The
huge ships arrive in the functional modern docks, and the smart folk
are now computerized buyers bidding in nanoseconds as the mech-
anically sorted catch lurches past on conveyor belts. It is a relief to
escape to the quayside where small shops still sell fine fresh fish, tiny
shrimp and plump prawns, mussels, smoked mackerel and eel, and
the traditional 'green herring' (almost raw after its short cure in
brine), which can be whisked home to the far from picturesque
modern apartment blocks in Scheveningen, where women still dust
and polish in their long cotton aprons, as neat and trim as Adriana's.

Baked Fish   SERVES 4

1 kg (generous 2 lbs) cod or haddock fillets, skinned
The juice of 1 lemon
1 tsp salt
6 tbsps soft white breadcrumbs
8 black peppercorns and 4 blades of mace ground together with ½ tsp
   grated nutmeg
50 g (4 tbsps) or more unsalted butter

Sprinkle the fish with the lemon juice and a pinch of salt and set aside for 20 minutes. Mix the breadcrumbs and seasonings together. Generously butter an ovenproof dish that will take the fish in one layer and cover with half the breadcrumbs. Lay the fish on them, cover with the remaining breadcrumbs and dot lavishly with the remaining butter.

Bake in a hot oven for 10 to 15 minutes until the fish is only just done; it will go on cooking in the dish as you take it to table. (If overcooked the fish exudes its juices, becoming dry and fibrous as the flavour loses itself in the by now soggy breadcrumbs.)

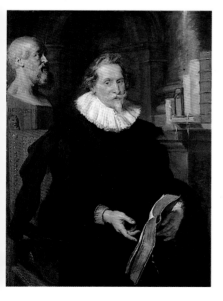

Herrings, the pride of the Low Countries, were not known to the ancient Greeks and Romans. This did not prevent the physician Ludovicus Nonnius from including them in his book about the eating habits of the ancient world, *Ichtyophagia sive Piscium esu commentarius* published in Antwerp in 1616. Nonnius, or Nuñez, from a family of Portuguese descent, must have been one of the earliest food historians, writing with enthusiasm and discrimination, plundering classical poets and dramatists for snippets of information about diet and health. The book he is holding in this portrait by Rubens might be his work on diet, *Diaeteticon*; a bust of Hippocrates, the father of medicine, looms in the background. When Nonnius came to write about herrings and salmon, too, his staid Latin becomes quite bubbly as he enthuses about these versatile, delicious fish – 'sweet, tender and tasty'. Salmon, he explained, were exported all over Europe, salted, smoked and fresh. Thick raw steaks do indeed glow in many genre and still life paintings, the warm colour adding gaiety to the monochrome contents of fish stall and kitchen table, matching the red jacket of the Amsterdam fishwife.

Although the rumour, from a perhaps overcredulous English tourist, about uppity servants in Ghent refusing to eat the vulgar salmon more than once a week has been dismissed by historians, there survive a fair number of interesting recipes for this versatile fish. Fresh wild salmon is best enjoyed simply cooked, but today's farmed fish will benefit from the ideas in this chapter. Mackerel or salmon trout would work well, too.

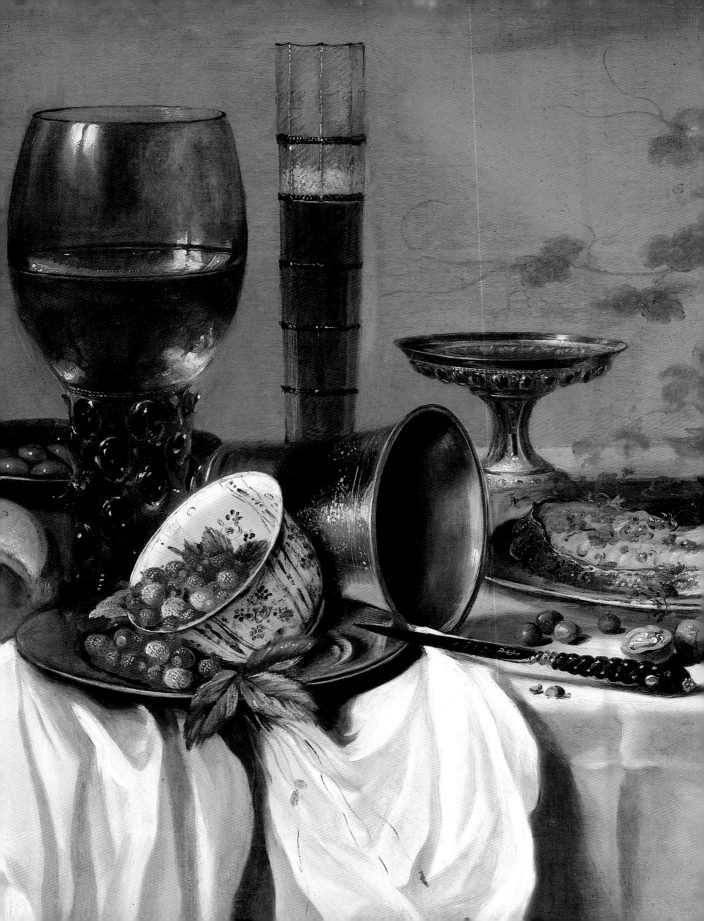

Spiced Salmon   SERVES 4

A salmon tail, about 1 kg (generous 2 lbs), scaled and boned
6 cloves
4 blades of mace, 6 black peppercorns, ½ tsp freshly grated nutmeg
  ground together with 1 tsp coarse rock salt
25 g (2 tbsps) unsalted butter
1 tbsp Seville or other sharp orange juice
1 tsp redcurrant jelly or, better still, 2 tbsps fresh destalked red
  currants, crushed

With the help of a sharp knife, stick the cloves into the outside of the
salmon tail, three on top, three underneath. Spread the salt and
ground spice mixture into the cavity left by the bone. Arrange the fish
in an ovenproof dish, cover with foil and bake in a moderate oven until
done, about 30 to 40 minutes. When cooked, remove the cloves and
skin from the salmon. Soften the butter in a small pan and whisk in
the orange juice. Stir in the jelly or crushed redcurrants and pour the
lot over the fish to give a spectacularly decorative sauce. Serve at once,
with plenty of good bread and a green salad.

Pieter Claesz. shows a cooked salmon cutlet in a subdued shade of
pink, swimming in its sauce of butter and capers, a rather rich dish.
The redcurrant sauce above is perhaps more appropriate, and indeed
a happier combination for rich fish than the traditional gooseberries
and mackerel, which also aims at a balance between acidity and
richness, for if the mackerel is rank and fatty and the gooseberries
acid and tasteless this can be a miserable partnership.

  The strawberries in this painting were probably intended to be
eaten on their own, not cowed by sugar and cream. This salad,
exploiting their tartness and perfume, goes well with the next
salmon recipe.

Strawberry Salad   SERVES 4

½ cucumber, peeled and sliced
1½ tsps salt
500 g (generous 1 lb)
  strawberries, hulled
6 spring onions (scallions),
  chopped
2 tbsps extra virgin olive oil

1 tsp sherry vinegar, or genuine
  traditional balsamic vinegar
  from Modena
1 tsp sugar
Freshly ground black pepper
Mint or purple basil leaves, to
  garnish

Lay the cucumber slices in a layer on a baking sheet and sprinkle over
1 teaspoon of salt. Set aside for 20 minutes. Rinse under cold running
water and pat dry with paper towels. If the strawberries are big cut
them into quarters, otherwise halve some and leave the rest whole.
Mix everything together and allow the flavours to develop for 5 or 10
minutes. Do not chill. Decorate with the mint or basil leaves.

Pieter Claesz., *Still Life with Drinking Vessels*, 1649.

The happy combination of grappa and fish in North Italian cooking does not seem to have its counterpart in Holland, but here is a recipe inspired by the possibilities of using London gin or *jenever*, the fragrant, cheap and ubiquitous Dutch gin.

Salmon with Gin   SERVES 4

A salmon tail, about 1 kg (generous 2 lbs), scaled and boned, or 4 salmon steaks
1 tsp juniper berries, lightly crushed
1 garlic clove, chopped
1 tsp salt
1 tsp sugar
2 tbsps gin

Stuff the cavity of the boned fish with the juniper berries, garlic, salt and sugar, and dribble in the gin. Leave to absorb the flavours, preferably overnight or for at least several hours. Bake covered in foil in a moderate to hot oven until done, about 30 to 40 minutes. Remove the skin and serve hot or cold, with good bread and asparagus with butter and Parmesan.

The crabs and lobsters which look so decorative piled among fruit, silver gilt and musical instruments in many a still life (a messy combination perhaps intended to foster guilt) are difficult to handle at table. This contemporary recipe is an agreeable way of preparing crab or lobster, especially when served in small individual pots.

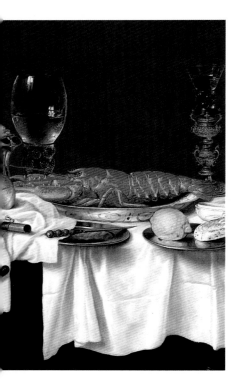

Potted Crab   MAKES 4–6 POTS

30 g (2 tbsps) butter
A large crab, about 1 kg (generous 2 lbs), freshly boiled, the inedible parts removed
8 black peppercorns
3 blades of mace
1 tsp freshly grated nutmeg
The juice of ½ lemon
Salt to taste

Leave the butter to come to room temperature while you deal with the crab. Crack the claws and body with a heavy pestle in a mortar or with a nutcracker and extract the meat, taking care to get rid of all bits of shell. Grind the peppercorns and mace together and add the grated nutmeg; shake through a coarse strainer into a bowl. Add the crab meat, butter and lemon juice. Taste for saltiness (this will depend on the amount of salt in the butter). Mash together with a fork – this is better than using a processor, unless you prefer a smooth paste. Pot up into separate containers. There is no need to float melted butter on top unless the crab has to be kept a day or two in the refrigerator.

The quality of butter is critical in this recipe; some commercial brands may seem too bland and oily so choose a regional or organic product. It is a good idea to add it to the crab bit by bit to get the balance to your taste.

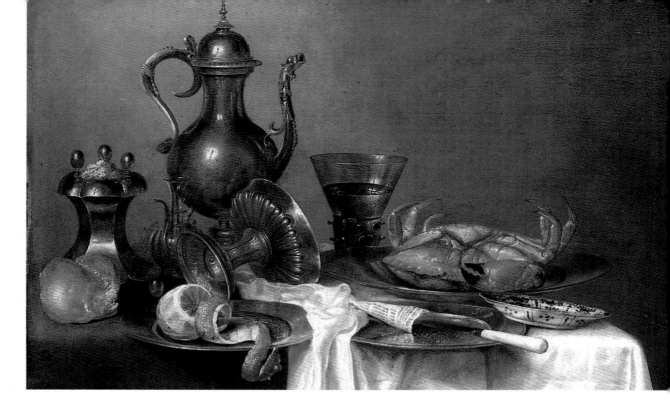

Willem Claesz. Heda,
*Still Life: Pewter and Silver
Vessels and a Crab,*
probably about 1633–7.

Mussels and French fries with mayonnaise are today one of the glories of Nonnius' city, Antwerp. Mussels are less popular in Holland, but in the past their shells littered the floors of taverns and untidy homes, where they might have had lascivious undertones but on a practical level simply implied messy manners and a gross profusion of this delectable shellfish. A recent campaign to revive their popularity in the Netherlands produced this recipe from chef Albert Tickmans, winning him the title 'nationale Mosselman' in 1995.

Mussels with Orange   SERVES 4

2 kgs (4½ lbs) mussels, scrubbed clean
2 garlic cloves, chopped
1 small onion, chopped
2 celery stalks, stringed and chopped
25 g (2 tbsps) butter
250 ml (1 cup) aromatic beer

2 or 3 small, sharp oranges,
    cut into wedges peel and all
A handful of whole leaves of
    sweet cicely, broad-leaved
    parsley or chervil
Salt & pepper

Discard any damaged or open mussels. Soften the garlic, onion and celery in the butter in a capacious pan. Tip in the mussels and beer and bring rapidly to the boil, covered, until the mussels open. Throw away any that remain closed. Do not overcook or they get tough and stringy. Add the oranges, herbs and seasoning, and stir in well.

   Serve at once, garnished with a few reserved sprigs of greenery. Wash the mussels down with the beer left over from cooking; you need a pungent, mellow beer rather than a pallid lager for this dish.

Opposite: Willem Claesz.
Heda, detail from *Still Life
with a Lobster,* 1650–9.

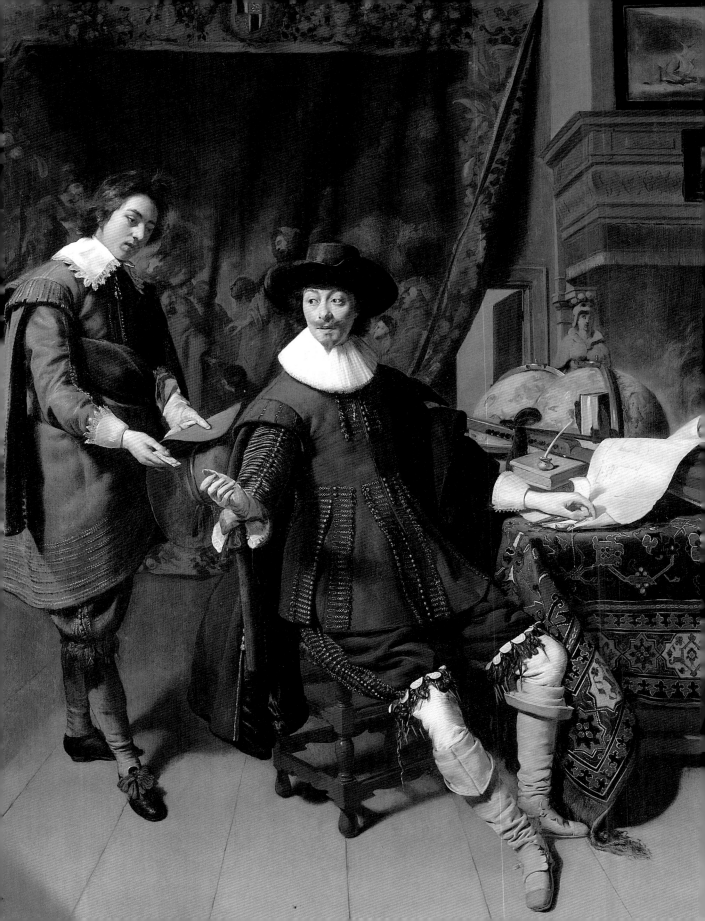

Constantijn Huygens
& THE COUNTRY HOUSE KITCHEN

KING JAMES the First of England led a restless, somewhat unstructured social life, descending at short notice with numerous retinue to enjoy the hospitality of his loyal subjects. Good housekeeping for him, disastrous for his delighted hosts. One fine day in June 1618 he dropped in on Sir Noel de Caron, the Netherlands' ambassador, in his mansion across the Thames in Lambeth – not to bother him with affairs of state, but to visit the walled garden and enjoy the new crop of sweet ripe Dutch cherries, which the greedy monarch insisted on eating as he grabbed them from the tree, perched on a specially constructed ladder. This must have been the highlight of Constantijn Huygens's first visit to London. The young man, not yet the suave, polyglot diplomat of later years, sang to the lute as His Majesty partook of an impromptu collation in the gardens, and was invited to perform again at a similar festivity in far-flung Wimbledon.

At first glimpse Constantijn Huygens, portrayed here in conversation with his clerk, seems too good to be true – with his cool good looks and elegant posture, surrounded by the attributes of a cultivated and upwardly mobile man of letters. His autobiography tells of the comprehensive and highly enjoyable education planned by his father, a respectable member of the Dutch ruling class. As well as the usual grasp of the classics young Constantijn was fluent in several European languages, a brilliant musician and poet, skilled in dancing, fencing and sport, a talented draughtsman and calligrapher, patron of the arts and an enthusiastic participant in the new sciences of optics and astronomy. What endears this paragon of all the virtues to us is the way Huygens focused all his skills and achievements on the thing that meant most to him: life at home with his wife Suzanna. He wrote a poem, *Dagh-werck* (*The Daily Round*), in which her everyday life is the framework for their shared enthusiasms. Suzanna's death in childbirth in 1647 brought the poem to a tragic end.

House and home were central to the culture of Holland in the Golden Age. Domestic and civic virtues found their perfect expression in the order and harmony of a well-run household. A society without monarchy or court was not without its landed, monied aristocracy, and it was to this that Huygens aspired. In the portrait his left hand smooths out the plans for the country house he planned at Hofwijck, which like so many of the time was a comparatively modest building (unlike *The House in the Woods*

Thomas de Keyser, *Portrait of Constantijn Huygens and his (?) Clerk*, 1627.

designed by the same architect, Pieter Post, for the wife of the Prince of Orange, the head of state). Originally surrounded by a moat in well-wooded parkland, the Hofwijck house seems today surprisingly tiny, a little doll's house of a mansion, almost swallowed up in the grim concrete and tarmac outskirts of The Hague. But the scale and endearingly modest rooms still evoke the domestic pleasures of this idyllic rural retreat.

Two of the luxuries of a new place in the country would have been a fine garden and a spacious kitchen. Back in town the houses of the rich were often built on tiny sites with kitchen and larder tucked away in odd corners, but in the country there was room for a light, spacious kitchen with that splendid innovation, the elegant tiled stove. Marcus Doornick, the publisher of a series of books on estate management, included a volume on cooking, *De Verstandige Kock* (*The Well-informed Cook*), with an engraving on the title page showing all the appurtenances of a bright modern kitchen: a nice tiled floor, tall windows, the usual open fire with spit, an adjacent bread oven and the fine upstanding new stove on the left. The author thoughtfully includes instructions for building the stove.

Huygens's interest in the natural world was far from theoretical. He and Suzanna set up a miniature apothecary's cabinet in their home, with every spice, herb, root, bark, mineral, drug and potion known to science. Together they wielded pestle and mortar, still and alembic, knife, fork and spoon to produce remedies, cordials, perfumes, sweetmeats and delicious food. Here is a version of a delicate steamed pudding flavoured in the original with ambergris (an aromatic substance from the intestines of sperm whales, used in both perfumery and cooking), and musk (extracted from the abdominal scent glands of the male musk deer), for which I have substituted cinnamon and mastic (a resinous gum, a version of which is sold in chewable form in little packs in most Turkish stores).

Huygens's Pudding   SERVES 4

50 g (¼ cup) sugar
50 g (4 tbsps) butter
2 eggs
75 g (½ cup) soft white breadcrumbs
50 g (½ cup) ground almonds
1 tsp freshly ground cinnamon
½ tsp ground mastic
2 tbsps orangeflower water, more or less
50 g (⅓ cup) whole peeled almonds

Cream the sugar and butter until light and fluffy and beat in the eggs. Fold in the breadcrumbs, ground almonds and flavourings, moistening with the orangeflower water. Stir in the whole almonds. Put the mixture into a buttered basin, cover with foil and steam for 45 minutes. Unmould and serve with plenty of cream.

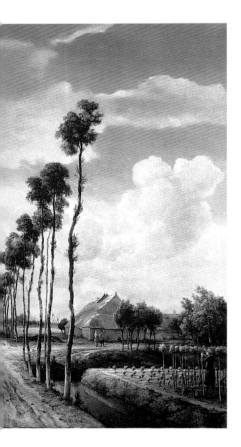

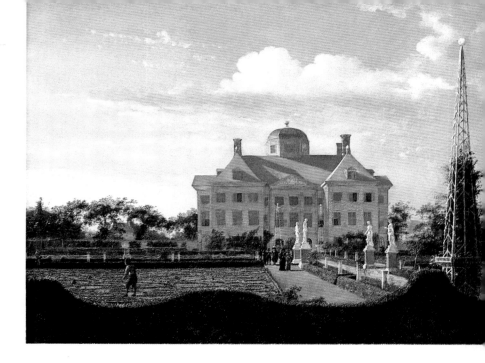

Jan van der Heyden, *The Huis ten Bosch at The Hague*, 1665–75.

It is pleasant to imagine Huygens making pastry in his new kitchen, perhaps this delicate pie, in the new gastronomic style that went with the modern country house lifestyle.

Artichoke & Chicken Pie   SERVES 6

450 g (1 lb) shortcrust pastry
6 free range chicken pieces, lightly fried in butter
6 small cocktail sausages
6 small meatballs made from 200 g (7 oz) ground veal or pork mixed with 1 egg, chopped fresh parsley and salt & pepper
6 artichoke bottoms, cooked and cut into quarters
6 asparagus spears, peeled if necessary, and lightly cooked
12 chestnuts, cooked and peeled
Salt & pepper
1 tsp each of freshly ground nutmeg and mace
30 g (2 tbsps) butter

FOR THE SAUCE:
150 ml (½ cup) chicken stock
The juice of 1 lemon
2 egg yolks
1 tbsp butter

Roll out the pastry on a floured surface and use half of it to line a 25 cm (10 in) pie dish. Lay the filling ingredients, including the salt and spices, over it, distributing them evenly, and dot generously with the butter. Cover with the rest of the pastry, carefully seal the edges and make a hole in the centre. Bake in a moderate oven for 1 hour.

Make the sauce by beating the ingredients together at just under boiling point until thick, stirring in the butter at the last minute. When the pie comes out of the oven tip it into the hole in the lid and shake gently to amalgamate with the filling. Put into the oven for 5 minutes to 'set' slightly and serve hot or tepid.

Opposite: Meindert Hobbema, detail from *The Avenue at Middelharnis*, 1689.

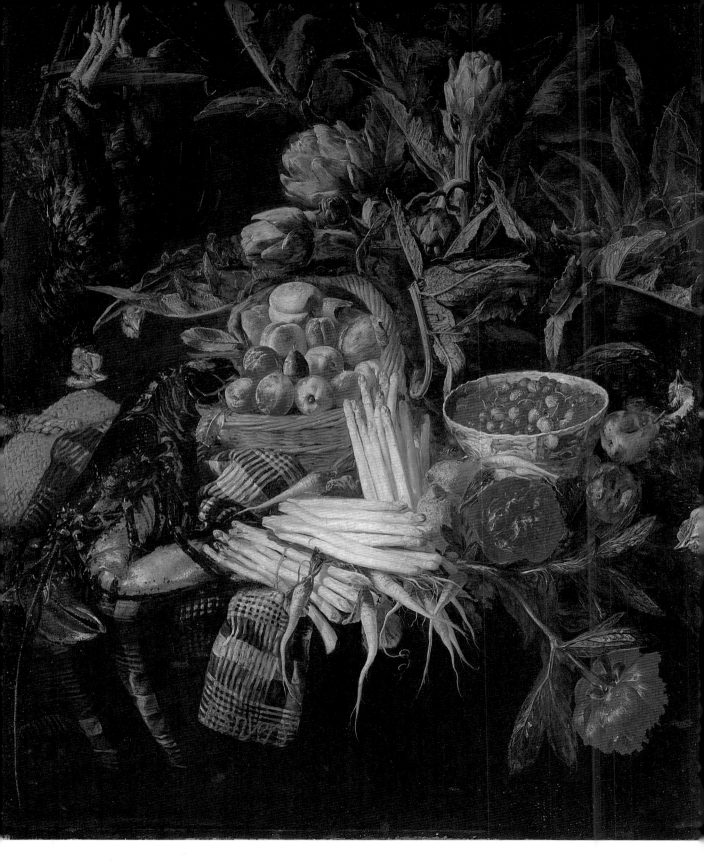

The Dutch reputation for tasteless watery vegetables is recent and unfair. In the Golden Age the Netherlands were in the forefront of horticultural innovation and experiment. Novelties like asparagus and artichokes were grown in kitchen gardens and hothouse fruit graced the tables and still lifes of the wealthy. Oranges and lemons, imported luxuries, were also carefully tended in pots and in specially constructed houses. Grapes hang, fraught with symbolism, all over market scenes and interiors, indicating the lavish fecundity of a fruitful wife as well as being a sign of virginity and also a reference to the wine of the Eucharist. They were not as commonplace as one might think from their appearance in so many paintings, but they proclaim, displayed in a tumble of peaches, nectarines and rare and precious blooms glowing among Venetian glass and oriental carpets, the wealth and taste of these patrician households, with their keen practical interest in collecting and growing rare fruit and plants.

Asparagus with Butter   SERVES 6

1 kg (generous 2 lbs) fresh asparagus
30 g (2 tbsps) unsalted butter, or more
A pinch of freshly grated nutmeg
Salt

Cut away all the woody and inedible parts of the asparagus and peel the remaining stem, keeping the shavings for soup. (Very young green asparagus need not be peeled.) Simmer the asparagus in a little lightly salted water until just soft, about 5 to 10 minutes, lying them flat in a wide shallow pan. By this time the water should have evaporated, leaving a little flavourful liquid. Into this tip the butter and freshly grated nutmeg, and shake the asparagus over a low heat to absorb the flavours.

Chicken with Orange   SERVES 4

1 medium free range chicken, cut into pieces (keep the carcass for stock)
Plenty of unsalted butter
2 small blades of mace

1 wine glass of dry white wine
The zest of ½ bitter orange or 1 tbsp marmalade
Salt & pepper
1 tsp freshly ground cinnamon

Fry the chicken pieces in butter until golden. Add the whole mace, wine, orange zest or marmalade and salt and pepper and simmer, uncovered, until tender, about 30 to 40 minutes. Add more wine if it seems to be drying out, cook more fiercely if it seems too liquid. The chicken pieces should be bathed in a thick, aromatic sauce.
Sprinkle on the cinnamon before serving.

Pieter Snijers, *A Still life with Fruit, Vegetables, Dead Chickens and a Lobster*, 1707–52.

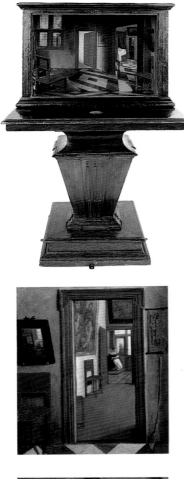

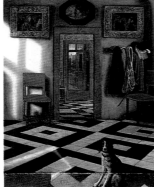

Samuel van Hoogstraten, *A Peepshow with Views of the Interior of a Dutch House*, about 1655–60.

Huygens had a passionate interest in optics – new ways of seeing, observing, recording nature. The camera obscura was a magical way of looking at the world, a sort of window on reality. When this became a popular attraction in the form of the peepshow, the chosen subject in the Netherlands was not some high drama or heroic escapade but an idealized domestic interior. The National Gallery in London has an enchanting example by Samuel van Hoogstraten, who combined serious studies of perspective and optics with a wicked sense of humour, littering his home with trompe l'œil panels of things like old shoes or fruit and a dried fish hung on the back of a door. His 'perspective box' offers at keyhole level oblique glimpses into a calm home, with its black and white tiled floor, red velvet upholstered chairs; not a speck of dust, not a thing out of place, from the docile little dog on the threshold to the discarded broom. This feeling of eavesdropping on the private life of people like oneself, waiting in the wings about to enter the room in a bustle of chatter, music, tobacco smoke and cooking smells, is a sort of sanitized voyeurism, the twitching of lace curtains before their invention, profoundly reassuring. We can walk through rooms like these in museums in Holland, but few have the immediacy of this peepshow home, with its tantalizing fragments of domesticity lurking on the edges of vision.

Women and children, calmly busy peeling carrots or preparing fish, are present in so many domestic interiors, where the daily round is as vital as the music party or polite conversation. The next recipe would surprise modern Dutch cooks; demoted to cattle food in the nineteenth century the parsnip became obsolete and is now an exotic rarity.

This goes well with a plain, lean roast or ham and a green salad.

Buttered Parsnips SERVES 6

1 kg (generous 2 lbs) parsnips, peeled and sliced vertically
4 cloves
A good handful of chopped fresh herbs such as parsley, mint, sage, rosemary and chervil
Plenty of butter

Cook the parsnips with the cloves in a little salted water until they are soft and all the water has evaporated. Discard the cloves, stir in the herbs and butter and shake or gently stir the pan from time to time to allow the parsnips to absorb the flavours. Serve very hot. The amount of butter depends on a balance between greed and prudence; the parsnips will absorb a great deal more than many would consider wise, much depends on how rich the rest of the meal is.

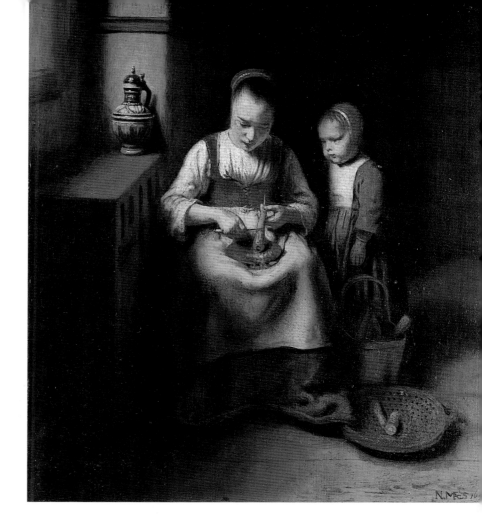

Nicolaes Maes, *A Woman scraping Parsnips, with a Child standing by her*, 1655.

Veal with Green Herbs SERVES 6

1 kg (generous 2 lbs) shin (shank) of free range, humanely reared veal, cut into 2 cm (1 in) cubes (failing veal, try lamb shanks or leg of pork)
2 garlic cloves, chopped
1 small onion, chopped
150 ml (⅝ cup) dry white wine
150 ml (⅝ cup) veal or chicken stock
500 g (generous 1 lb) spinach, washed and chopped
200 g (½ lb) sorrel, washed and chopped
200 g (½ lb) chervil, washed and chopped
A handful of basil leaves, roughly torn (the anise-flavoured Thai or Holy basil is anachronistic, but good)
30 g (2 tbsps) unsalted butter
Salt & pepper

Simmer the meat, garlic and onion slowly in the wine and stock until tender, about 1 hour. Adjust the heat towards the end to get a very small amount of concentrated juice. Put in the vegetables and herbs and wilt gently until lightly cooked. Stir in the butter and season as required.

A different texture can be got by processing the herbs in a little stock before adding them to the meat.

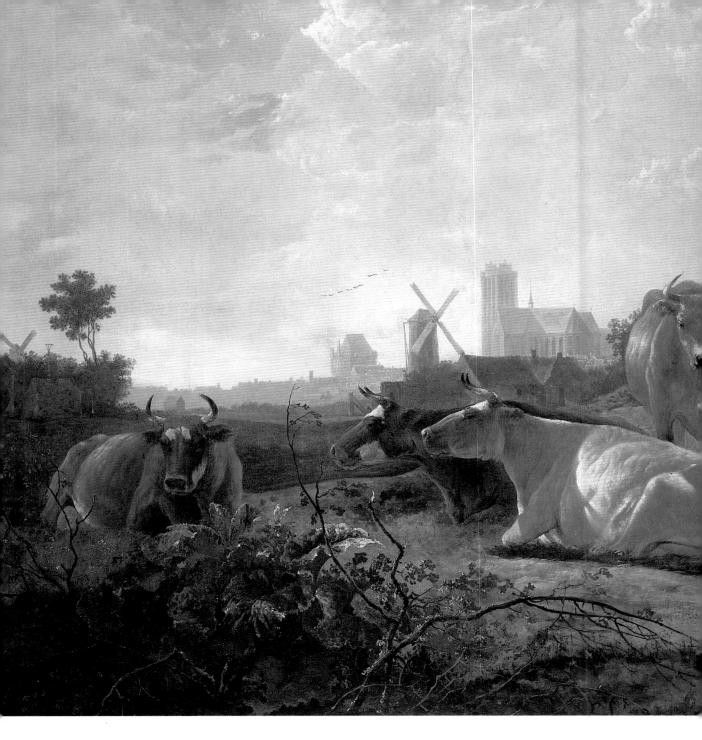

Aelbert Cuyp, *A Distant View of Dordrecht, with a Milkmaid and Four Cows and Other Figures*, about 1650.

The country house kitchen also enjoyed superb quality cheese, butter and cream – the rich pastures of reclaimed land were grazing for the noble cattle immortalized here by Aelbert Cuyp. They browse in a golden, buttery light, sleek rotund bellies and glossy flanks reminiscent of the warm tones of the opulent cheese-stacks in paintings. Here we see a milkmaid, buxom charms quite eclipsed by

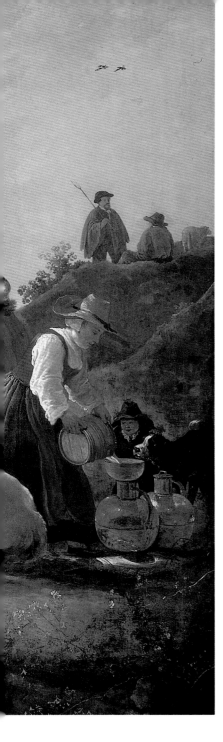

her herd, pouring the milk into rotund pots. We can smell the cattle's fragrant breath, the crushed grass, the creamy milk, and look forward to the lush tide of cholesterol which enriched the prosperous little town of Dordrecht in the background, where Cuyp lived and worked.

Seascapes and watermeadows hung comfortably side by side in patrician and bourgeois homes, happy reminders of the sources of Holland's wealth. Cheese, herrings, bread and beer made a patriotic and satisfying meal, and although depicted as 'humble' fare, the modest meal in so many genre scenes shows quite a lot of capital locked up in the cheese and ham on the simple table. Worthy folk but by no means poor.

Cheese recipes do not abound in seventeenth-century recipe books. However the powerful Dutch colonial presence gave rise to some exotic ways with exported cheeses; perhaps the most unexpected is this recipe for stuffed cheese from Curaçao.

Keshy Yena SERVES 6

500 g (generous 1 lb) shell-on prawns (shrimp)	1 tbsp salted capers, soaked for 1 hour and drained
1 small Gouda or Edam cheese, about 750 g (1¾ lbs)	2 tbsps fresh breadcrumbs
	1 egg, beaten
1 medium onion, chopped	2 tbsps cheese from the cavity (see method)
1 tbsp butter	FOR THE STOCK:
4 medium tomatoes, chopped	The prawn (shrimp) shells and debris
Salt & pepper	
1 fresh hot chile, chopped	1 garlic clove, smashed
1 tbsp raisins	3 bay leaves
12 pitted black olives	1 wine glass of white wine

First make the stock by combining all the ingredients in a large pan and boiling, covered, for 10 minutes. Crush with a wooden spatula and strain into a bowl. Now remove the red or yellow outer covering of the cheese. Cut off the top and reserve to use later. Scoop out the inside, leaving a 2 cm (¾ in) shell. Grate the scooped-out cheese to add to the stuffing.

Fry the onion in the butter until soft. Add the tomatoes, salt, pepper and chile and simmer for about 10 minutes. Add the stock, raisins, olives, capers and breadcrumbs and simmer for 15 minutes until thick. Stir in the egg, prawns (shrimp), and grated cheese and heat through. Stuff the cheese shell with this mixture, cover with its lid and put into an ovenproof dish that will just hold it. Bake in a moderate oven until the cheese is melting but not too runny, about 15 to 20 minutes, checking carefully from time to time to make sure it does not fall apart. Serve while hot and bubbling.

It was not patriotism alone that called for delicate concoctions of butter, cream and fruit. Fashion played a part, and fashion meant France, technically a papist superpower, but nevertheless the arbiter of taste. Huygens learnt French calligraphy and dancing, as well as the language, and French fashions in gastronomy were reinforcing the general trend towards lighter, less pungent food. Suzanna's kitchen probably offered the best of all worlds.

Rosewater Cream   SERVES 4

250 ml (1 cup) thick cream
1 tbsp rice flour mixed with 2 tbsps of rich milk
1 egg
1 tsp rosewater, or to taste
4 tbsps sugar
2 cm (½ in) stick of cinnamon ground with 1 tbsp sugar

Mix all the ingredients except the cinnamon and sugar together and cook slowly in a non-stick saucepan or double boiler, stirring all the time until thick, about 10 to 15 minutes. Pour into a bowl and cool. Before serving sprinkle with the cinnamon and sugar.

Redcurrant Cream   SERVES 6

200 ml (scant 1 cup) each of crème fraîche, live yoghurt and double (heavy) cream
150 g (5 oz) redcurrants, hulled
4 tbsps sugar, depending on the sweetness of the fruit
1 tsp rosewater, or to taste
1 wine glass fragrant dessert wine, such as Frontignac, Beaumes de Venise, Madeira or a fizzy Malvasia
2 cm (¾ in) stick of cinnamon ground with 2 tbsps sugar

Mix the creams and yoghurt together and leave at room temperature for an hour or so to thicken. Meanwhile crush the redcurrants with the sugar and stir in the rosewater, keeping back a spoonful of fruit. Swirl the rest into the cream mixture and serve in a glass bowl to show off the pretty marbled appearance. Before dishing up pour over a generous slug of the dessert wine you will be drinking with the cream, add a sprinkling of cinnamon sugar and decorate with the reserved crushed fruit.

The exotic fowl in Melchior d'Hondecoeter's barnyard were as unlikely to end up on the spit as the bulbs of the convoluted, multi-coloured tulips were to be sliced into a *hutspot*, but perhaps some of the eggs may have served to bind these enigmatic little dumplings, which could accompany a roast, or be served as a dessert with the sweet sauce given here.

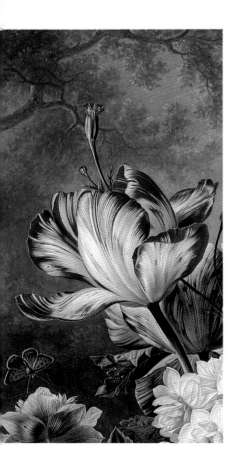

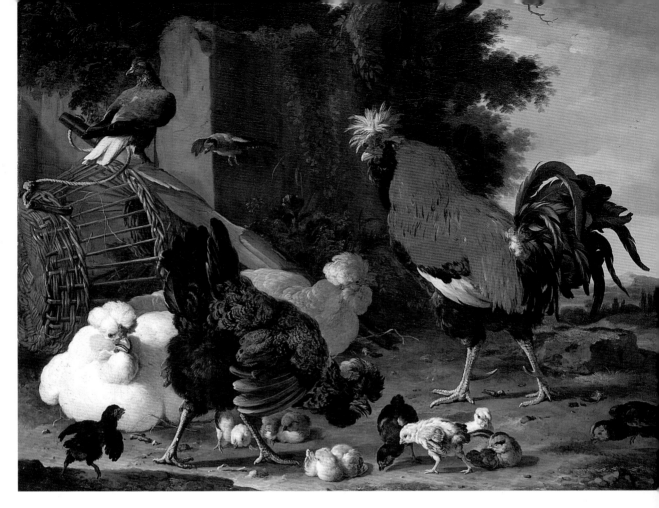

Melchior d'Hondecoeter,
A Cock, Hens and Chicks,
about 1668–70.

Pennyroyal Dumplings   SERVES 4

100 g (4 oz) suet
200 g (1⅓ cups) fresh white
   breadcrumbs
2 eggs, beaten
2 tbsps raisins
1 tbsp candied peel
1 tbsp chopped fresh pennyroyal
   (*Mentha pulegium*), or mint if
   pennyroyal is unavailable
1 tbsp chopped fresh parsley
½ tsp grated nutmeg

1 tsp orange zest
Sugar to taste (1 tsp if savoury,
   2 tbsps if sweet)
2 tsps dry sherry
Plain white flour (all-purpose
   flour)

FOR A SWEET SAUCE:
100 g (½ cup) sugar
100 g (8 tbsps) unsalted butter
A pinch of grated nutmeg
Dry sherry to taste

Mix all the dumpling ingredients together except the flour and make
up into little balls the size of walnuts. Roll these in flour. Simmer,
covered, in a pan half filled with boiling water until light and fluffy,
about 30 minutes. Serve with melted butter if accompanying a lean
roast, or with a sweet sauce if they are to be a dessert.

To make the sweet sauce, cream the sugar and butter until light and
fluffy and flavour with the nutmeg and dry sherry.

Opposite: Paulus Theodorus
van Brussel, detail from
Flowers in a Vase, 1792.

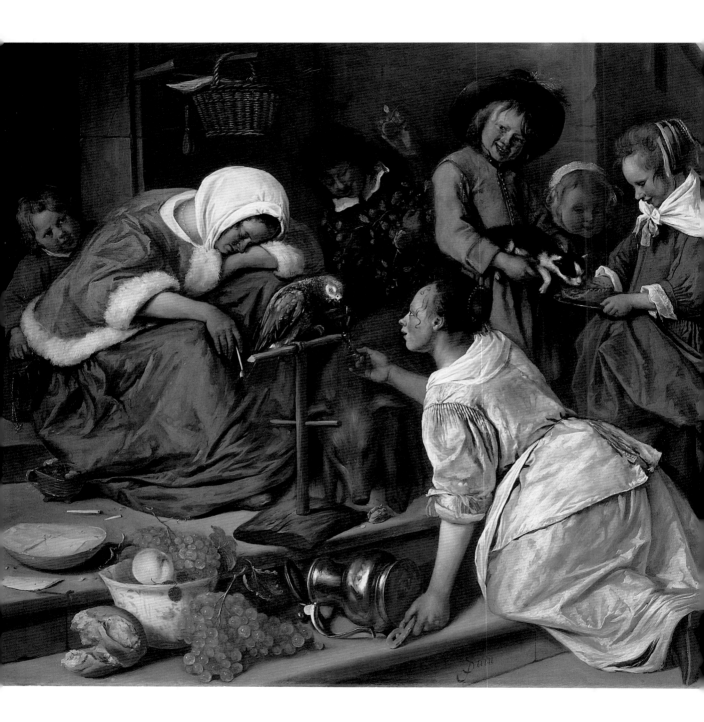

Morality & Merrymaking

SHOT SILK & SHEEP'S SHANKS IN THE GOLDEN AGE OF THE NETHERLANDS

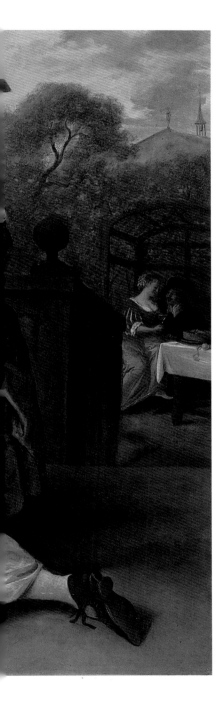

Jan Steen, *The Effects of Intemperance*, about 1663–5.

Maria van Egmond, widow of an unsuccessful bookseller, kept her family together by selling cooked mutton and sheeps' offal in Leiden market. She prudently kept the job on when she remarried. Her new husband was the widowed artist Jan Steen, with his brood of unruly children and irresponsible lifestyle. She once complained to a painter friend, Cavel de Moor, that she was fed up being the model for whores, procuresses and drunken sluts in so many of Jan's paintings. Cavel kindly did a portrait of her in her Sunday best, which pleased Maria but provoked her husband into adding to it a basket of sheeps' feet and innards, the tools of her trade. This affectionate send-up of respectability was characteristic of Steen's mocking and sometimes not very kind treatment of his subjects. But his skills in rendering the silks and satins of his richly dressed women and the pots and pans of his peasant hovels were appreciated by his discriminating patrons, who could decipher without difficulty the symbolism scattered among the decorative mayhem of the dissolute, rich household in *The Effects of Intemperance*. They were amused to recognize Steen's wife and children on the rampage, while deploring the mess, waste and rampant mischief, with mother slumped in drunken apathy, her shot-silk skirt singed by the charcoal footwarmer, and father disporting himself in gluttonous dalliance in the background.

The expression 'a Jan Steen family' has become a sort of social worker's summing up of messy domesticity toppling into dissolution. As spectators we enjoy a frisson of horror and delight at the enviably awful behaviour of parents and children. Misuse of food was often part of this – a wanton waste of luxuries, peaches and grapes, and basics like bread and cheese, scattered all over the floor, with naughty children feeding a fine pie to the cat.

Steen also teased and delighted his clients by working outrageous self-portraits into his paintings. We see him as a sozzled peasant tormenting a woman in a tavern, or as an irresponsible father giving a small boy a puff of his noxious tobacco. This apparently raucously bad behaviour, together with that of his long-suffering wife and children, amused and shocked people into endorsing the moral messages of Steen's canvases – that the survival and security of the nation depends on the maintenance of order and discipline in the home. Drunk and disorderly parents produce wayward and destructive infants; sober and industrious ones create a calm, prosperous commonwealth.

By contrast this somewhat smug peasant household is secure in the decent sufficiency won by the hard-working man and his wife. He cuts the loaf bought with the sweat of his brow, while the small girl leaves her toys and pet dog (emblem of fidelity) and says grace before tucking into the *hutspot*, the meat and vegetable stew that symbolized the heroic struggle of the Protestant Netherlands against the tyrannous Spanish invaders. The story goes that when in 1574 the agonizing decision to flood the recently reclaimed land around Leiden broke the long siege of the city, the Spanish army fled, and first into their deserted camp were some bold and starving little boys who seized from the dying embers a huge pot of stew, which is recreated every year at cheerful street parties in Leiden. The seventeenth-century hotchpotch or *olla podrida* would certainly not have featured the potatoes which go with carrots and beef into this unassuming dish today.

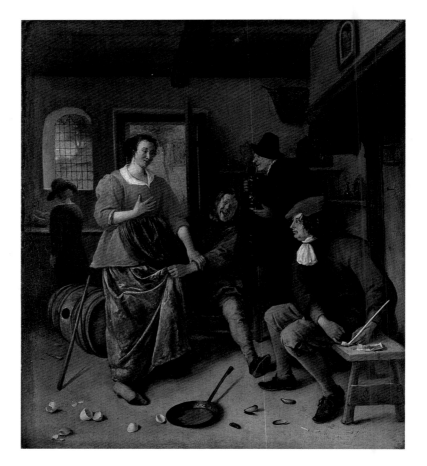

Jan Steen, *The Interior of an Inn*, about 1665–70. The lecherous man in the middle might well be a self portrait.

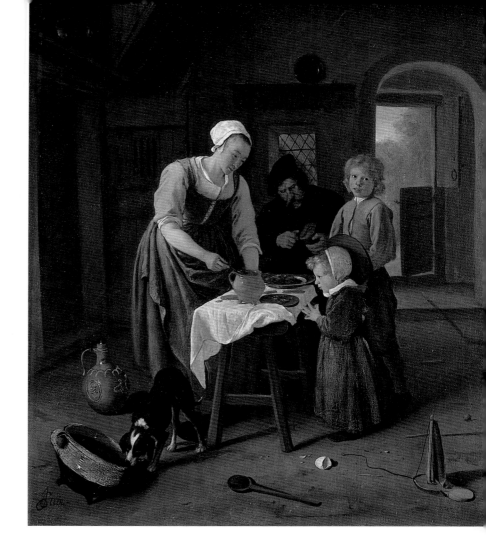

Jan Steen, *A Peasant Family at Meal-time*, about 1665.

Hutspot SERVES 6

250 g shin of beef (½ lb blade of beef)
250 g (½ lb) pork belly
100 g (4 oz) fatty bacon
500 ml (2 cups) meat or chicken stock
2 garlic cloves, smashed
6 cloves, 4 blades of mace, ½ tsp grated nutmeg, 1 tbsp chopped fresh ginger
Salt & pepper
6 chicken thighs

6 small pork sausages
1 savoy cabbage, chopped and blanched in salt and water
1 large carrot, chopped
1 heaped tbsp chopped fresh herbs: parsley, mint, lemon balm, marjoram, rosemary, sage, whatever is to hand
15 g (1 tbsp) butter, or more
Lemon juice to taste

Cut the meat and bacon into 2 cm (¾ in) cubes and simmer them in the stock with the garlic and spices until almost done, about 1½ hours. Add the chicken and sausages and cook for 15 minutes. Add the cabbage and carrot to the pan and cook for another 15 minutes. Keep testing and tasting, and when ready to serve add the herbs, butter and lemon juice.

The puritan conscience has perhaps been unfairly blamed for the decline of gastronomy in Protestant countries. But although Calvin was against sin he could not totally disapprove of eating and drinking, which after all happens quite a lot in the Bible. The depressing thing is that he was indifferent to the pleasures of the table, and sadly this hardened into dogma in the hands of his followers and created an intolerance he would not himself have professed, an 'eat to live, not live to eat' mentality. In spite of this travellers in Holland in the Golden Age were amazed at the roistering and guttling enjoyed at every level in this prosperous society, where even a labourer's minimum wage would buy fresh meat and fish to go with the bread, cheese and vegetables of an ordinary household. Paintings of gross merriment in murky smoke-filled taverns hung alongside decorous vignettes of elegant gentlefolk sipping wine in calm, sunlit interiors. In both we detect a pride in this abundance of good things and the possibility of a decent life for the deserving, at all levels.

A fruit tart would have been enjoyed in either environment.

David Teniers the Younger, *An Old Peasant caresses a Kitchen Maid in a Stable*, about 1650.

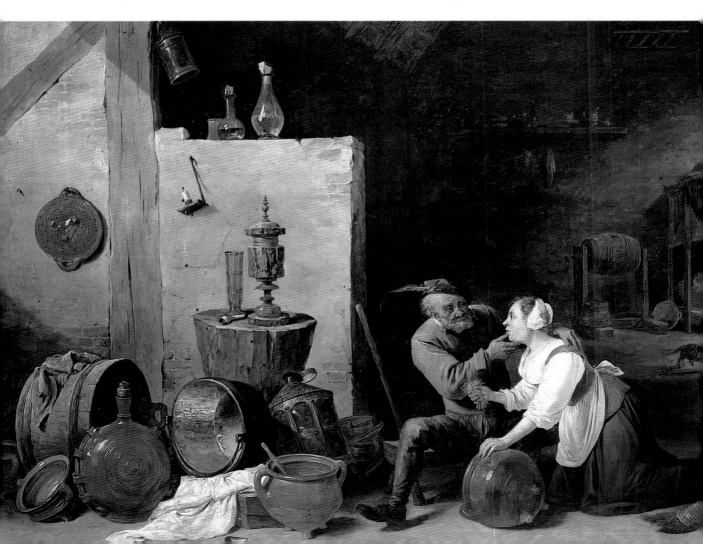

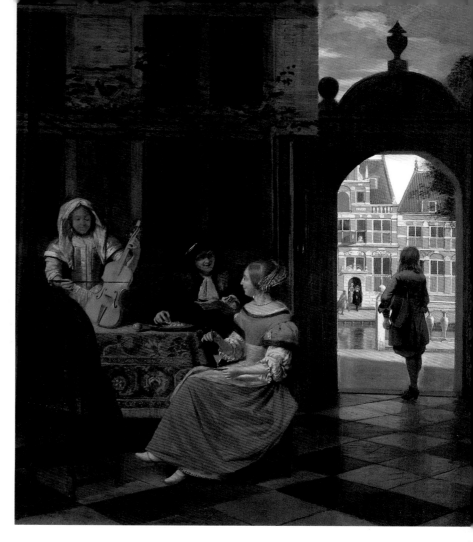

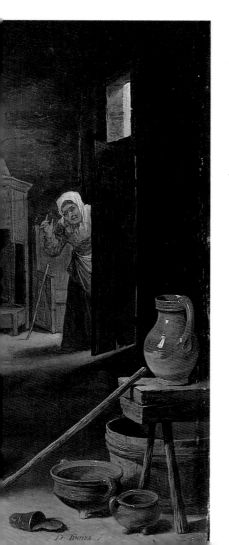

Pieter de Hooch, *A Musical Party in a Courtyard*, 1677.

Pear Tart SERVES 4

FOR THE RICH SHORTCRUST PASTRY:

100 g plain white flour (1 cup all-purpose flour)
75 g (6 tbsps) butter
1 egg yolk
1 tbsp sugar
2 tbsps rosewater
½ tsp salt

FOR THE FILLING:

4 ripe pears, peeled and cored
3 cm (1¼ in) stick of cinnamon ground with 3 tbsps sugar
2 tbsps raisins soaked for 30 minutes in 2 tbsps rum and drained
1 tbsp grated fresh ginger
2 tsps butter

To make the pastry, process or mix all the ingredients together and leave the mixture to rest for 30 minutes. Roll out on a floured surface to 3 mm (⅛ in) thick and line a 23 cm (10 in) tart or pie dish. For the filling, slice the pears and put half on the pastry base. Strew with half the cinnamon sugar, all the raisins and ginger, and half the butter. Add the rest of the pears, dot with the remaining cinnamon sugar and butter and bake in a moderate oven until golden on top, about 30 minutes.

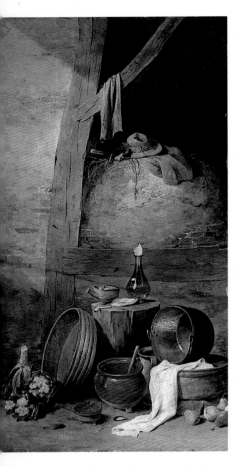

Follower of Teniers, detail from *An Old Woman peeling Pears*, after 1640s.

Guilt at the excessive indulgence in life's good things is a fairly natural reaction, and the prosperity of the Netherlands produced plenty of scope for this. A homely painting of domestic comforts was often loaded with opportunities for moralizing, preaching how the luxuries enjoyed by a hardworking, godfearing trading nation might, if taken in excess, corrupt and lead astray. And then there are lessons to be drawn from the contrast between flighty youth and world-weary old age, symbols in profusion, from caged birds to dead ones (innocence and defilement), keys, jugs, onions (more of the same), so that we turn with some relief to enjoy at its face value Teniers's accurate, loving portrayal of everyday earthenware pots and pans, bowls, jugs and platters, as meticulous as Heda's rendering of sumptuous silver goblets, Venetian glass, Chinese porcelain and white linen (hours of painstaking laundrywork crumpled carelessly beneath a drooling lobster or over-ripe melon). Snijers's humble vegetables are honoured alongside hothouse fruit and exotic asparagus and artichokes, painted with the same virtuoso skill with which Jan Steen depicted furs and shot silk. Later in the century it became fashionable to paint a sort of idealized shop or kitchen in a classical niche, a far cry from Adriana's fishmarket or Maria's offal stall. Perhaps the old woman is explaining a recipe, not a moral homily, to the cheerful young woman in Gerrit Dou's poultry shop, surrounded as she is by emblems of mortality and corruption – which we can thankfully also read as good things to eat.

Casserole of Pheasant   SERVES 3–4

1 pheasant, cut into pieces
100 g (4 oz) fatty bacon, cut into small cubes
1 medium onion, chopped
50 g (4 tbsps) butter
1 wine glass each of white wine and meat stock
150 g (scant 1 cup) mushrooms, chopped

1 tbsp dried mushrooms (*funghi porcini*), rinsed and soaked in some of the stock
2 garlic cloves, smashed
2 tbsps fresh white breadcrumbs
1 tbsp chopped fresh parsley
1 tbsp salted capers, soaked for 1 hour and drained

Brown the pheasant, bacon and onion in the butter. Add the wine, stock, mushrooms and garlic and simmer, covered, until almost done, about 40 to 60 minutes depending on the age and condition of the pheasant. Stir in the breadcrumbs, parsley and capers and simmer for 10 minutes until the sauce thickens. Serve hot, perhaps with the Buttered Parsnips on page 92 and a plain green salad.

The fat on a well hung pheasant may taste a bit rank, so you might wish to skin the pieces before frying them. This recipe works well with wild rabbit or hare, too, but give the hare an hour's more cooking time.

Opposite: Gerrit Dou, *A Poulterer's Shop*, about 1670.

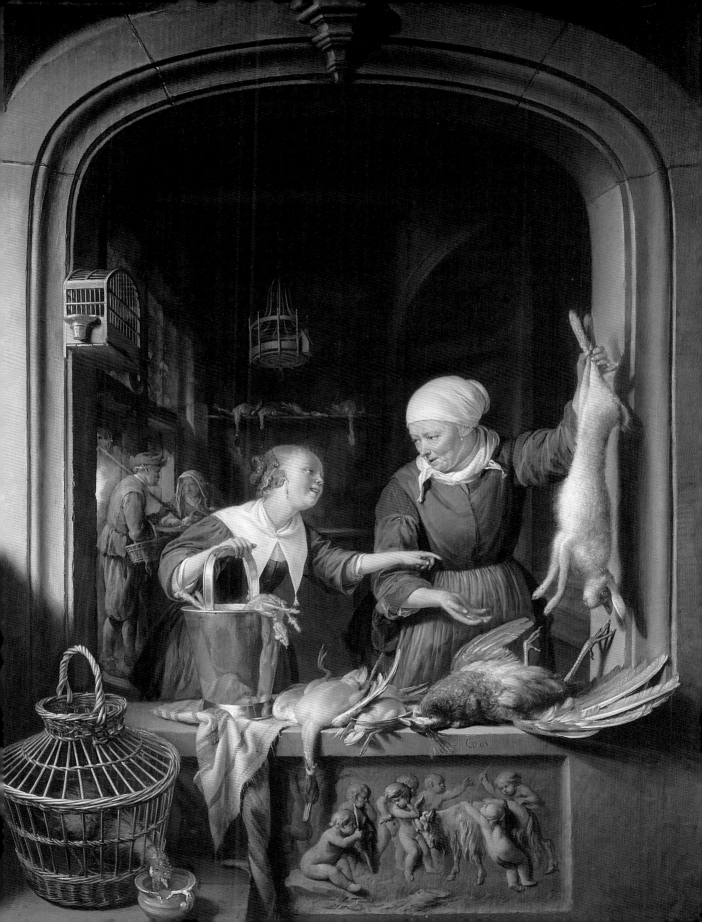

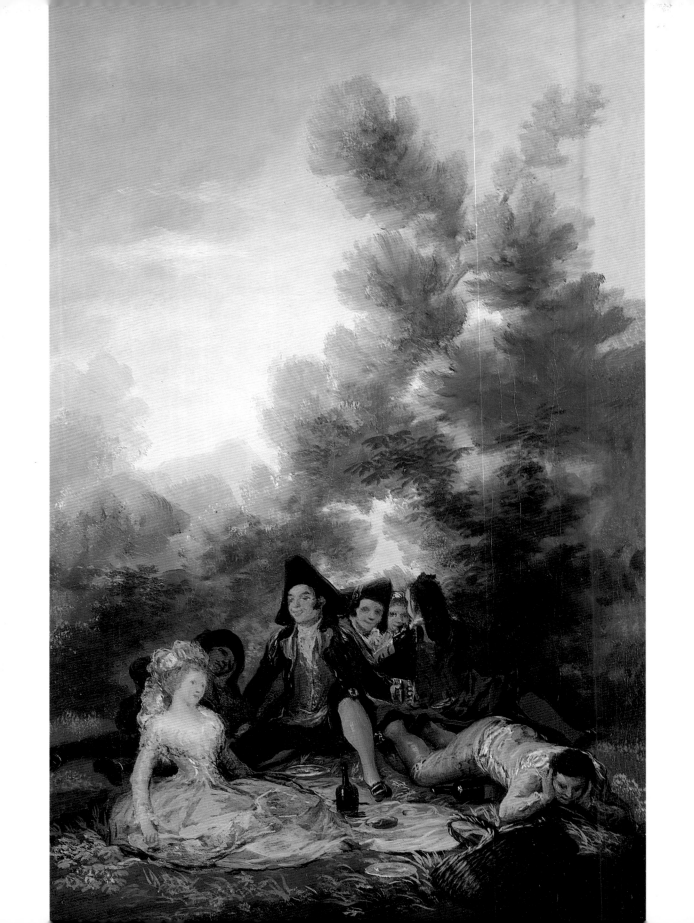

Darkness & Light
ASPECTS OF SPANISH GASTRONOMY

The painting of Goya, Spain's leading artist of the Enlightenment, is as full of contrasts as Spanish food. He veers from gaiety to gloom, from elegant picnic to sombre witches' brew, revealing the light and dark sides of his own nature, just as the food of Spain offers ethereal pastries, pale, refreshing gazpachos and heavy, dense stews and casseroles; light, cooling drinks like *horchatas* or thick, sweet, dark chocolate, like the *sol y sombra* of the bullring.

This lighthearted sketch for a tapestry was commissioned in the 1780s to decorate a room in the royal palace in Madrid. 'Picnic' is an inadequate word for the charming *merienda* that can grace almost any hour of the day in Spain, taken indoors or out, an elegant light meal or insubstantial snack. Some cured mountain ham, a little cheese, a few tiny empanadas, a small portion of the classic tortilla, fruit, one or two exquisite pastries, light wine, thirst-quenching liquid to banish dehydration – a gazpacho, say – all served on immaculate linen with every civilized appurtenance. That is the theory, but perhaps here Goya is reminding us of how even the most decorous of events may sometimes topple towards insobriety, as indeed the bolt-upright young maiden shows every sign of doing.

The austere and sober aspects of the Spanish character are a response to climate and resources. The many fine wines of Spain enhance the cuisine, but it would be unwise to quench the parching summer thirst with them and so a tradition of cooling, non-alcoholic iced drinks flourished alongside the dubious blessings of tea, coffee and chocolate in the seventeenth and eighteenth centuries. Perhaps the most popular survivor is *horchata de chufas*, a pale, semi-sweet drink made from the ground-up tubers of the tiger nut (*Cyperus esculentus*), welcome chilled at any hour of day or night. A similar brew can be made with almonds or pumpkin and melon seeds, but like so many chilled drinks based on nuts and seeds it is now presented as a soup.

The heart and soul of the chilled soup we know as gazpacho is bread soaked in water, allowed to mature, then pounded in a mortar with salt, garlic, oil and vinegar to which other ingredients are then added. The quality of the bread is paramount, as in the preparation of a Tuscan *ribollita*.

Although classic recipes for gazpacho have well-defined boundaries there is scope here, helped by history, for some creative and

Francisco de Goya, *A Picnic*, 1785–90.

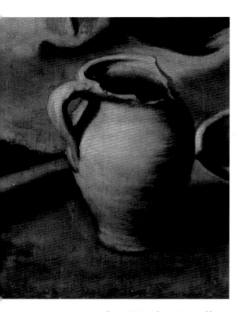

Bartolomé Esteban Murillo, detail from *Christ healing the Paralytic at the Pool of Bethesda*, 1667–70.

Opposite: Francisco de Zurbarán, *Saint Margaret of Antioch*, 1630–4. Margaret was of noble birth but had a rustic upbringing and is here setting off to market with her capacious saddle-bag.

unexpected combinations. As performance art there was nothing to beat the panache with which Alicia Ríos, food historian and philosopher, on the hottest day of a sweltering Madrid summer, finely sliced a lettuce, mixed it with yoghurt, olive oil, a few drops of vinegar and salt, sprinkled in some chopped herbs and ate it elegantly with exquisite lacquered chopsticks. She explained how the gazpacho belongs to an ancient, empirical tradition of combining elemental ingredients to achieve a nutritional balance that is almost perfect. The salt breaks down the cell walls of the vegetables incorporated into the liquid, releasing vitamins; the oil contains unsaturated fatty acids and more vitamins; the vinegar is medicinal and like the oil zaps undesirable micro-organisms as well as being refreshing. Salt is fundamental to this hot-weather beverage, together with cool, fresh water from the well, creating the perfect re-hydration fluid.

The classic gazpacho from Andalucia incorporates peeled tomatoes and sweet green peppers into pounded bread, olive oil and garlic, sometimes diluted with water, and is served with a garnish of chopped onion, cucumber, hard-boiled (hard-cooked) egg, and so forth. A green version can be made using green bell peppers, cucumber and green chile and a selection of green herbs, but no tomatoes. Here is yet another variation that makes an agreeable first course before a rich roast or stew.

Strawberry Gazpacho   SERVES 4

1 thick slice of stale white bread, soaked in water and
    squeezed dry
1 tsp rock or sea salt
500 g (generous 1 lb) strawberries, hulled, and cleaned
    if necessary
2 or 3 tbsps extra virgin olive oil
1 or 2 tsps sherry vinegar or genuine traditional balsamic
    vinegar from Modena
1 tsp sugar
100 ml chilled (scant ½ cup) mineral water
A garnish of fresh mint leaves, chopped chives or
    diced cucumber

Pound the bread and salt together in a mortar and go on pounding while adding the strawberries. Do not overdo it and make a frothy mush, the strawberries should retain some of their texture. Add oil to taste in a slow dribble, pounding as you go, and flavour with the vinegar and sugar, tasting carefully to get a pleasant balance between sweet and savoury. Chill. Dilute with chilled mineral water before serving, decorated with the garnish.

White Gazpacho   SERVES 4

250 g (1½ cups) almonds, peeled
1 slice of stale white bread, soaked in water and squeezed dry
1 or 2 garlic cloves
½ tsp rock or sea salt
2 tbsps extra virgin olive oil
Sherry vinegar
About 750 ml (3 cups) chilled mineral water
250 g (9 oz) muscat grapes, peeled, halved and deseeded, or cubed melon

Pound the almonds, bread, garlic, salt and oil together in a mortar or processor, adding a little water as you go to get a smooth paste. Season with the vinegar and check the salt. Chill for at least 2 hours or preferably overnight. Dilute with the chilled water to taste before serving, garnished with the grapes or melon.

Goya's picnic would have been incomplete without some empanadas. These little pasties have had a long and honourable existence; historians wishing to look on the bright side of the austere sixteenth-century king Philip II always mention his fondness for empanadas, an example of his humanity and discernment. Here is a recipe for empanadas with a filling that the king might well have enjoyed.

Spinach Pasties   MAKES ABOUT 16–18

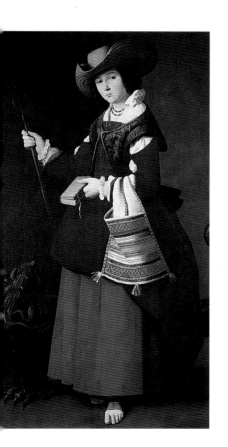

FOR THE FILLING:
500 g (generous 1 lb) spinach, washed and picked over
150 g (scant 1 cup) pine nuts
3 tbsps raisins
3 tbsps candied peel, diced
1 anchovy, cut up small
2 tbsps grated hard cheese
1 very small egg
Salt & pepper
Freshly ground cinnamon

FOR THE PASTRY:
250 g strong white flour (2½ cups all-purpose or bread flour)
½ tsp dried yeast
4 tbsps beer
A few drops of lemon juice
1 beaten egg
4 tbsps olive oil
4 tbsps milk, plus a little extra for glazing
½ tsp salt

First make the filling by cooking the spinach in its own juices. Drain well and chop. Add the rest of the filling ingredients and mix well. To make the pastry, mix all the ingredients together in a processor or by hand, kneading until the dough is springy and leaves the sides of the container. Let it rest for 30 minutes.

Roll out the pastry on a floured surface until very thin and, using a pastry cutter or small bowl, make into circles about 11 cm (4½ inches) in diameter. Put some of the filling into one half of each circle and fold over to make the pasties, curving them to make little half moon shapes, with the edges firmly closed with a frilly pattern. Glaze with the extra milk and bake on a greased baking sheet in a moderate oven until browned, about 20 to 30 minutes. Eat warm or cold.

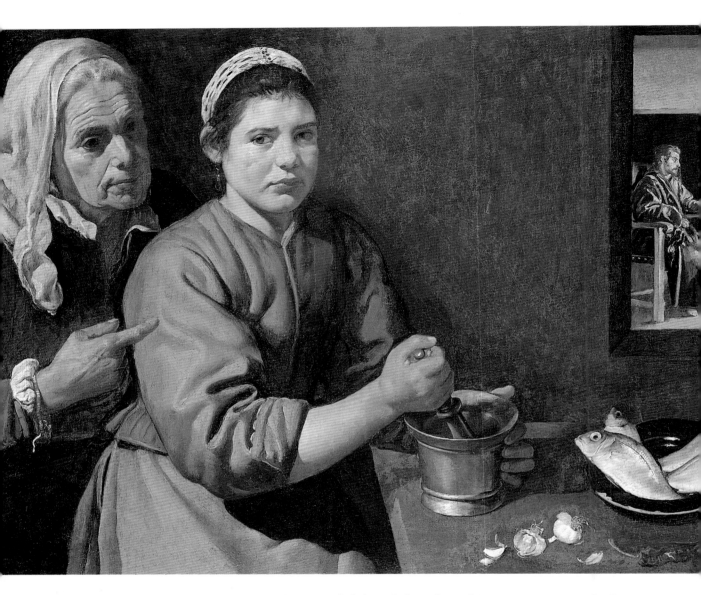

Diego Velázquez, *Kitchen
Scene with Christ in the
House of Martha and Mary*,
probably 1618.

By the time of Philip's father, the Holy Roman Emperor Charles V,
the jovial medieval banquet had become fossilized in an irrational
parade of ostentatious wealth, dominated by unbending ritual and
formality. When the Emperor retired from his creation – the greatest dominion in the world – to the austere monastery at Yuste to
pray for his soul, he renounced all the sins of the flesh except
gluttony. Couriers sped from the outermost confines of his empire
bearing rare and seasonal luxuries, and the fires in the monastery
kitchens were stoked day and night to assuage the emperor's
invincible appetites.

Philip's tastes in food were less gross, but he, too, insisted on a
rigid court etiquette with a cast of thousands performing the tedious

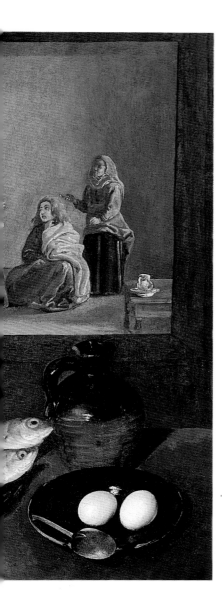

rituals which accompanied every act of the monarch. It took a multitude of functionaries to get the King to table, waft napkins before him, pass the wine from hand to hand, open it, taste it, offer, pour, and hand the goblet, deftly flourishing with prescribed gestures a damask cloth to catch the non-existent drips. No wonder the dehydrated monarch pined for the simple food of his childhood in Aranquez, where nightingales sang in the woods and from where his old nurse, remembering his young days, would send baskets of fresh strawberries.

This kitchen scene by Velázquez reminds us of food in the real world, the everyday cooking of most people in Spain in the seventeenth century, during the reign of Philip II's grandson, Philip IV. The sulky young woman is about to fry some fish and appears to be making one of the traditional sauces using egg, garlic and oil. The surprise ingredient is the chile pepper, an early sighting of this import from the New World which, together with the tomato, was to add a red, warm glow to the Spanish kitchen.

Fish fried in good olive oil is one of the common pleasures of Spanish cuisine, whether eaten straight from the pan or made into *escabeche*, a wonderful way of prolonging the life of an otherwise ephemeral dish; after cooking quickly in oil the fish is simmered in a light wine vinegar, with plenty of garlic and some sliced lemon, bayleaves and saffron, then left to cool in the cooking juices, and eaten cold. Since a quick fry-up in oil is both costly and hazardous in a small northern kitchen, better serve the fish grilled or baked in the oven, anointed with a trickle of the best Spanish extra virgin olive oil and garnished with Romesco sauce. This famous sauce from Tarragona claims to be of Phoenician origin, though how the Phoenicians managed it without tomatoes and chiles is unclear. But the idea of pounding basic aromatics with elements that give body and unctuousness to make a fine sauce is surely quite universal.

Romesco Sauce   SERVES 4

1 hard-boiled (hard-cooked) egg, shelled and chopped or 1 tbsp peeled almonds	2 garlic cloves, chopped Salt Olive oil
1 slice of good stale bread, soaked and squeezed dry	2 medium tomatoes, skinned, deseeded and chopped
1 dried chile, deseeded and soaked in a little hot water	Vinegar

Pound the egg (or almonds), bread, chile, garlic and salt in a mortar or processor. Gradually add enough oil to make a smooth paste. Mix in the tomatoes. Season with vinegar to taste.

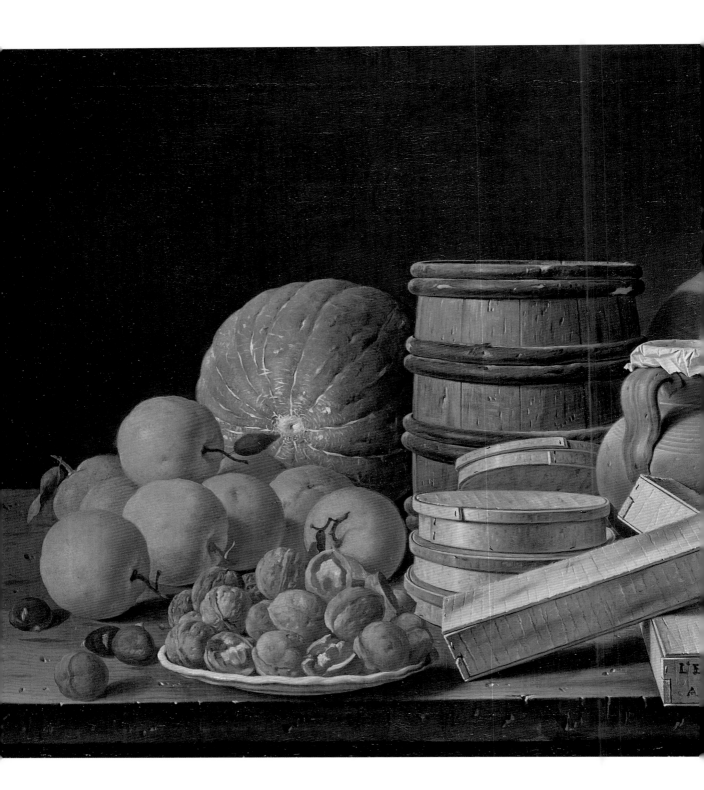

Luis Meléndez, *Still Life with Oranges and Walnuts*, 1772.

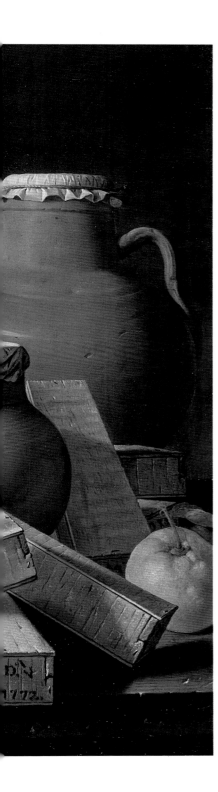

Bottles of cordials and fruit liqueurs glow in the background of many of the still lifes by Luis Egidio Meléndez. His aspiration was to produce the grandiose history paintings that were fashionable in eighteenth-century Madrid. He had the virtuoso technique, the ambition and the pride – but he also had a contentious and overbearing old father who quarrelled with the Royal Academy of Painting (where his son was a pupil), and got them both expelled. Young Luis studied abroad and came home to eke out a living as best he could.

The series of still-life paintings which delight us today brought him neither fame nor fortune. He and his wife, Maria Redonda, died in poverty in 1780. Her kitchen seems to have provided both consolation and inspiration. Meléndez, by training and temperament, needed a theme; his still lifes are not just a random selection of domestic objects, the faultless geometry of his compositions is more than an arrangement of planes, circles and rectangles – these paintings tell a story, and in most cases the story is a recipe or a meal.

This one is a celebration of Maria Redonda's winter storecupboard, the dark treasure trove of good things laid down during the summer to see her family through the winter months: *membrillo*, quince paste, in circular wooden containers, boxes of nougat, a dish of walnuts, fruit preserved in syrup in earthenware jars neatly sealed ‚with paper covers, a barrel of pickled olives, a melon kept fresh in sawdust or hung in the rafters, and the vitamin-packed joyful orbs of the first oranges of the season. Darkness and light again, the sombre depths of the storeroom yielding a bright hoard of comfort.

Membrillo was never an exclusively Spanish speciality, for quinces can flourish in a wide range of climates, and quince recipes are to be found as far apart as Seville and Edinburgh. Quinces from southern Europe are easier to find today than the fragrant native ones, but from October onwards it is possible to buy or beg enough of this under-appreciated fruit to make jelly, paste and jam and countless puddings and savoury dishes.

Quince Paste

6 quinces, peeled and cored
A little water

Sugar, see below
Dried bay leaves

Simmer the quinces until soft in the water; this may take quite a long time, about 45 minutes. Strain or process the fruit and put in a kilo of sugar (about 2¼ lbs) to every litre (2 quarts) of pulp. Boil gently, stirring all the time, until the paste is thick and leaves the sides of the pan. Tip out on to an oiled, shallow baking pan and let it cool. Cut into cubes. Dust them with very fine sugar and store in airtight boxes, interleaved with dried bay leaves.

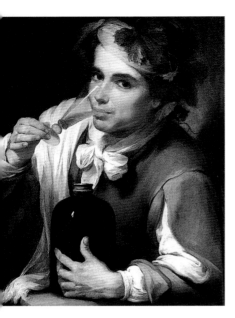

Style of Murillo, *A Young Man Drinking*, 1700–50.

Storecupboards also contained spirits distilled from wine; as cordials with healing and restorative powers, they had many uses in that hinterland where medicine and gastronomy coincide. Gin or vodka are a reasonable substitute for the *aguardiente*, literally firewater, that Maria Redonda would have used to make many flavoured fruit liqueurs.

Quince Vodka

4 quinces, as ripe and fragrant as possible, wiped clean and grated
2 cm (¾ in) stick of cinnamon
2 cloves (optional)
150 g (⅝ cup) sugar (to make a medium sweet liqueur)
1 litre (2 quarts) vodka

Half fill wide-necked glass jars with grated quince. Add the spices with restraint and sugar to taste (some like a sweet, almost sticky drink, others prefer a drier result). Top up with vodka, close tightly and hide away in a dark place for 3 or 4 months. Taste to see how the flavour has matured, and eventually strain off the liquor into clean dry bottles.

Chickpeas & Quinces   SERVES 6

200 g (1⅓ cups) dried chickpeas
2 bay leaves
Salt
500 g (generous 1 lb) quinces, weight when peeled and cored, sliced into 1 cm (½ in) wedges
1 medium onion, chopped
100 g (8 tbsps) butter, plus more to taste
50 g (¼ cup) sugar
1 tsp red wine or sherry vinegar
Freshly ground spices from:
    1 tsp anise seed, 8 cloves, 4 cardamom pods, 4 cm (1½ in) stick of cinnamon, shaken through a strainer
100 g (4 oz) pasta such as *paglia e fieno*

Cook the chickpeas and bay leaves in plenty of water until soft; this could take anything from 1 to 3 hours, depending on the quality of the chickpeas. Salt them right at the end of cooking. Meanwhile cook the quinces and onion in half the butter until soft. Season with salt and sugar (to mitigate the sharpness of the quinces) and flavour with the vinegar and some of the spices. About 15 minutes before serving cook the pasta in salted water until just done, *al dente*, and drain. Arrange a layer of drained chickpeas in a large ovenproof casserole, then add a layer of quinces and some of the pasta; dot with bits of the remaining butter and sprinkle on some of the remaining spices. Continue layering in this way until you end up with a well-buttered layer of chickpeas. Put the casserole in a moderate oven for 5 to 10 minutes to warm through, and serve with roast lamb or pork, or some cooked ham and a green salad. Alternatively this substantial dish would be very agreeable with a Middle Eastern lamb stew.

Milk Ice SERVES 4

500 ml (2 cups) full-cream milk
5 cm (2 in) sliver of lemon peel
150 g (⅝ cup) sugar

2 egg whites
Freshly ground cinnamon

Heat the milk, lemon peel and sugar together for 2 minutes, stirring all the time. Cool and freeze until starting to thicken. Beat the egg whites to meringue consistency (they should form stiff peaks) and fold into the mixture. Freeze until soft and creamy stirring from time to time to break up the ice crystals. Serve sprinkled with cinnamon.

A single, unblemished rose speaks of purity and restraint, but in April the estates of Ibn al Awam in the fertile plains of Guadalquivir must have burgeoned with roses which he harvested to fill the tear-shaped flasks of his specially constructed still, with its dome and ogival apertures reminiscent of the great mosque of Seville. He produced fifty vessels of distilled rosewater in a day and a night. Add to this the perfumed oil, the preserves and syrups, the salves and ointments and the dried blossoms which were kept in sealed jars to scent linen and banqueting halls, and the simple calculation that it takes 10,000 pounds of rose petals to make one pound of oil, and we are given some idea of the extent of this huge twelfth-century rose garden.

The darkness and light of Zurbarán's tiny still life evoke the complexities of the culture of southern Spain, and the sombre and lighthearted aspects of its cuisine.

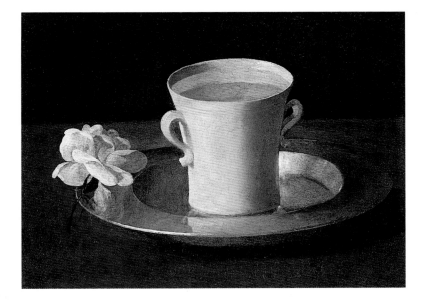

Francisco de Zurbarán, *Cup of Water and a Rose on a Silver Plate*, about 1627–30.

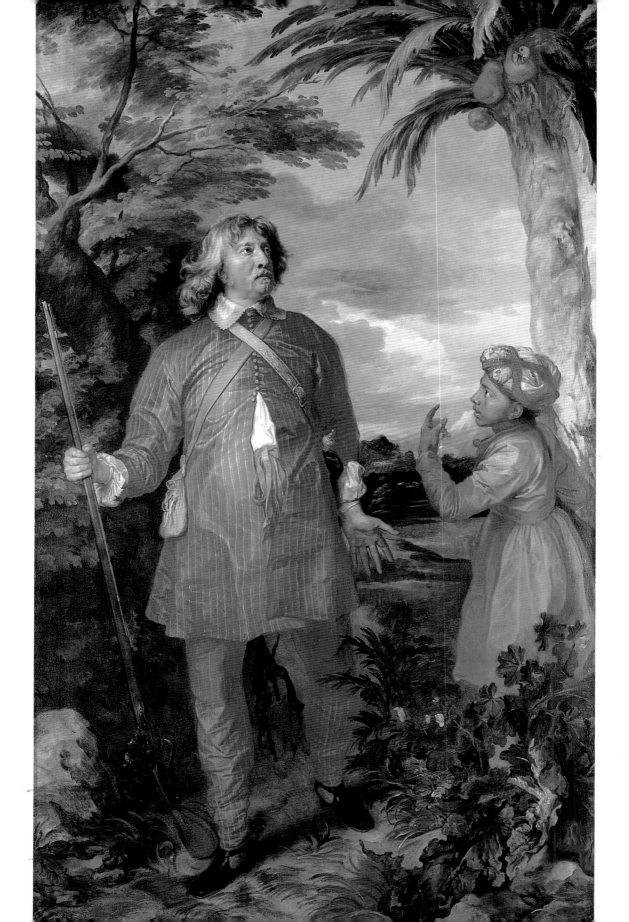

Breakfast, Sunshine, Marmalade
& STRIPED SILK PYJAMAS

Su Villiers married for love, which was just as well since her unassuming young husband William Feilding, a small landowner in Warwickshire, had few prospects of wealth or advancement. Her brother George Villiers, soon to become Duke of Buckingham, changed all that. Groomed by an ambitious mother he rose with a speed described as 'rather a flight than a growth' to become the close confidant and quaffing partner of King James I of Great Britain. His family rose with him. William was Master of the Wardrobe and 1st Earl of Denbigh by 1622, his wife and mother-in-law glittering and scheming at the steamy Jacobean court, but there is a sense that the cares of a by now large estate and the strains of promotion beyond his capacities (he had the misfortune to be the admiral in charge at the time of Britain's humiliating retreat from La Rochelle in 1630) were too much for this decent, unambitious man. In 1631 he took off for a period of wanderings in India and Persia, with exquisitely inscribed credentials but no official position, to 'better my understanding'.

This portrait was painted to celebrate his return. It must have been a welcome change from the smirking vanities and lush satins of the sitters whose demands wore the painter almost to death during his stay in England. Here the good Sir William lurches across the canvas, clad in Indian garments – a light silk shirt and comfortable matching drawstring pyjamas, his grey hair tousled and his searching gaze looking far beyond the parrot and native boy on his left. The family legend that he was lost in a forest and rescued by the small child may be close to the truth. However, lost or found, he returned home with the desire to commemorate the experience, and with the judgement to use one of the finest painters of his age.

The family were loyal supporters of Charles I and Henrietta Maria during the Civil War. William died as the result of head wounds at the siege of Birmingham on 3 April 1643 and Su survived to comfort her friend the queen in exile.

A close royalist friend of Van Dyck and the Denbighs was Sir Kenelm Digby, whose wide-ranging interests included medicine and cooking. His book, *The Closet of the Eminently Learned Sir Kenelm Digby Kt, Opened* . . . includes a potent recipe for metheglin from the Earl of Denbigh and this delicious recipe for little iced almond cakes.

Anthony van Dyck,
William Feilding, 1st Earl of Denbigh, about 1633–4.

My Lord of Denbigh's Almond Marchpane
MAKES ABOUT 15–20

250 g (2 cups) almonds, shelled,
   peeled and ground in a mortar
   or processor
50 g (¼ cup) sugar
1 tbsp orangeflower water
A pinch of ground cinnamon

FOR THE FROSTING, COMBINE:
1 egg white
100 g icing sugar (⅔ cup
   confectioner's sugar)
1 tbsp lemon juice
A little water if necessary

Mix all the non-frosting ingredients together and form into little flat
rounds about the size of walnuts. Put them on a non-stick baking sheet
and dry out in a very low oven for an hour or so. They should become
quite solid. When cold, cover thinly with the frosting.

The original recipe has complicated instructions for coating the
cakes with a brilliant, almost silver, finish, perhaps a reminder of
some of the oriental sweetmeats decorated with gold leaf enjoyed
by William Feilding on his travels.

The spiced food of the East may have been less of a novelty to Sir
William than the rice which accompanied it. Contemporary recipes
for 'Turkish' or foreign food are mildly seasoned and owe their
exoticism to the use of rice. A mild 'Pulao' is made from boiled lamb,
trimmed of fat and sliced, and rice cooked in the degreased cooking
liquid, the meat layered with dried fruit among the rice, spiced with
cinnamon and cloves, each layer anointed with butter and warmed
through in a moderate oven.

Spices continued to enhance English cooking for some time before
becoming discredited by a puritanical, chauvinistic vaunting of plain
not-messed-about-with food. The eighteenth century perhaps enjoyed the best of both worlds, the huge roasts and sizzling steaks of
London taverns and the delicately flavoured breads and buns of the
domestic kitchen.

Young James Boswell, hell bent on getting as far as possible from
both his father and his fatherland, aspired on his second trip to London to a genteel lifestyle he could barely afford. He found cheap but
respectable lodgings in Downing Street and economized on food and
drink, but allowed himself the luxury of calm, comfortable breakfasts, writing up his journal and enjoying 'fine muffins with a good
taste of flour' presented on a neat white napkin. 'Words come skip-
ping to me like lambs upon Moffat Hill,' he gloated, intoxicated with
tea and his own verbosity. 'Breakfast, sunshine, marmalade' sum up
one idyllic February morning with uncharacteristic succinctness.

Another fine meal was a lunch with Dr Samuel Johnson in Green-
wich, after a boat ride down the Thames 'charmed with the beautiful
fields on each side of the river'.

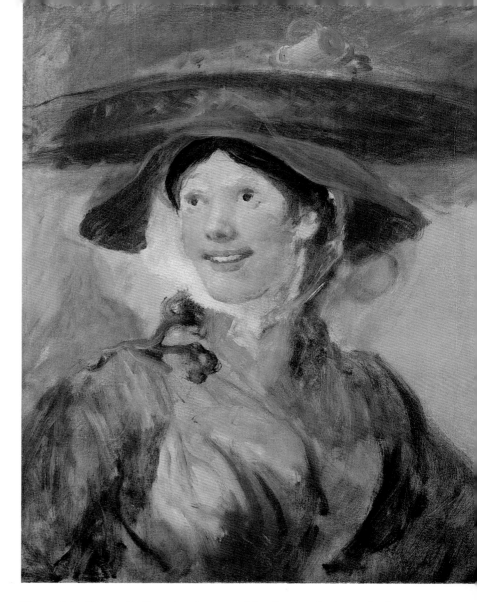

William Hogarth, *The Shrimp Girl*, about 1745.

Hogarth's *Shrimp Girl* has the charm and freshness of a fine July day on the water, her wares probably best eaten simply, with a squeeze of lemon and some pepper, but this recipe for shrimp butter makes a good sauce for any plainly cooked fish.

Shrimp Butter MAKES ONE LARGE POT

500 g (generous 1 lb) cooked shell-on shrimps (or 250 g/½ lb peeled)
250 g (½ lb) unsalted butter
Salt, pepper, nutmeg & mace to taste

Shell the shrimps and whizz the debris in a processor or blender. Boil this mush up with the butter and while still warm pass through a strainer. Stir in the shrimp, whole or pounded to a paste, and season well. Put up into one large pot and cool.

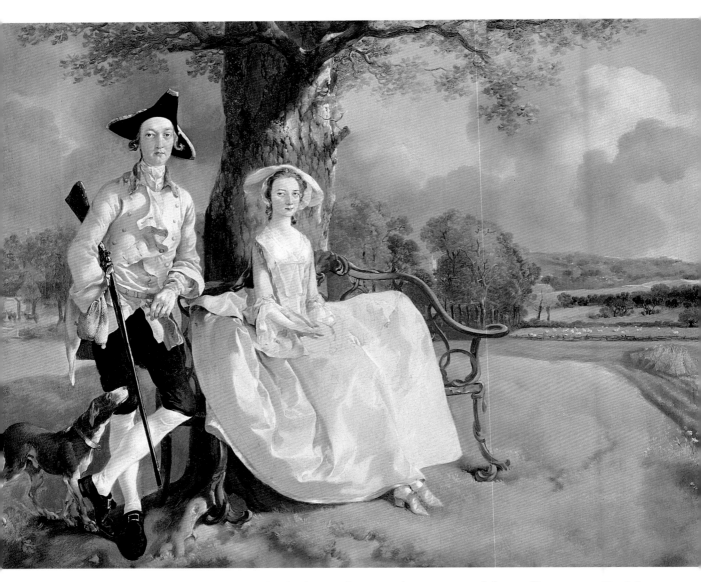

Thomas Gainsborough,
Mr and Mrs Andrews,
about 1748–9.

Elizabeth David's masterly overview of the muffin scene in *English Bread & Yeast Cookery* includes a phrase of Boswellian exuberance from a master baker in 1937: 'the batter requires attacking with vivacious turbulence' and her recipe, a distillation of several professional versions, bears him out.

Muffins MAKES 8

500 g strong white flour (4 cups all-purpose or bread flour)
450 ml (scant 2 cups) milk & water mixed
3 tbsps olive oil or butter

15 g (1 tbsp) wet yeast
½ tsp sugar
1 tbsp salt
Rice flour or cornflour (cornstarch) for forming the muffins

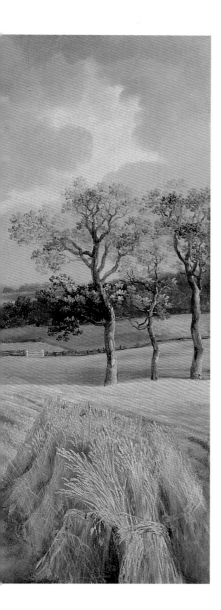

Warm the flour in an ovenproof bowl in a low oven. Meanwhile, heat the milk, water and oil or butter until warm. Mix some of this with the yeast and sugar and wait for 10 minutes for it to start to froth. Take the heated bowl out of the oven, add the salt and yeast and mix in the warm liquid. This is more of a batter than a dough and needs to be beaten with the 'vivacious turbulence' recommended, using your hands or a wooden spoon. Then leave the bowl, covered, in a warm place for 45–60 minutes for the batter to rise. Divide the dough into eight pieces. Form each one into a squarish shape and put on a non-stick surface sprinkled with rice flour, using the flour to keep everything unstuck. Cover and leave to rise for about 30 minutes while you heat up a cast-iron griddle on a low to medium heat. Lay as many muffins on it as will fit and cook on one side very slowly. Then turn gently over and cook the other side, taking about 15–20 minutes in all. Best eaten hot off the griddle, split, with a lot of butter inside.

The muffin man liked a rainy day, when housewives and servants hated to go out in the wet, and bought hot muffins from his basket, swathed in flannel, fresh from the baker. The price of butter had a knock-on effect on these entrepreneurial street vendors; the cheaper it was the more muffins they sold.

The good flour Boswell so enjoyed must have accounted for the complaisant smirks on the faces of Mr and Mrs Andrews of Sudbury, Suffolk, contemplating their broad acres of wheat and totting up the pleasant prospect of flour at 33s. 3d. the bushel and a sliding scale of bread prices that kept waged manual workers fit and hearty and their own bank balance as rotund and gleaming as their cornfields. The early East Anglian enclosure of common land had not yet produced the unrest and bitterness which fomented at the end of the eighteenth century, when labourers deprived of grazing and kindling, poorly paid and undernourished, took to burning ricks and upsetting the calm tranquility so serenely evoked by Gainsborough.

Some fifty years later William Cobbett blasted off on behalf of the rural labourer, castigating the social and economic climate that deprived him of life's two essentials – a fat pig and a rosy-cheeked, bread-making wife. 'Without bread all is misery!' he thundered and poured scorn on the lazy slut who bought, at huge expense, the vastly inferior baker's bread, adulterated with whiteners and improvers. 'Servant women in abundance appear to think that loaves are made by the baker, as knights are made by the king; things of their pure creation. . .' Cheaper and more nutritious, and more economic with fuel (three hours' work a week at the most instead of the mucky business of scraping, peeling, boiling and dishing up the despised potato and poisonous tea), bread and home-brewed beer were endowed by Cobbett with an aura of moral and physical virtue which today's nutritionists are now happy to endorse.

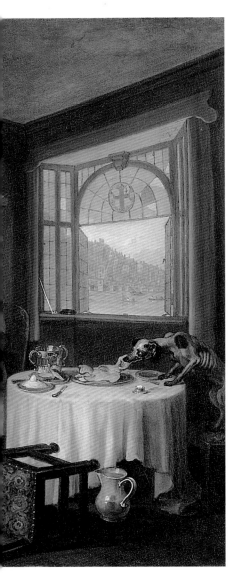

William Hogarth, detail from *Marriage à la Mode: VI, The Suicide of the Countess,* before 1743.

Opposite: William Hogarth, detail from *The Graham Children,* 1742.

The baking of bread is indeed a labour of love, and even stale scraps ask to be used rather than thrown away. Two traditional English puddings owe their success to the goodness of well-made bread.

Summer Pudding SERVES 4

8 slices of good white bread, crusts removed
250 g (generous ½ lb) redcurrants

500 g (generous 1 lb) raspberries
50 g (½ cup) each of gooseberries and blackcurrants
400 g (1⅔ cups) sugar, or to taste

Line the bottom and sides of a shallow, circular pudding dish or basin with half the bread. Top and tail the berries and warm gently through in an enamelled pan with sugar to taste, depending on the sweetness of the fruit. Pour into the bowl and cover with the rest of the bread. Cover with a plate or saucer that fits with room to spare over the bread and weigh it down with something heavy, like a can of beans. Chill for some hours or overnight, and serve with rich, thick cream.

Here is a savoury version of the classic bread and butter pudding.

Savoury Bread & Butter Pudding SERVES 6

6 eggs
300 ml double cream (1¼ cups heavy cream)
300 ml single cream (1¼ cups light cream)
Salt & pepper
A little milk
A scraping of nutmeg

12 slices of good stale white bread, retaining the crusts if not too hard
6 tbsps freshly grated Parmesan
6 canned or salted anchovies in oil, chopped
18 pitted black olives
2 tbsps butter

Beat the eggs, creams, and seasoning together into a custard, thinning with a little milk if it seems too thick. Butter an ovenproof dish about 24 x 18 cm (9½ x 7 in). Arrange a layer of bread slices, cutting them to fit if necessary. Dribble over some of the custard mixture, sprinkle generously with the Parmesan and dot with anchovies and olives. Carry on in layers until all the bread is used up, but with no cheese on the final layer, which should be plastered lavishly with butter. Bake in a moderate oven until golden and well risen, about 45–50 minutes. Eat at once before it collapses, with some lean cold ham and a plain green salad.

Boswell followed his comfortable breakfasts with social calls, walks in the park and hours of conversation in taverns and coffee houses, equally at home at a fashionable rout at Lady Northumberland's or dining off a simple steak at Child's (where the conversation was political or downright weird: 'What is the reason that a sole is not a good fish?' 'Why, it is a good fish if you dress it with a plain butter

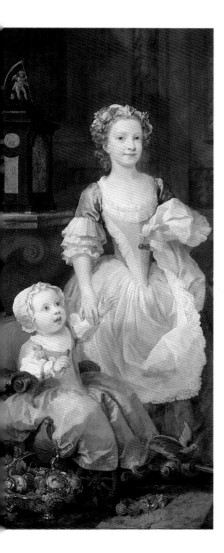

sauce. But you must have something so dev'lish high-seasoned. You might as well have a sauce of fire and brimstone.'), reading the subversive *North Briton* hot from the press. He avoided the company of brash Scottish tourists (metheglin louts) and the overly raffish theatrical crowd, but enjoyed the diverting company at Ranelagh and Battersea pleasure gardens, scorned years later by Cobbett in his eulogy of the home bread-maker: 'Talk indeed of your pantomimes and gaudy shows, your processions and installations and coronations! Give me, for a beautiful sight, a neat and smart woman, heating her oven and setting in her bread! And if the bustle does make the sign of labour glisten on her brow, where is the man that would not kiss that off, rather than lick the plaster from the cheek of a duchess?' The egregious Boswell fantasized about both possibilities over his delectable muffins, pitying his Edinburgh friends back home, 'gaien down to Halkerston's Wynd and wigs and roundabouts.'

Hogarth caught the downside of British eating in his series *Marriage à la Mode* where the rich city merchant combines pretentious table setting with execrable food. The arms of the City of London glow in costly stained glass in the window, but the fine silver loving cup holds small beer, while only a wretchedly miserable cur could covet the unappealing soused pig's head.

The smilingly wholesome portrait of *The Graham Children* is a welcome contrast to the corruption and squalor of Hogarth's London, the bowl of fresh fruit implies a healthier diet, in spite of its load of symbolism (the transient freshness and innocence of youth), and reminds us of the creamy fruit fools and pies of traditional English food.

Gooseberry & Elderflower Fool   SERVES 4

500 g (generous 1 lb) gooseberries, topped and tailed
100 g (½ cup) sugar, depending on the sweetness of the fruit
1 tbsp unsalted butter
2 or 3 heads of elderflower blossoms, washed, dried but kept on the stem (alternatively use a few drops of orangeflower water, if fruit and flowers do not coincide)
2 eggs plus 1 extra yolk
250 ml (1 cup) thick cream

Simmer the gooseberries, elderflowers, sugar and butter briefly until the fruit is soft. Beat the eggs and egg yolk with the cream and add to the fruit, stirring well on a very low heat until the mixture thickens. Serve cool or chilled. It is as well to adjust the sugar and cream to achieve a nice balance between acidity and fruitiness. Some eighteenth-century versions include raw spinach juice to mitigate the sludge-like appearance of this dish, or you could add a flavouring of sherry or muscat dessert wine.

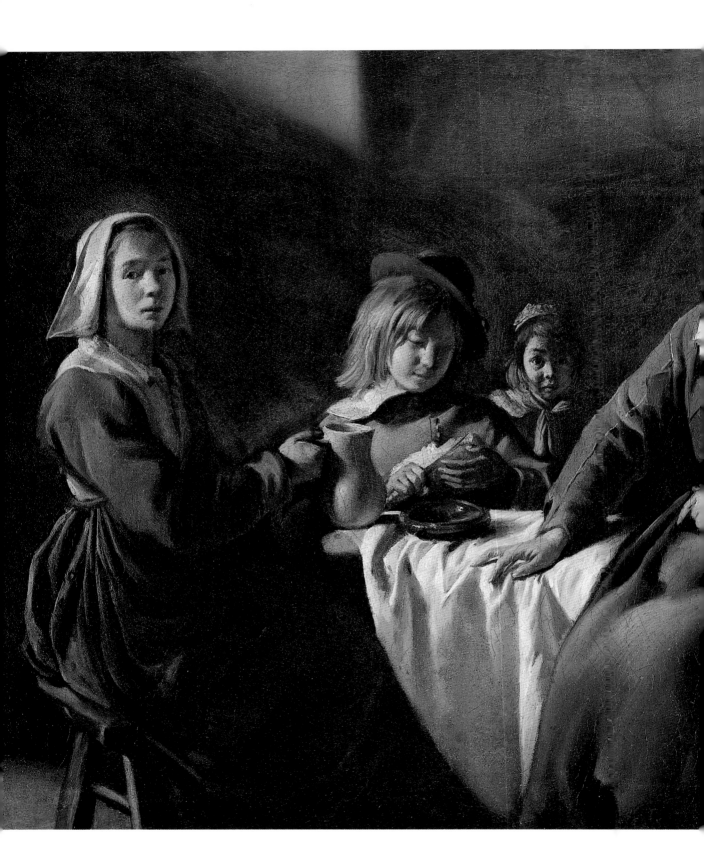

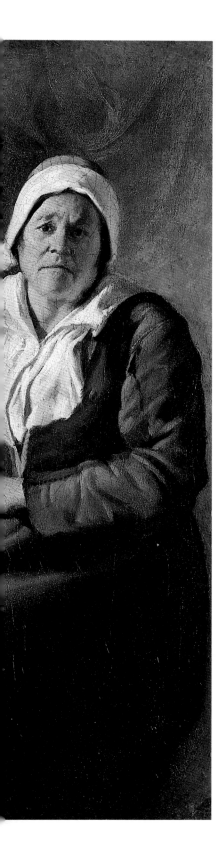

Calories & Champagne
IN PARIS & THE PROVINCES

The dignity, resignation and exhaustion of the people in this group portrait by the Le Nain brothers have nothing to do with any political agenda, or moral theme. No cheap laughs or nostalgia here, no picturesque squalor, vulgar merriment, or slogans. We have to go back to the roots of the Le Nain family to find an answer to the puzzle – who were these humble folk and what did the clients who bought the paintings see in them?

When Isaac Le Nain died in 1636 his four sons did not divide their inheritance, houses and property in and around the city of Laon in northern France, but held it jointly, managed by the brother who stayed at home while Antoine, Louis and Mathieu remained in Paris and carried on with their successful careers as painters. The dashing young men about town on the next page might be an unfinished portrait of the three brothers. Very different from the pale, almost stunted, personalities of their genre scenes. But these brothers never got so caught up in the bustle and excitement of Paris that they lost touch with the life of the small town functionaries and property owners that they remained. Perhaps they identified closely with their subjects, for there exists at least one 'peasant' scene in which the three brothers appear, barefoot but well-dressed, in a simple but far from poor interior, drinking with some satisfaction what could be their new season's wine and clutching a loaf of freshly baked bread.

The wine and the bread are significant in most of the Le Nain genre scenes, not as symbols of the sacraments, but as a statement about the way of life of small landowners and country people of the time. The word that hangs unspoken over accounts of the glories of the *Grand Siècle* is 'famine', a threat that ebbed and flowed with the price of grain, the availability of bread, and created desperation, riots and mayhem. Bread and wine are cheap calories, enough of them and the equation that it takes one hundred hours of work to earn a hundredweight of grain, makes sense. But if it takes many more hours of work for the same result then malnutrition and starvation loom. These people are sitting down, tired but at rest, and they possess with dignity the wine and bread that they need to survive. They are a sort of middling, rural peasantry, typical of the northeast of France at the time. Life was hard, but the toil was honourable, and one wonders if clients who bought these paintings were from

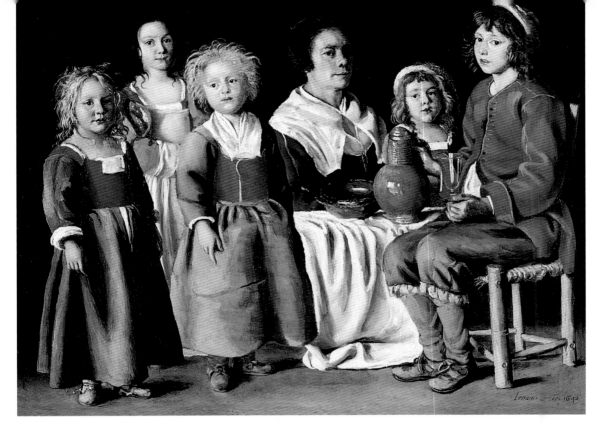

The Le Nain Brothers, *A Woman and Five Children*, 1642.

Opposite: The Le Nain Brothers, detail from *Three Men and a Boy*, probably 1640s.

Previous page: The Le Nain Brothers, *Four Figures at a Table*, perhaps 1630s.

the same stock as the Le Nain brothers, proud to contrast their decent sufficiency with the shallow glitter of Paris and, even worse, the corrupt world of intrigue and speculation based on the court at Versailles.

Sometimes a bowl of food is on the table, too, one of the porridges of pulses and grains often dismissed as boring but part of the tasty tradition of basic country food which, the moment something extra is available to add a touch of luxury – herbs, a bit of bacon, some goose fat, a ham bone – becomes a fine stew or pottage.

Stewed Beans   SERVES 6

500 g (generous 1 lb) dried white haricot beans
4 garlic cloves, smashed
2 bay leaves
6 whole black peppercorns
100 g (8 tbsps) butter
1 tbsp chopped fresh parsley

Wash the beans well in a strainer to get rid of any dust or grit. Do not soak; young beans of the same year will soften as they cook. Put them in a large heavy pan, cover with plenty of water and add two of the garlic cloves, the bay leaves and the peppercorns. Bring to the boil and cook vigorously for 2 minutes; then turn the heat down and simmer, uncovered, for 1 to 2 hours, depending on the quality of the beans. Check, cook some more if necessary, adding water if needed. There should be no need to drain the beans, for the cooking water is tasty and gets more so as it reduces. When the beans are soft but not mushy cook the remaining garlic cloves in the butter until pale gold and add to the beans. Taste and salt as necessary. Serve with the parsley.

Try a good extra virgin olive oil instead of butter. A non-vegetarian version could include the knuckle end of a Parma ham from a friendly delicatessen or a few garlic sausages added to the simmering beans 20 minutes before serving. The elaboration of this dish into the cassoulet of the south-west, with the beans and a variety of meats cooked separately and finally brought together into one unctuous, fragrant mass in an earthenware pot in the oven, stirring in the savoury crust as it forms, is peasant food raised to a romantic art form, a long way from the subsistence stews of the Le Nain families.

These people of the north-east, their wide, bleak fields racked by the to-and-fro of armies, Spanish, Austrian, French, impoverished by iniquitous taxation, a harsh centralized regime and periods of dearth and famine, compensated for the rigours of life with as many feasts and festivals as could be crammed into the liturgical and family year, when weddings, births, saints' days and holidays stimulated a riot of entertainment and jollity. Genre paintings of scenes of gluttony and merrymaking often show filled tarts, sweet or savoury custard enriched with cheese, bacon, onions, or whatever, contained within a casing of pastry or crisp bread dough. This universal baked tart is by no means confined to the north, and dogmatism about the origins and composition of quiches, flans and pies is best avoided. Here is a recipe characteristic of Picardy.

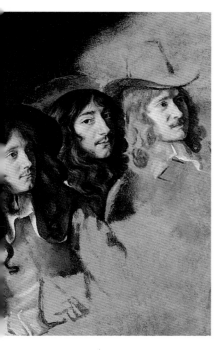

Flamiche SERVES 4

225 g (½ lb) flaky pastry
4 medium leeks, well washed and finely sliced
125 g (10 tbsps) butter
4 eggs
150 g (1½ cups) Gruyère cheese, grated
50 g (½ cup) Parmesan, grated
2 tbsps crème fraîche or thick cream
Salt & pepper

Roll out the pastry on a floured surface to fit a 20 cm (8 in) quiche pan. Cover with foil and weigh down with dried beans. Bake 'blind' in a moderate oven until the pastry is browned, about 20 to 30 minutes. Remove the beans and foil and set aside to cool. Meanwhile sweat the sliced leeks in half the butter, covered, until soft, stirring occasionally to keep from sticking. Cool, then mix in the other ingredients and the rest of the butter. Tip the mixture into the pastry case and cook in a moderate oven until the filling is set, about 20 minutes. Serve hot or at room temperature.

A favourite dish for a family festival was rabbit. Here is a version using red wine and aromatics: a wild rabbit would be best, nearer to the herb-fed creatures of a northern farmyard.

Rabbit with Prunes   SERVES 4

1 rabbit, cut into pieces
1 bottle of good red wine
4 garlic cloves, smashed
2 bay leaves
Thyme, rosemary & sage
6 juniper berries
1 onion, chopped
100 g (4 oz) unsmoked fatty bacon or pancetta, diced
A little oil or butter for frying
Salt & pepper
20 pitted prunes
1 tbsp dried fruit – raisins, currants, sultanas (golden raisins),
    mixed peel
Beurre manié, made by mixing 1 tbsp of butter into 1 tsp of flour
    and forming into little blobs the size of a pea

Marinate the rabbit overnight in half the wine, the garlic and seasonings. Next day cook the onion and bacon in the oil or butter until pale gold, add the rabbit pieces and the marinade and simmer for 30 minutes. Meanwhile soak the prunes and dried fruit in the rest of the wine. Add the prunes and their soaking liquor to the rabbit and simmer, uncovered, for another 20 minutes. Cook longer if necessary, then adjust the seasonings and thicken the juices with the beurre manié.

Another characteristic dish is this gentle treatment of red cabbage.

Sweet-sour Red Cabbage   SERVES 6

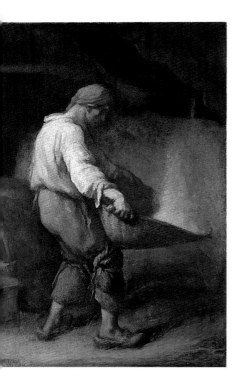

1 kg (generous 2 lbs) red cabbage
1 large onion, chopped
2 tbsps butter
2 garlic cloves, smashed
3 cloves
3 bay leaves
250 ml (1 cup) red wine
1 large tart apple, peeled, cored
    and sliced
Salt & pepper
1 tbsp honey, or more

Cut the cabbage into quarters and slice away the thick parts of the stem. Chop the quarters roughly. Cook the onion in half the butter until soft, then add the cabbage, garlic, cloves and bay leaves. Pour in the wine and simmer for 30 minutes. Add the apple and cook for another 30 minutes. Season with salt, pepper and honey and stir in the rest of the butter. The cooking time can be prolonged on a low heat if necessary.

Cooking the onion in lard instead of butter, and adding some chopped fatty bacon is a non-vegetarian option.

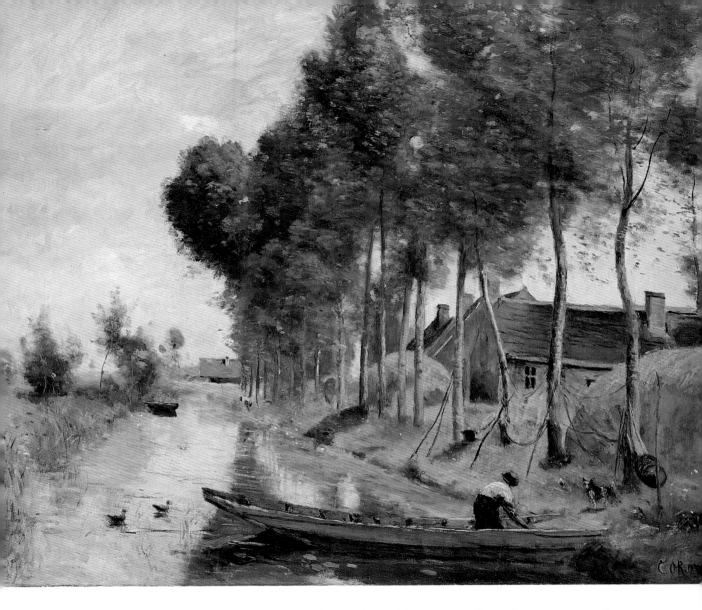

Jean-Baptiste-Camille Corot, *Landscape at Arleux-du-Nord*, 1871–4.

Opposite: Jean-François Millet, *The Winnower*, about 1847–8.

Two hundred years later other painters brought passionate political convictions to their scenes of country life; Millet's peasant, twisted in an ungainly and back-breaking pose, winnows grain, reminding us of how our daily bread is the result of someone else's cruelly unrewarding toil. The painting was bought by Ledru-Rollin, a revolutionary politician who fled soon after its purchase in 1848, and it was only discovered recently in an attic in the United States.

It was to escape the upheavals of political unrest that Corot left Paris in 1871 to stay with a friend in Douai, where he came under the spell of the tranquil farmland and wide windy plains of Artois, the formative influence on the Le Nain brothers. These unchanged landscapes and people figure in many of his open-air studies.

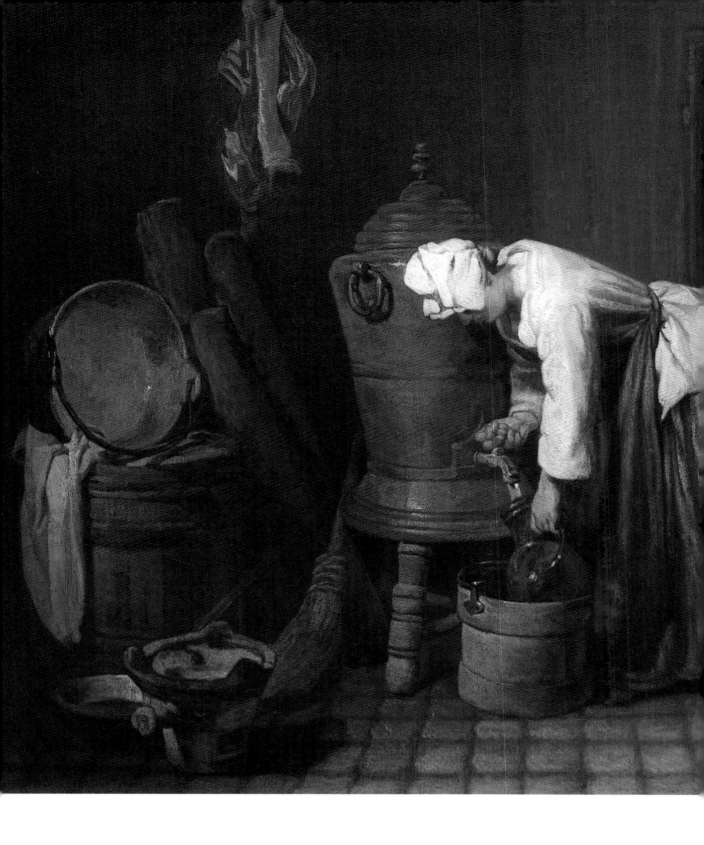

But although country food remained very much the same throughout the centuries the Le Nain brothers would have been aware in Paris of a gentle change of emphasis rather than a revolution in the cuisine of France. In 1651, La Varenne's *Le Cuisinier françois* tells more of continuity than innovation, his light sauces and mild seasonings were common to other countries as well, particularly England and Holland. The landscape twitched at some point and French fashions became predominant throughout Europe. Food succumbed to the strict rules of behaviour applied to manners and taste, and the gentle, almost universal, changes of the seventeenth century became codified in the conventions of *haute cuisine*. By the time of Chardin, a century later, this new style of cooking was the dominant influence on the rest of Europe. His paintings tell of a comfortable domesticity, with calm family life continuing beyond the scullery where a maid draws water from a copper cistern. A simple omelette, or *aumelette* as La Varenne called it, might have been more appropriate to this bourgeois family than the complex dishes garnished with the inevitable asparagus, truffles, artichokes and coxcombs of the nobility. Delicate egg dishes have been around for time out of mind – Pontormo was whipping up a deft rolled omelette in sixteenth-century Florence – but La Varenne was the first to use the term *baveuse* in print, and explain the technique of a light, moist, quickly cooked omelette.

Herb Omelette   SERVES 4

1 tbsp each of fresh finely chopped spinach, sorrel, parsley and the chopped tips of any fragrant young herbs – thyme, basil, marjoram, as you wish	Salt Some freshly grated nutmeg and ground cinnamon 4 eggs, lightly beaten Butter

Beat the herbs and seasonings into the eggs. Melt the butter in a medium frying pan or skillet and add the eggs, tipping the pan and gently coaxing the uncooked egg to the edge and middle to get a soft, lightly cooked mass. Cook until just set. Sprinkle with a very little sugar, roll up and serve cut in slices.

La Varenne's omelettes were in the old tradition, perfumed with sugar and rosewater. One version consists of slices of apple cooked in butter and sugar then added to a lightly cooked plain omelette which is rolled and served dusted with sugar; another of pine nuts, chopped candied fruit and raisins added to the egg mixture and, when nicely cooked and rolled, sprinkled with cinnamon and rosewater.

Jean-Siméon Chardin,
The Cistern, 1733 or later.

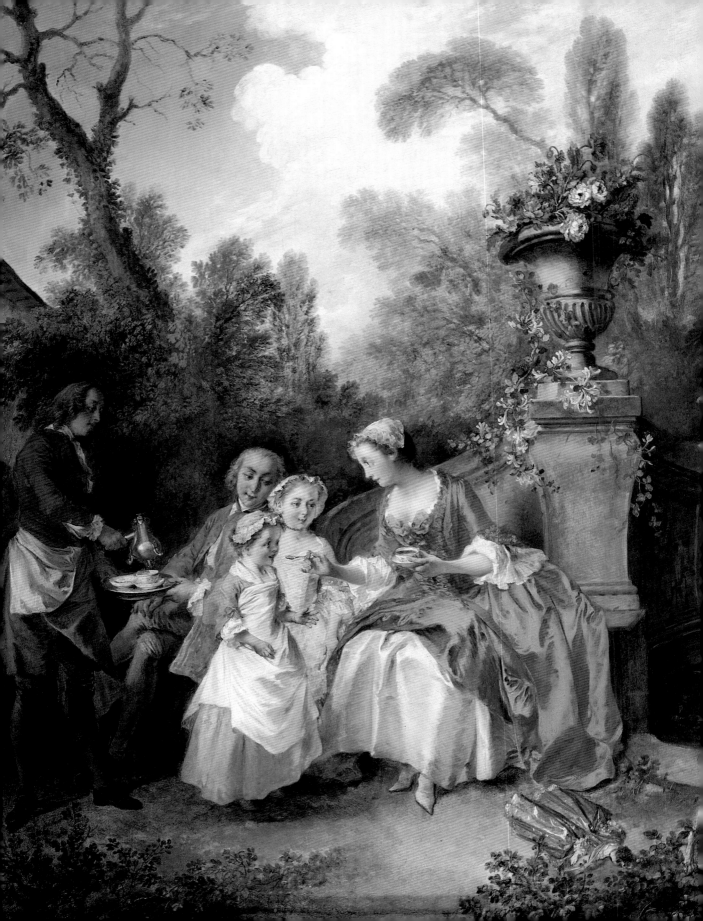

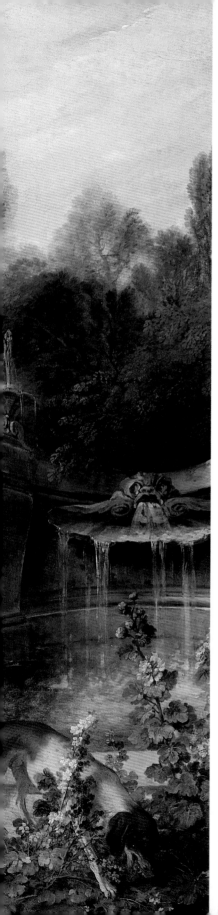

Meanwhile, a long way from Artois and in a very different climate, another family is enjoying a tranquil afternoon snack on the terrace of a country villa. The little girl, enveloped in a massive napkin, is about to become addicted to that sophisticated modern indulgence – chocolate. Little did she or her fond parents know that cocoa in its native land, Mexico, was a psychotropic substance so potent that it was reserved for priests and god-kings only. By the time it reached eighteenth-century France chocolate had lost touch with its origins and become a fashionable beverage.

The idea of adding a little bitter chocolate to a stew of hare or rabbit came to Europe from the New World where perhaps its most celebrated use is in the turkey stew enriched with nuts, spices and chiles, *mole poblano*. An infinitesimal amount of chocolate gives the dish a wonderful richness, too much can be disconcerting. In this chocolate cake the pepper has a similar role, merging with the spices to enhance the flavour.

Spiced Chocolate Cake

MAKES A FLAT CAKE ABOUT 23 CM (9 IN)

½ tsp each of cardamoms, anise seed & cloves	50 g plain flour (½ cup all-purpose flour)
2 peppercorns & a pinch of coarse chile powder	50 g (½ cup) potato flour
8 cm (3 in) stick of cinnamon	½ tsp baking powder
3 cm (1¼ in) piece of vanilla pod (vanilla bean)	2 tbsps unsweetened cocoa powder
100 g (½ cup) sugar	150 g (10 tbsps) butter, softened
A pinch of salt	2 medium eggs, separated
50 g (scant ½ cup) whole unpeeled almonds	1 tsp orange zest
50 g (2 squares) bitter chocolate	2 tbsps rum
	Orange juice if needed
	Cream and rum to serve

Line a greased 23 x 18 cm (9 x 7 in) cake pan with buttered paper or foil. Grind the spices, sugar and salt together, reserving 2 teaspoons. Coarsely grind the almonds. Pound the chocolate into uneven lumps about the size of peas. Sift the flours, baking powder and cocoa together. Cream the spiced sugar and butter together until light and fluffy. Beat the egg whites until stiff and lightly mix the yolks. Beat the yolks into the sugar and butter, then mix in the flours and orange zest, moistening with the rum and orange juice to get a loose but not sloppy batter. Stir in the nuts and chocolate. Work in about a third of the egg whites, then deftly fold in the rest. Put the mixture into the prepared cake pan and bake in a preheated moderate oven until done, about 40 minutes. The cake is cooked through when a skewer inserted into the centre comes out clean. Serve with plenty of whipped cream flavoured with the reserved spiced sugar and more rum.

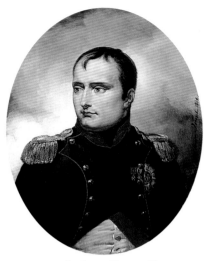

Emile-Jean-Horace Vernet,
The Emperor Napoleon I,
1815.

If the clients of the Le Nain brothers identified with their sitters, it is not unreasonable to suppose that those of Lancret identified with this innocent, happy family in its arcadian setting of lush greenery and outsize garden furniture, blotting out the disturbingly close world of riots and unrest. This idealized image of security and wealth must have helped the uneasy aristocrats of pre-revolutionary France to ignore the social ferment bubbling away beyond their elegant garden walls, where the frightening correlation between effort, the price of bread and desperation was an ever present menace.

After the French Revolution the cooks of defunct noble establishments found employment feeding the crowds of citizens and deputies drawn to Paris from the provinces without households of their own. This new set of masters were comforted and restored by the brand new restaurants offering aristocratic cuisine.

Napoleon, too busy getting ahead to enjoy his food, left gastronomy to one of his more devious ministers, Talleyrand, who adroitly survived several unsavoury regimes; perhaps his most steadfast loyalty was to Brie, his favourite cheese, which he did a lot to promote. He might have enjoyed this on one of his visits to England.

Toasted Cheese & Asparagus SERVES 4

8 asparagus spears
250 g (9 oz) young Brie
4 rounds of home-made white
   bread, toasted

100 g (8 tbsps) butter
Freshly grated nutmeg
Black pepper

Cook the asparagus spears in a very little water. Cut off the tips and reserve, crush the rest of the spears in the cooking liquid and boil up with the butter to make a few spoonfuls of concentrated liquid.
Cut away any hard parts of the Brie crust and slice the cheese. Toast the bread, butter generously and cover with the sliced cheese. Melt under the grill (broiler). Season with nutmeg and pepper and a dribble of the asparagus cooking liquor. Serve very hot, decorated with the asparagus spears.

Napoleon's insensitivity gave rise to what must be one of the odder dishes of the classical tradition. Once, in mid campaign, his long-suffering chef offered him a variety of local produce – a chicken, some crayfish, new-laid eggs, ham, a handful of tomatoes, some olives, anchovies. 'Cook them as fast as you can and bung them all on the same dish, I've no time to waste while you mess around. . .' was the gist of the emperor's instructions. He scoffed the lot then strutted off to win the battle of Marengo. Versions of this dish abound. Here is one which mercifully omits the fried eggs.

Previous page: Nicolas Lancret, *A Lady in a Garden taking Chocolate (?) with some Children,* probably 1742.

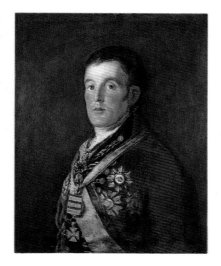

Francisco de Goya, *The Duke of Wellington*, 1812–14.

Chicken Marengo   SERVES 4

250 g (9 oz) shell-on prawns (shrimp)
250 ml (1 cup) dry white wine
5 garlic cloves, 4 smashed, 1 chopped finely
2 bay leaves
Lemon juice
Freshly ground black pepper
1 free range chicken, cut into pieces

100 g (4 oz) fatty ham or bacon, cubed
Olive oil for frying
2 medium ripe tomatoes, chopped
2 anchovy fillets, drained and boned
12 pitted black olives
12 triangles of home-made white bread fried in butter

Peel the prawns (shrimp) and reserve the flesh. Put the debris in a saucepan with the wine, 2 cloves of smashed garlic and the bay leaves. Boil to get a small amount of concentrated stock. Marinade the prawns (shrimp) in the chopped garlic, lemon juice and black pepper. Meanwhile fry the chicken pieces and ham or bacon in olive oil until golden. Add the tomatoes and cook quickly to evaporate the juices. Pound the remaining 2 smashed cloves of garlic in a mortar with the anchovies and put the paste in a bowl. Strain the prawn (shrimp) stock into the bowl, mix and add to the chicken. Cook fast for a few minutes and serve on an oval dish decorated with the olives and the reserved prawns (shrimp), with the triangles of fried bread tucked around the sides of the dish.

A nod towards authenticity might be an embellishment of lightly fried quails' eggs, glistening like the meretricious medals, the *Légion d'Honneur* for one, invented for himself by our hero in this portrait by Vernet.

Goya's sketch, made in 1812, the same year as the portrait of Napoleon, shows the Duke of Wellington flushed with success after winning the battle of Salamanca and equally encrusted with decorations, added by the artist over the years as the Golden Fleece joined the Peninsula Medallion, later to be replaced by the Military Gold Cross, jostling for position on the manly chest with the Order of the Bath, the Order of the Tower and Sword of Portugal and the Order of San Fernando of Spain.

In 1815, when the allied armies passed through Epernay (not far south of the Laon home of the Le Nain brothers), they liberated six thousand bottles of champagne from the cellars of a distressed M. Moët, who cheered up the following year when the barbarian hordes despatched orders for more of the same, thus doubling his output. Brillat Savarin came up with equally comforting statistics – the crushing defeat of the French armies at Waterloo resulted in a treaty imposing a fine of fifteen hundred million francs, most of which he claims trickled back into the exchequer through the restaurants and traiteurs catering to the victors which, during the peace, turned Paris into a veritable refectory.

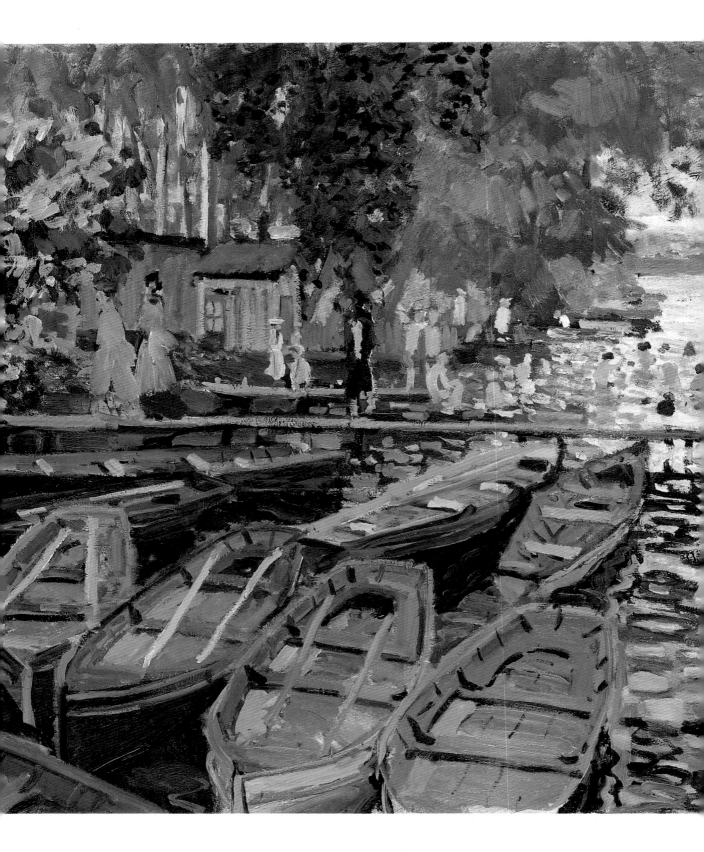

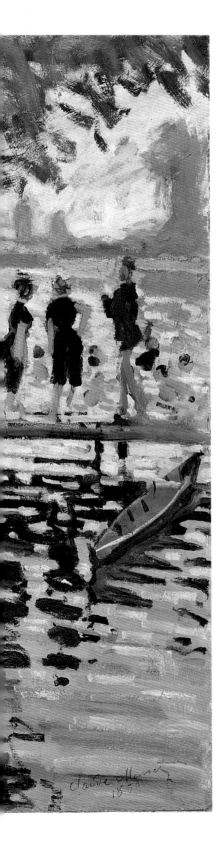

Gastronomic Impressions
IN & AROUND 19TH-CENTURY PARIS

Fresh air and new horizons generated healthy appetites in the raffish young people who took the train out of Paris at weekends to mess about in boats and bathe in the river Seine near Bougival. Just out of the picture on the right was a funny little round island affectionately known as the Camembert, off to the left a riverside restaurant. Two forward young women in provocative bathing suits make the most of the freedom and lack of restraint, ogling possible partners for the next meal.

At first impoverished young painters ate at country inns serving basic country food, depicted with stark realism by young Monet in his youthful enthusiasm, but a decade later shrewd entrepreneurs moved in to offer the smart food enjoyed by Renoir and his friends in an iridescent haze of reflected light and enticing aromas at posh boating establishments.

Monet used to come to Bougival with his friend Renoir, keen to pin down in paint transient sensations of light and colour and hedonistic enjoyment. Their experimental sketches are as universally loved now as they were execrated then, and it is hard to imagine the shocking impact on conventional taste of the wild rush of feckless youth in and out of the new suburban rail stations, and the slither and slap of soft oil paints laid with eager flat brush on canvas by these enthusiastic, irreverent young men. Of course artists had sketched outdoors for some time, bringing neat little 'impressions' home to be worked up with impeccable finish in the studio, but not with subjects as modern and evanescent as these. It was not so much the outdoors as the 'here and now', the apparent glorification of trivial contemporary frivolity which upset serious academic critics.

The railways opened up the regions of France to a swathe of society that had never travelled before. The young and impoverished could live cheaply in a small seaside hotel or a country cottage, so while fashionable resorts catered for the rich and famous, young painters like Monet could survive on next to nothing in unknown seaside towns in Normandy, working like his master Boudin on beach and seascapes, merging the swirl of petticoats in the sharp sea breezes on the sands of Trouville with the surge of wind and wave over the rocks at Etretat. Monet returned all his life to the light and atmosphere of these northern skies and the robust food of Normandy.

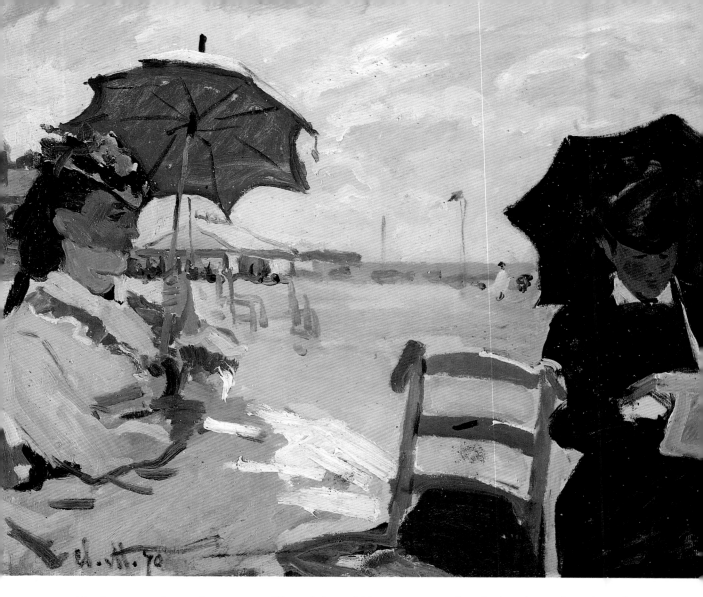

Claude Monet, *The Beach at Trouville*, 1870.

Opposite: Eugène Boudin, *Beach Scene, Trouville*, 1873.

The celebrated Norman recipe for chicken braised with apples, cream and calvados is almost too much of a good thing but a pheasant cooked breast down on a bed of quinces, then carved and served with a sauce made from the strained quince and cooking juices, with a little butter and calvados (or whisky, or indeed any honest spirit to hand) is fragrant and not too rich. Served with a 'last minute' potato gratin like the one that follows, this can be a modest reminder of Normandy's rich cuisine.

Potato Gratin SERVES 4

1 kg (generous 2 lbs) potatoes, cut into thin slices	Bay leaves and garlic if wished
	Salt & pepper
250 ml (1 cup) milk	200 g (scant ½ lb) butter, or more

Previous page: Claude Monet, *Bathers at La Grenouillère*, 1869.

Simmer the potatoes in the milk in a non-stick pan until almost done, about 15 minutes. Add bay leaves and garlic and season with salt and pepper. Tip them into a buttered ovenproof dish and dot with the butter. Bake in a hot oven until brown and bubbling, about 20 minutes.

This does not have the unctuousness of a slow-cooked gratin starting from raw potatoes and taking much time, cream and butter, but its lightness is a blessing with the pheasant and would allow for this rich apple custard as a dessert.

Apple Custard   SERVES 4

1 kg (generous 2 lbs) tart apples, peeled, cored and sliced
100 g (8 tbsps) butter
175 g (¾ cup) sugar
250 ml (1 cup) rich cream
4 eggs
Freshly ground cinnamon and nutmeg

Brown the apples in the butter in a heavy pan. Add the sugar and cook quickly to caramelize. Tip the mixture into an ovenproof dish and allow to cool a little. Mix the cream and eggs together and pour over. Bake in a low oven until the custard sets, about 30 to 40 minutes. Serve warm, dusted with the spices and more sugar if necessary. A few cloves among the apples would be fine, or a slug of calvados poured over just before serving.

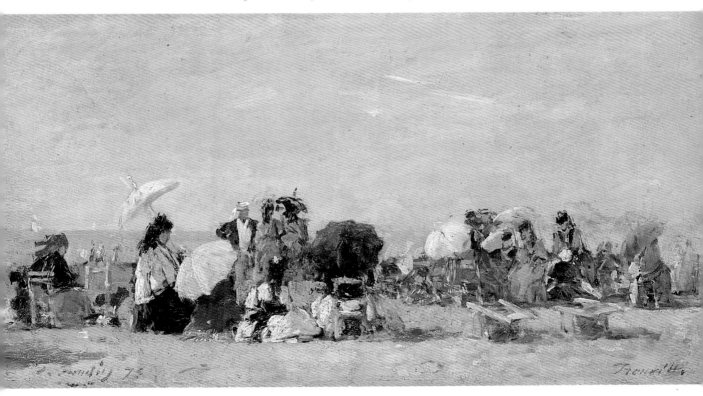

Zizi the cat would curl up as cats do in the middle of Edouard Manet's letter. He retaliated by drawing the animal in the centre of the page, fitting the words in around her intrusive presence. In this slightly larger than life portrait of the painter's wife Suzanne, Zizi, a big puss, is quite cut down to size, peacefully ensconced on Madame Manet's vast pink bulk. Gentle but firm, sweet but with an inner strength like a well-composed raspberry bavarois, Suzanne's kind and comforting presence sustained the volatile and temperamental painter during thirty years of marriage. She was a gifted pianist, hired to give music lessons to the Manet brothers. Her liaison with the young Edouard produced a son who was brought up discreetly and lovingly as her baby brother. After the death of his disapproving father, Edouard married Suzanne, who performed brilliantly at his mother's fashionable soirées but kept well away from the studio, content to be a benign domestic influence.

Raspberry Bavarois   SERVES 6

500 g (generous 1 lb) raspberries
100 g (½ cup) sugar
15 g (1 tbsp) gelatine, dissolved in
   125 ml (½ cup) hot water

3 eggs, separated
300 ml (1¼ cups) milk
250 ml double cream (1 cup
   heavy cream)

Pass the raspberries through a strainer and sweeten the purée with a little of the sugar. Stir the dissolved gelatine into the purée. Make a custard with the egg yolks, the remaining sugar and milk by heating gently in a heavy non-stick pan, stirring all the time until it thickens. Beat the egg whites until stiff. Beat the cream until stiff.

Stir the raspberry purée into the custard. Fold in the beaten egg whites. Chill until almost set, at least 45 minutes. Finally fold in the cream and chill some more. This can be made in a mould and presented, unmoulded, as miracle of soft coherence and almost weightless bulk; a simpler solution is to serve it in a decorative glass or china bowl.

Manet missed Suzanne terribly during the siege of Paris in 1870; letters came and went by carrier pigeon or balloon and the starving Parisians ate cats, dogs, rats and animals from the zoo. Zizi must have been safe with Suzanne and the artist's mother in the Pyrenees and so escaped the fate of the maid's cat, who vanished one night.

Manet's portraits of his women friends and models have a vibrancy quite lacking in his paintings of his wife; Berthe Morisot smoulders and glows, Victorine Meurent has the poise and sparkiness of a Parisian working girl, Méry Laurent radiates good humour and vitality, while Suzanne exudes a mild, bland benevolence, comforting rather than stimulating. Even Zizi seems to have a stronger personality than his kind mistress.

Opposite: Edouard Manet, *Woman with a Cat,* about 1880–2.

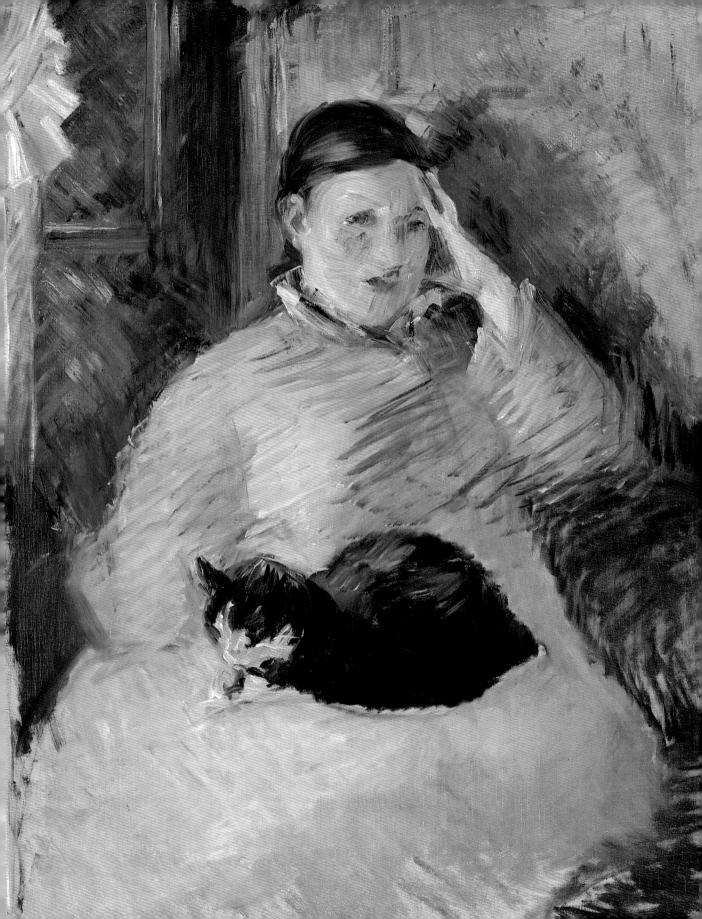

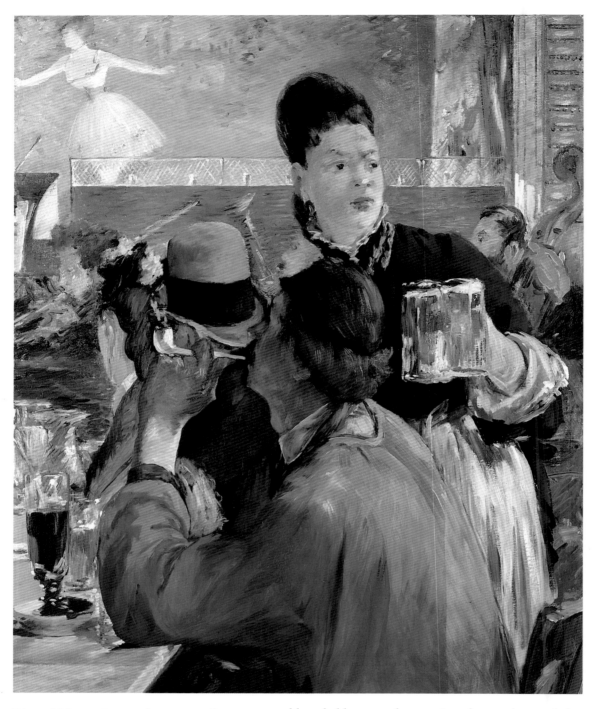

Edouard Manet, *Corner of a Café Concert*, probably 1878–80.

Suzanne would probably never have enjoyed or understood the charms of the Café Guerbois, where the iconoclastic young painters gathered every afternoon, or the steamy café concerts or music halls to which her husband, the worldly *flâneur*, could escape when the elegant respectability of his home life became too stifling. It is unlikely, though, that Manet did any gastronomic slumming – his tastes in food were conventional – on a trip to Spain he was intoxicated by Goya and Velázquez but rejected the finest food in Madrid, the olive oil and vibrant seasonings just too much for his refined Parisian palate.

Toulouse-Lautrec on the other hand enjoyed exploring the bistros and restaurants of Paris for regional dishes and unusual recipes. He regaled his special friends, the 'happy few', with this casserole of tender young pigeons, a recipe discovered in a pastry-cook's in the rue de Bourgogne.

Pigeons with Olives   SERVES 6

6 tender young wood pigeons or
  squabs
2 medium onions, chopped
4 shallots, chopped
2 slices of fatty bacon, chopped
1 tbsp butter
1 tbsp flour
250 ml (1 cup) stock
3 bay leaves
1 tsp chopped fresh thyme
1 tsp chopped fresh rosemary
36 pitted green olives

2 tbsps cognac
Salt & pepper
FOR THE STUFFING:
250 g (about ½ lb) sausagemeat
  from Toulouse sausages
½ tsp freshly ground black
  pepper
½ tsp freshly grated nutmeg
And, failing the truffles specified
  by Lautrec, 1 tbsp dried mushrooms, soaked for 20 minutes,
  rinsed, drained and chopped

First make the stuffing by combining all the ingredients in a bowl. Use to stuff the pigeons. In a flameproof casserole large enough to hold all the birds, cook the onions, shallots and bacon in the butter. When the onions are soft, stir in the flour and cook for 2 minutes, then pour in the stock and herbs and stir well. Add the birds, breasts down, and simmer uncovered until tender, about 1 hour for young birds, but longer if you have older ones; less for small birds. About 20 minutes before serving add the olives and cognac and taste before adjusting the seasoning; the bacon and olives may have supplied all the salt you need.

Toulouse-Lautrec was well supplied with luxuries from his family's properties in the south, but his contemporary Camille Pissarro was content with the humble products of the kitchen gardens he loved to paint. When the cabbages which figured in so many of them were in danger of acquiring profound and portentous double meanings he gently defused the situation with characteristic good humour: 'Ah yes, the Symbolists are really quite amazing, deep down they dislike cabbages because they don't know how to cook them, not everyone can make a really good cabbage soup with bacon – wonderful when it's piping hot!'

Cabbage with Bacon   SERVES 6

1 medium savoy or hearted
   cabbage, coarsely chopped
250 g (about ½ lb) salt belly of
   pork or pancetta, in small
   cubes or in one piece (if in one
   piece cook first in water for 30
   to 45 minutes)
6 garlic cloves, coarsely chopped

1 parsnip, sliced
1 carrot, sliced
1 onion, chopped
1 litre (2 quarts) stock
1 wine glass of red or white wine
Bay leaves, thyme, sage and
   rosemary
1 Toulouse or pure pork sausage

Blanch the cabbage in salted water for 2 minutes and drain. Put into
a large pan with the salt pork, garlic, vegetables, stock, wine and herbs
and simmer for 30 minutes. Add the sausage and cook for 30 minutes
longer. Do not add any more salt, but season with pepper if desired.
The addition of an elderly partridge at the start of cooking transforms
this peasant dish into a luxury.

Pissarro never idealized the French peasant – after all he was married
to one. His political beliefs and sense of humanity made him aware of
the deep divisions in French life (an ancient rural past co-existing
with a dynamic modern industrial society) and he may have used the
techniques of Impressionism and Pointillism to reconcile the two in
his own benign way. His formidable wife Julie had been his parents'
parlourmaid, and he made no secret of his preference for her warmth
and robust common sense to the stuffy conventions of his bourgeois
family. Throughout his long life he was plagued by money problems
but gave his six children generous financial support, gently subvert-
ing their mother's attempts to prod them away from the arts towards
more stable professions. The family usually spent winters in Paris
and lived cheaply in the countryside for the rest of the year, ending
up in Eragny when Julie badgered him to borrow from their friend
Monet to buy a house and settle down. But the reluctant anarchist
property owner kept his cabbage tastes and enjoyed pottering round
the markets of Normandy in search of the patterned cotton hand-
kerchiefs and aprons that brightened his peasant girls at work in
meadow and farmyard, and possibly bringing home some of the rich
cream, perfumed apples and plump fowls of the region.

   Pissarro loved the coarse texture and weave of peasant clothing.
He did not render them with the slick virtuosity of Jan Steen's shot
silk, but used this pleasure in rough repetitive patterns in his laying
on of paint, like the repetitive rhythms of agricultural work and the
pattern of furrow, stubble and vegetable plot. Rough, honest
country food like cabbage stew and duck with lentils co-existed with
refined Parisian cuisine just as the worlds of peasants and factory
workers continued only a short train journey away from the glitter
of Haussmann's boulevards.

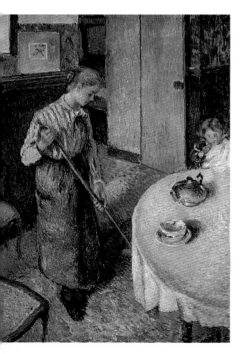

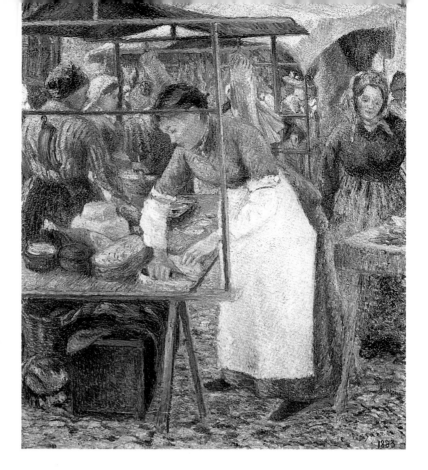

Camille Pissarro, *The Pork Butcher*, 1883.

Duck with Lentils SERVES 4

2 whole ducks, legs and breasts removed
250 ml (1 cup) red wine
2 bay leaves
1 tsp chopped fresh thyme

5 garlic cloves, 4 chopped and 1 smashed
2 onions, chopped
3 celery stalks, stringed & chopped
1 carrot, chopped
200 g (1⅓ cups) Puy lentils

Make some stock with the duck carcasses, half the wine and 500 ml (2¼ cups) of water, the bay leaves, thyme and smashed clove of garlic. Put half the onions, the celery and carrot into a roasting pan and pour over the remaining wine. Arrange the duck pieces, skin side up, over the vegetables and cook in a moderate oven until done, about 45 to 60 minutes. The meat is done when a skewer inserted into the legs comes out clean.

Meanwhile, simmer the lentils until just soft in twice their bulk of the stock with the remaining onion and the chopped garlic. Adjust the liquid as they cook, you should not need to strain off any. Towards the end of cooking top the lentils up with any fat and juices from the duck and adjust the seasoning. If necessary crisp the duck skins in a medium hot grill (broiler).

Serve the duck pieces and vegetables on top of the lentils, with plenty of home-made bread and a crisp green salad.

Opposite: Camille Pissarro, detail from *The Little Country Maid*, 1882.

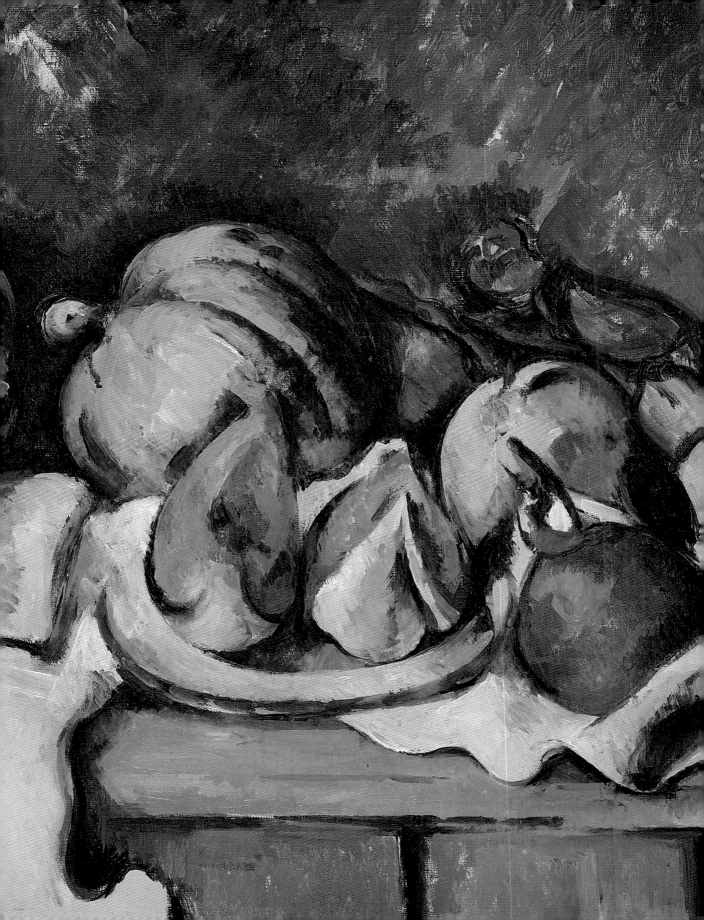

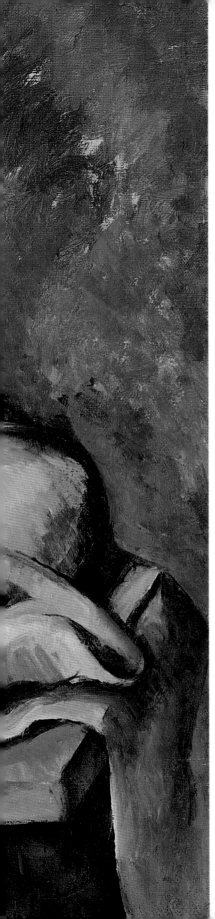

Lusting after the Warm South

WITH CÉZANNE & FRIENDS

'I shall astonish Paris with an apple,' affirmed the young Paul Cézanne. He rose above the scepticism of friends and critics to assert his power to delight us with the glorious attributes of every apple in the world. The luscious flavour, crisp texture, glowing rotundity, which transcend geometry, colour theory and symbolism make Cézanne's fruit more than paint on canvas and very much more than mere things to eat. Paris was indeed astonished and not entirely won over by this uncouth young artist with his uncompromising vision expressed in the strong earthy pigments of the south. He would have no truck with the sophisticated fashionable world and soft pale charms of the grey northern city, turning his back on the conventional existence of his Impressionist friends and his respectable family back home in Aix-en-Provence. Later Paul Gauguin, who revered Cézanne, would also reject the glittering modernity of Paris, the cult of the here and now. Cézanne strove to understand and paint the motif, the landscape or still life under his nose, while Gauguin searched for ancient beliefs and mystic forces in the harsh landscape and primitive cults of Brittany and the lush islands of the South Seas.

The teapots, jugs and bowls of Cézanne's canvases seemed to him to have a stubborn life of their own, they talked to one another and probably moved around, like all kitchen clutter... It is unlikely that Cézanne had a gastronomic agenda for this still life – it does not seem like part of a meal. The fruit simply exist, at the peak of evanescent glory, bursting with ripeness, their fleeting bloom and sensuous aroma poised on the verge of dissolution. One cannot help wondering what became of them. We know how carefully Cézanne composed these arrangements and the long, titanic struggles he had to get them on to canvas. There must have come a time when, over the top, they were sent back to the kitchen and replaced. Perhaps they found their way into the sumptuous compote overleaf. The basket of fresh fruit which makes the ideal end to a rich meal in Provence is unlikely to contain blemished or over-ripe fruit. Surprisingly, all this ripe fruit does not cook to a mush; the strong sugar syrup keeps it intact.

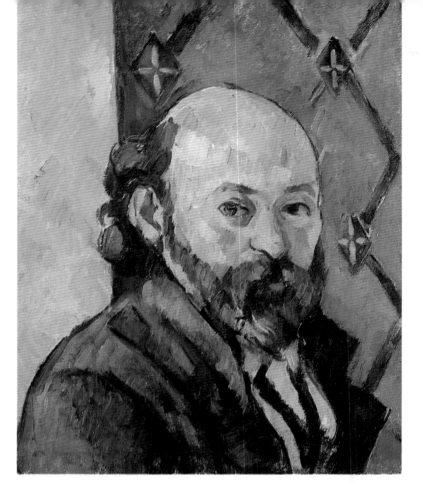

Paul Cézanne, *Self Portrait*, about 1880.

Provençale Compote   SERVES 6

1 ripe quince
1 apple
1 ripe pear
½ very ripe melon
1 ripe mango
Sugar to taste, about 300 g (1¼ cups) depending on
    the sweetness of the fruit
12 pitted prunes
1 lemon
1 Seville or sharp orange
3 cm (1¼ in) stick of cinnamon
3 cm (1¼ in) piece of vanilla pod (vanilla bean), which can
    be dried and reused
Sprigs of mint, to decorate

Peel, core and cut up the quince and cook it gently in a very little water
until soft. Peel, core and cut up the apple and pear. Cut up the melon,
discarding seeds and skin. Peel the mango and cut the flesh off the
stone in slices. Tip the sugar into the quince juices and stir until it

Previous page: Paul Cézanne,
detail from *Still Life with Apples
and Melons*, about 1890–4.

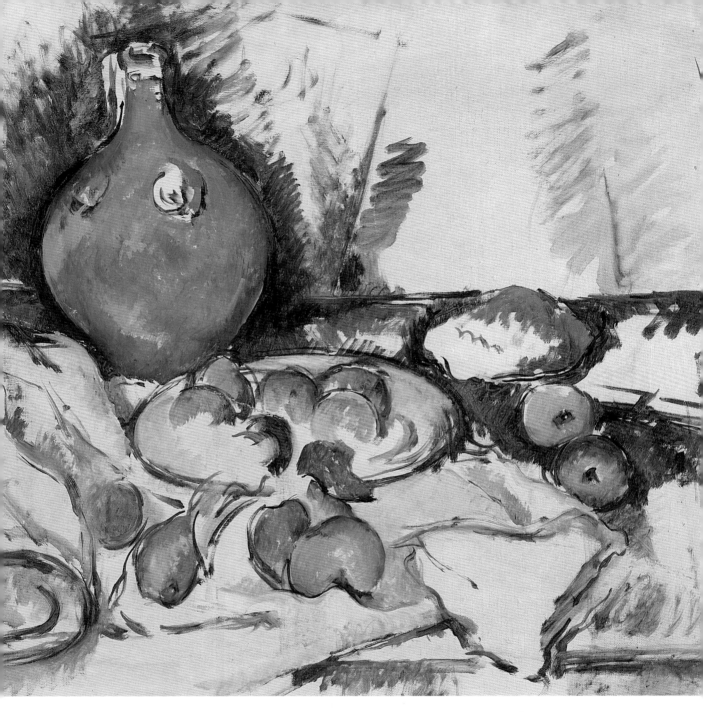

Paul Cézanne, detail from
Still Life with Water Jug,
1892–3.

dissolves into a nice thick syrup. Add the prepared fruit to the quince, together with the prunes, the juice of the lemon and orange and some of their zest, the cinnamon and vanilla. Taste for sweetness and add more sugar if you need it. Simmer gently until the fruit is soft. Keep tasting and take out the spices when the flavour seems right. Excessive sweetness can be mitigated with a little more lemon juice. Just before serving, chilled or at room temperature, decorate with a few sprigs of mint and add a slug of the Quince Vodka on page 114.

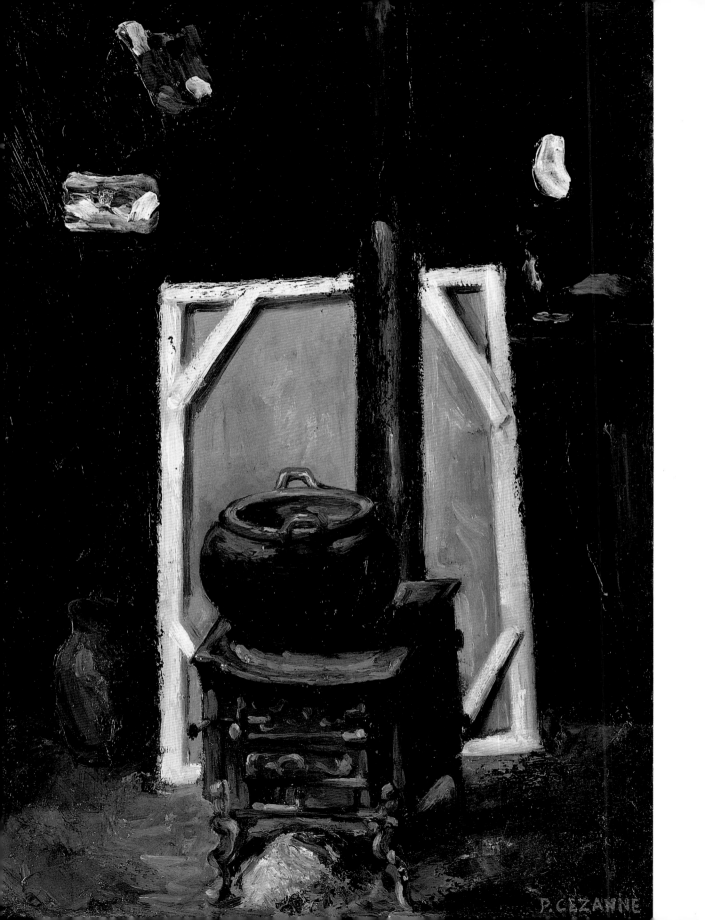

Cézanne's happy childhood roaming the Provençal countryside with his friend Emile Zola, was a time for the carefree enjoyment of the tastes and scents of the south. The lads wandered for days on end in the countryside, sleeping rough on beds of lavender and thyme, and dreaming of the heroic creative exploits with which they would take the world by storm. Their student years in Paris were full of nostalgia for the food of home and this wild hot landscape, their poverty mitigated by parcels of food from Cézanne's wealthy family. Olive oil, sausages and preserved fruit brightened up their humble meals, sometimes a simple pan of potatoes cooked on the studio stove.

Zola treasured this painting, *The Stove in the Studio*, until the day he died. Although he and Cézanne drifted apart it is unlikely to have been because of *L'œuvre*, the novel in which the depressingly two-dimensional character of the artist Claude Lantier was thought to be based on Cézanne. In fact the hero of the novel was Zola himself, beating the painters at their own game with virtuoso descriptions of the atmosphere and moods of Paris, a topographical and verbal *tour de force*. There is an affectionate vignette of a tiny canvas by a farouche young painter. *'Dites donc, il est joliment exact, votre poêle!'* A nicely detailed rendering of a lugubrious rusty little stove, with perspective askew and dying embers.

Cézanne's letters rarely mention food, he would have scorned to descend to chat about inessentials. He wrote about his work with a lucid intelligence, even when despairing and discouraged, and his friends replied in the same tone.

Zola, though, writing in 1860 to a mutual friend, extols the 'blue sky and bouillabaisse' of their native Provence, and confesses, 'Another sad result of the life I lead is that I have become terribly gluttonous. "You were that before", you tell me; I agree, but not quite so damnably. Drink, food, everything, fills me with longing and I take the same pleasure in devouring a good morsel as in possessing a woman. . .'

The aspiring young artists and writers in *L'œuvre* meet for modest but riotously enjoyable meals which Zola describes with affectionate care. One began with a fine onion soup followed by skate with black butter, livened with a tinge of vinegar, then a pink, juicy leg of mutton, barely enough bread to go round, a nice Brie, and torrents of talk into the small hours, intoxicated with hope rather than the watered *vin ordinaire* which the guests sipped with frugality.

Cézanne and Zola cooked simple meals together. An authentic bouillabaisse would have been out of the question, but a *bourride* could have been assembled without difficulty in the pallid north,

Paul Cézanne,
The Stove in the Studio,
probably 1865–70.

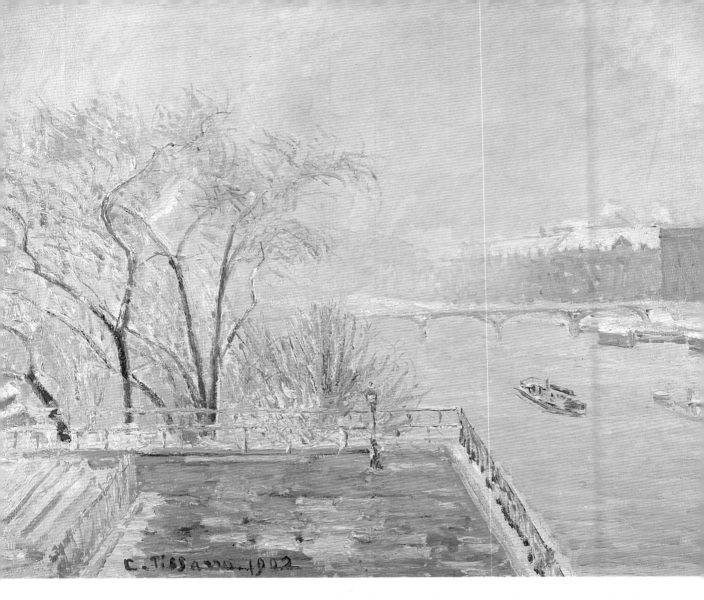

Camille Pissarro, *The Louvre under Snow*, 1902.

appealing as their friend Camille Pissarro's luminous winter landscape, snow tinged with pink, the sun setting beyond the Louvre and the boulevards. The pale, soft colours of Parisian winter echoed in the muted tones of this richly satisfying fish stew, with its hidden reminder of the south in the hint of orange zest and the blast of garlic from the *aïoli*.

Bourride   SERVES 6

1.5 kg (3¼ lbs) firm-fleshed fish such as halibut, haddock, cod, monkfish, swordfish, all filleted and skinned (keep the bones and trimmings)
1 salmon steak, boned and skinned
500 ml (2 cups) good quality dry white wine

3 bay leaves
A pinch each of fennel and anise seeds
½ tsp chopped fresh thyme
6 black peppercorns, salt
1 Seville or sharp orange
2 large leeks
2 large potatoes
4 celery stalks
1 carrot
25 g (¼ cup) ground almonds
Aïoli

Cut the fish into pieces. (The salmon steak is not traditional but adds delicate touches of pink to the finished dish.) Simmer the fish bones and trimmings in the wine for 20 minutes with the aromatics, salt, a strip of orange zest and a little juice, and a little water to make a strong fish stock. Prepare the vegetables and cut them into chunks. Cook them in the strained stock with the ground almonds and additional seasonings if needed. When almost done put in the fish and simmer very gently for a few minutes until just cooked.

The horror of curdling the stew by adding the *aïoli* when it is too hot is avoided by first thickening it with the ground almonds. Most unorthodox. Stir in a dollop of the *aïoli* when the stew is on the table and serve the rest separately. Have plenty of crisp French bread to mop up the juices. A simple green salad is an agreeable accompaniment.

Aïoli

3 garlic cloves, or more to taste
A pinch of salt
2 free range egg yolks

500 ml (2¼ cups) extra virgin olive oil from Provence

Pound the garlic in a mortar with the salt. Add the egg yolks and continue pounding. Add the oil gradually, a drop at a time, mixing each drop in thoroughly. When the oil and egg have amalgamated add larger quantities of oil, always stirring in well. Patience and calm will be rewarded with a thick, pungent sauce. A quicker but less thick version can be made in a blender or processor. Amalgamate the egg yolks, salt and garlic first, then add the oil, starting off with a tiny dribble and gradually adding more at a faster rate. (If you wish to avoid using raw eggs, boil them first for 2 minutes. This will bring the still runny yolks to a temperature that will kill off any lurking salmonella bacteria.)

Zola was not alone in his passion for the food of the south. Vincent van Gogh, in one of the manic states of mind which preceded his final breakdown in the 1880s, wrote to his brother Theo that he was painting furiously 'like a Marseillais devouring his bouillabaisse,

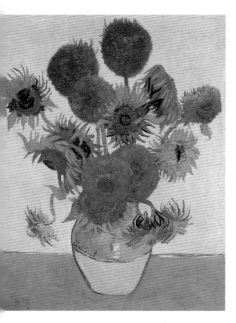

Vincent van Gogh,
Sunflowers, 1888.

which will come as no surprise when I tell you that the subject is sunflowers. . .' His companion during those fraught weeks was Paul Gauguin, whose own egocentric intensity could not have been the most soothing influence. But he took over the housekeeping '. . . such an interesting friend, and he's a marvellous cook, I do hope he will teach me. . .' Of course the economies thus achieved were frittered away in bars and brothels, but by and large it was a stimulating friendship in spite of poverty, bad weather and the inevitable bickering. The 'high yellow tone', symbol of friendship and hope, that Vincent craved with a mystic yearning materialized with the help of massive amounts of coffee and alcohol and conversations of electrifying intensity. Sadly, Vincent's attempt at soup was unkindly spurned by his friend: 'How he mixed it I don't know', wrote Gauguin, 'as he mixed the colours in his pictures I dare say. . .' Better housekeeping might have produced the stability that neither of them seemed to want. This high yellow pumpkin soup would have been the perfect restorative.

Pumpkin Soup   SERVES 6

200 g (1 cup) white haricot beans
2 garlic cloves, smashed
2 bay leaves
1 large onion, finely chopped

50 g (4 tbsps) butter or olive oil
250 g (about ½ lb) pumpkin
    flesh, diced
Salt & pepper

Simmer the washed but unsoaked beans in plenty of water until soft with the garlic and bay leaves. This will take about 1 to 2 hours, depending on the age and condition of the beans. Drain and reserve the cooking liquid. Cook the onion in the butter or oil until soft. Add the pumpkin and the beans and the reserved cooking water from the beans. Simmer until the pumpkin is done, about 30 minutes. Season with salt and pepper. Now the soup can be processed, strained or left as it is. It can then be enriched with cream and egg yolks, a sprinkling of chile flakes, or a slurp of olive oil.

Gauguin hoped to discover in Provence a complete contrast to the rugged landscape of Brittany where he found 'a certain wildness and primitiveness. When my clogs resound on this granite soil, I hear the dull, matt, powerful tone I am looking for in my painting.' But the wet plains around Arles were at times less radiant than this harvest scene at Le Pouldu, where Gauguin had lived for a time in a primitive bar on the beach. The sluttish landlady, Marie Henry, cooked superbly, and in return had the doubtful benefit of some wild murals executed by Gauguin and his friends in lieu of rent.

When the rigours of that dull, cold Provençal autumn prevented

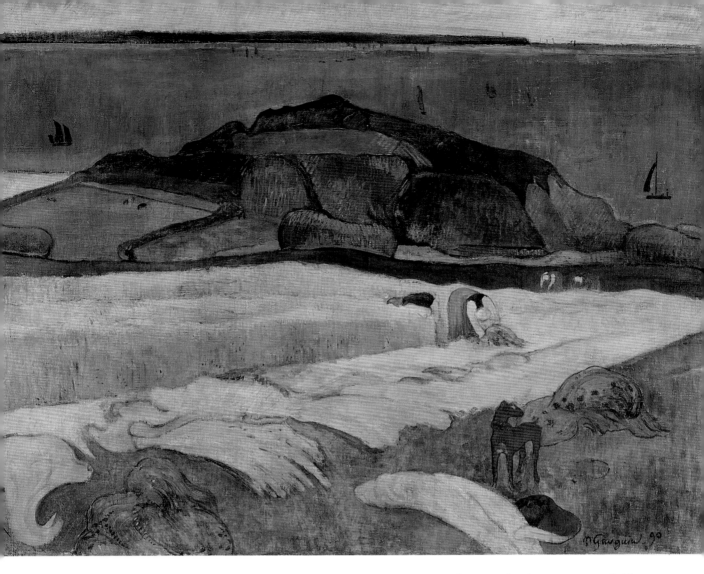

Paul Gauguin, *Harvest: Le Pouldu*, 1890.

outdoor work Gauguin and Van Gogh painted indoors. Vincent had fitted up his little yellow house with white wood tables and rustic chairs, plain tiled and wooden floors and whitewashed walls, which he intended to cover with sunflowers. He did a portrait of his own chair, true to life, with his pipe and tobacco, and some neglected onions sprouting in the background, ingredients perhaps for that sad soup. Gauguin's chair was less rustic, with the books, newspaper and reading lamp of the intellectual.

Gauguin later took the 'dull, matt, powerful tones' of Brittany with him to the South Seas where contrary to his imaginings, the lush tropical bounty of fish and fruit did not drop effortlessly on to his plate. Corned beef, indifferent red wine and the inevitable absinthe were his lot for much of the time, while back home his formidable Danish wife Mette brought up his five children single-handed in the bourgeois comfort she insisted upon.

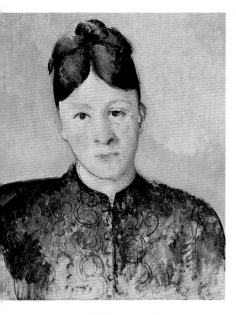

Paul Cézanne, *Portrait of Madame Cézanne,* about 1875.

Bourgeois comfort was what Cézanne's long-suffering mistress Hortense achieved at last when on the death of his father Cézanne was free to marry, but he chose all the same to spend as much time as he could in Provence, lovingly looked after by his mother and sister, escaping from the summer heat under the tree-lined avenue at their cavernous country house, the Jas de Bouffan. When they were together Hortense subdued her natural, perhaps rather irritating vivacity, to become Cézanne's model for innumerable portraits in which his harsh perfectionism and inherent kindness attempt to reconcile their increasing incompatibility, but she still exasperated him by preferring 'Switzerland and lemonade' to the hot and pungent south.

There is a touching passage in a letter from Renoir who staying in Provence in early March 1882, fell ill with pneumonia and was cared for by Cézanne and his mother: 'At lunch Madame Cézanne made me eat a ragout of cod; this is, I think, the ambrosia of the gods. One should eat this and die. . .'

He might have been referring to a *brandade de morue,* sturdy fare for an invalid but certainly ambrosial. An alternative might be one of the rich stews of salt cod and vegetables.

Aromatic Salt Cod   SERVES 4–6

1 kg (generous 2 lbs) salt cod, soaked for 24 hours with 3 or 4 changes of water
2 medium onions, chopped
3 or 4 garlic cloves, smashed and chopped coarsely
Extra virgin olive oil
500 g (generous 1 lb) ripe, tasty tomatoes, skinned and chopped
3 or 4 bay leaves
½ tsp chopped fresh thyme
A large wine glass of dry white wine
2 red and 2 green sweet peppers, skinned and chopped
500 g (generous 1 lb) firm new potatoes, sliced
Salt & freshly ground black pepper
18 pitted black olives
2 tbsps chopped fresh parsley

Put the fish in a pan with fresh water just to cover it. Bring gently to the boil and remove from the heat. Let it rest, covered, until cool enough to handle, then remove all the skin, bones and messy bits, keeping the pieces as large as possible. Cook the onions and garlic in some of the oil in a heavy cooking pan until soft. Add the tomatoes and cook rapidly until the moisture has evaporated. Add the bay leaves and thyme, the wine and the prepared fish. Simmer, covered, for 5 minutes. Now put in the peppers and potatoes and cook gently until the potatoes are done, adding a little water if necessary, about 30 minutes. Check for salt, it may need a little. Season with freshly ground black pepper.

Serve with a garnish of black olives and parsley. Have some fragrant olive oil on the table for guests to help themselves – this is the best way to enjoy the aromas of the rich fruity oil as it meets the pungent stew.

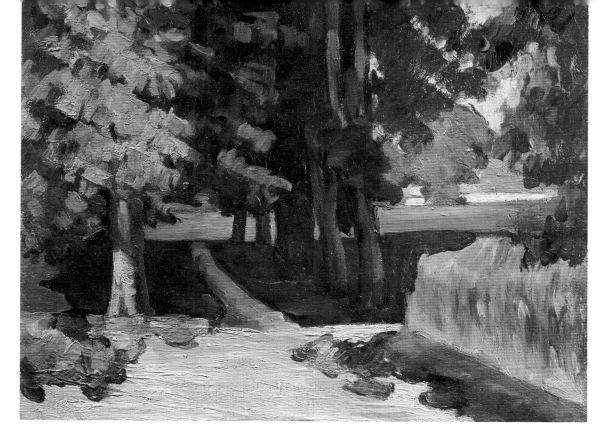

Paul Cézanne, *The Avenue at the Jas de Bouffan*, 1871.

A soupy version of this dish, *aigo-sau*, is said to be agreeable for invalids, churning up the fish in its sauce with the ferocity of a bouillabaisse. To do this, precook the salt cod as described above, then finish cooking it in a rich tomato sauce, with saffron, water and olive oil but without the potatoes and peppers, at a rolling boil. And what invalid could resist a dollop of *rouille*, to brighten the jaded palate?

Rouille

Pound 4 peeled cloves of garlic and 2 deseeded red chile peppers together with a little salt. Add 2 tablespoons soaked breadcrumbs and pound some more, then gradually incorporate as much olive oil as it will take (about 250 ml or 1 cup), thinning the sauce with concentrated fish stock to get the desired consistency. This can also be achieved by blending the lot in a processor until the mixture emulsifies, adding the oil slowly at the start.

Decades later between the two world wars, when traditional French cuisine was threatened by what he considered futurist 'caricatures' and unseemly foreign influences, the gourmet Prosper Montagné edited a little book of recipes compiled by an august body of doctors. *Le Trésor de la Cuisine du Bassin Méditerranéen* is perhaps the first sighting of that much abused nebulous term 'Mediterranean

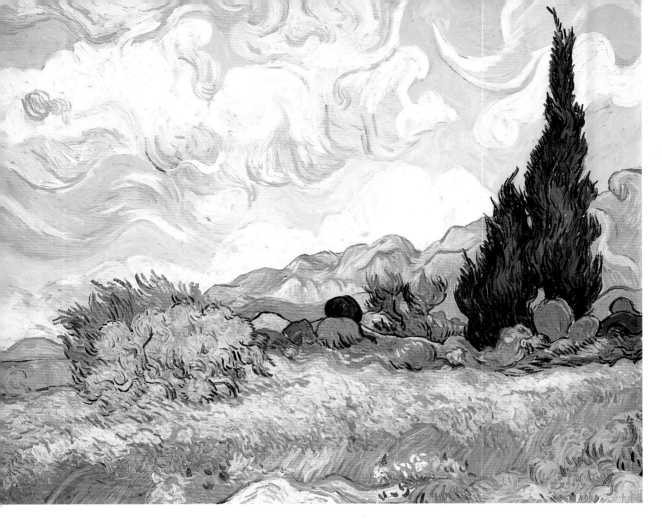

Vincent van Gogh,
*A Wheatfield, with
Cypresses*, 1889.

Opposite: Vincent van Gogh,
Van Gogh's Chair, 1888.

cuisine'. The cooking of the south had a powerful appeal to these medical men, with their network of contacts with colleagues in remote parts of France and their professional rapport with many different levels of society. It is cheering to see how their Hippocratic oath encouraged far from homeopathic doses of garlic, wine, goose fat, butter and good olive oil.

An inland version of the *bourride* or *pauchouse* is this pungent *paceronata* from Corsica, where in pre-phylloxera times the island was one vast vineyard; the old wine would be chucked out to make way for the new vintage with euphoric trout floating, pink and bemused, in the crimson waters of the Restonica. The kill-or-cure effect of this prescription would be the ruination of a fine wine or a noble fish but administered to farmed trout or salmon and cooked with a rough fruity syrah from the Pays d'Oc, it has enough clout to tame the inordinate quantities of chile, and has a most invigorating effect. You may want to remove the bones before serving this fish dish – they can be hard to spot since the fish and its skeleton both take on a claret hue during cooking.

Paceronata SERVES 6

12 garlic cloves, smashed
1 tbsp good olive oil
12 or 6 or 3 hot red chiles to suit
your taste
3 tbsps diced sweet red pepper

2 bay leaves
1 bottle fruity red wine
6 trout, cleaned and beheaded
6 thick slices of home-made bread
(white or mixed)

Cook the garlic in the oil in a large shallow pan which will take the fish side by side. When it starts to colour add the coarsely chopped chiles, sweet pepper and bay leaves, stir, and pour in the wine. Boil fast for a few minutes then put in the fish and simmer for about 20 minutes. Toast the bread until firm and put a slice in the bottom of each of six shallow soup plates. Lay a fish on each piece of toast and pour the cooking liquid over.

Garlic was a well-known folk remedy, a sort of universal theriac or panacea for all manner of ailments, and these wise old doctors knew how to learn from their hearty peasant patients. This way with partridges has an astonishing amount of garlic, which amalgamates with the gamey little birds to make a dense aromatic dish.

Catalan Partridge SERVES 2

2 slices of unsmoked bacon, diced
2 tbsps butter, goose or duck fat
2 partridges
24 garlic cloves, peeled

6 or 8 thin slices of lemon, skin
and all
2 wine glasses of dry white wine
Thyme and bay leaves

Cook the bacon in the fat in a heavy flameproof casserole and add the birds, browning the breasts slightly. Add the garlic and position the partridges breast down on top of the garlic and bacon, covering them with the slices of lemon. Put in the wine and herbs and bring to the boil. Reduce the heat and simmer, covered, for 45 to 60 minutes. Serve the birds garnished with the garlic and lemon.

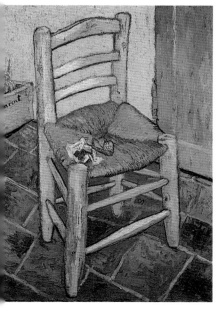

Our gastronomic medical men were passionate about traditional cooking at a time when food snobs abroad were emulating the more pretentious exclusivity of French cuisine. They kept a culinary broad church and their recipe collections were like the generous accretions of a wide-ranging art collection, with dishes to suit all tastes, a picture gallery where different flavours and aromas simmer and intermingle in a rich brew of colour and texture, as sustaining and enjoyable as grandmother's *pot au feu*.

Using the Recipes

QUANTITIES in ingredients lists are given in grams/millilitres. Quantities in parentheses are US equivalents *not* an alternative measurement for British cooks. Readers should use one set of measurements throughout and not try to mix them. Spoon measures are level unless otherwise indicated.

AMERICAN readers should use the descriptions in parentheses when cooking the recipes – for instance 250 ml double cream (1 cup heavy cream).

OVEN temperatures are given descriptively because ovens these days vary so much. As a guide, see the table below for standard gas/electric equivalents to the 'moderate', 'low', 'high' temperatures specified in the recipes. For other types of oven, such as fan ovens or cast iron ranges, refer to the instruction guidelines given with the stove.

	Fahrenheit	Celsius	Gas
Cool	175	80	
	200	100	
Low	225	110	
	250	120	1/2
	275	140	1
	300	150	2
Moderate	325	160	3
	350	180	4
Fairly hot	375	190	5
	400	200	6
Hot	425	220	7
	450	230	8
Very hot	475	240	9

COOKING times and quantities depend to a certain extent on the nature of the ingredients to hand, so are sometimes given as approximates, and 'some', 'a little', 'a drop' and 'until done' have their uses.

SPICES were used in the past to enhance rather than disguise or drown the taste of food. They were luxury items, expensive, exotic and an aristocratic indulgence rather than an everyday flavouring. Today every cook will wish to adjust the spicing of a dish to the tastes of the guests, known family preferences and decisions about the menu and wines, so use the spices and quantities here as guidelines not holy writ. Spices are best kept whole in a cool, dark place and ground just before use.

SUGAR was an expensive commodity until the eighteenth century, used medicinally and often more as a spice than a sweetener. Sprinkled over savoury dishes it can act as a catalyst, stimulating the taste buds without cloying.

SWEETNESS The distinction between sweet and savoury which dominates our menus today did not exist in the past – feasts often began with sugary sweetmeats and sweet tarts and the enigmatic *biancomangiare* (literally, white food) would appear alongside spiced or soured food as a pleasing contrast. The use of sugar and the so-called 'sweet' spices such as cinnamon, nutmeg, cloves and mace in sauces and in savoury dishes also created a taste which is sweeter than perhaps a modern palate is used to.

FINALLY AND MOST IMPORTANTLY it is agreeable to follow the spirit rather than the letter when cooking from early recipe books; to imagine the voluptuous luxury or spartan restraint of the dish described, and then recreate it to your own taste, remembering the two threads that run through the intricate web of the diverse cuisines of Europe – an insistence on the freshest top-quality ingredients and a respect for the craftsmanship needed to bring out the best in them.

Menu
Suggestions

Compatibility is more important than chronology in this eclectic offering of menus made up of dishes from late medieval Florence to pre-war Provence.

Trout with Lemon Stuffing (page 42)
Chicken with Sour Grapes (page 22)
Stewed Fennel (page 30)
Rosewater Cream (page 96)
A good Frascati or Tuscan Trebbiano

Spinach Priest-Stranglers (page 24)
Beef Olives (page 62)
Redcurrant Cream (page 96)
A Beaujolais-Villages and a slug of Fernet Branca

Strawberry Gazpacho (page 108)
Sea Bass with Sage and Grappa (page 73)
Apple Custard (page 139)
A Soave from the Veneto and plenty of foccacia
    might accompany this

Apostolic Broth (page 62)
Baked Red Mullet (page 74)
Summer Pudding (page 122)
A floral unoaked new-world Chardonnay and
    French bread

Paceronata (page 159)
Crisp French bread and a green salad
Provençale Compote (page 148)
No fine wines here, wash it all down with a fruity
    Syrah from the Pays D'Oc or a southern French
    rosé

White Gazpacho (page 109)
Salmon with Gin (page 84)
Gooseberry and Elderflower Fool (page 123)
An Australian Chardonnay-Semillon followed
    by a little Muscat de Beaumes-de-Venise
    dessert wine

Carciofi alla Romana (page 59)
Stuffed Guinea Fowl (page 38)
Castelvetro's Garlic Broccoli (page 70)
A lump of Parmesan sprinkled with genuine
    traditional balsamic vinegar
Plenty of Lugana, and some Nocino to settle
    things

Ribollita (page 28)
A meal in itself with a salty goats cheese and
    unsalted Tuscan bread
Chianti Classico, possibly from Querciabella
Panforte (page 16) and a glass of Vin Santo

Strawberry Salad (page 83)
Bourride (page 152)
Raspberry Bavarois (page 140)
Pink Champagne followed by a Syrah with the
    Bourride and a sweet Vouvray or Sauternes

Baked Fish (page 81)
Buttered Parsnips (page 92)
Purslane and Onion Salad (page 31)
Orange and Pistachio Tart (page 49)
Belgian Beer in abundance or an Alsace Riesling

Seafood Risotto (page 77)
Baked Courgette Mould (page 37)
Quince Paste (page 113)
Chablis followed by Quince Vodka (page 114)

Toasted Cheese and Asparagus (page 134)
Pigeons with Olives (page 143)
Pear Tart (page 103)
Hermitage or an Australian Shiraz with the meal
    and Muscat de Frontignan with the dessert

Chicken in a Spiced Cheese Overcoat (page 18)
Lemon Relish (page 50)
Creamed Ricotta with Coffee (page 63)
Macon Blanc Villages

Select Bibliography

Altamiras, Juan, *Nuevo Arte de Cocina*, Barcelona 1758.

Benporat, Claudio, *Storia della Gastronomia Italiana*, Milan 1990.

—, *Cucina Italiana del Quattrocento*, Florence 1996.

Boni, Ada, *Il Talismano della Felicità*, 1932.

—, *La Cucina Romana*, Rome 1983.

Casagrande, Giovanna, *Gola e Preghiera*, Foligno 1989.

Castelvetro, Giacomo, *The Fruits, Herbs & Vegetables of Italy*, trans. Gillian Riley, London 1989.

Cervio, Vincenzo, *Il Trinciante*, Rome 1593.

Cobbett, William, *Cottage Economy*, London 1831.

Coltro, Dino, *La Cucina Tradizionale Veneta*, Rome 1983.

Complete Illustrated Catalogue, National Gallery, London 1995.

David, Elizabeth, *English Bread and Yeast Cookery*, London 1977.

Davidson, Alan, *Mediterranean Seafood*, London 1972.

& Coquatur Ponendo, exhibition catalogue, Istituto Francesco Datini, Prato 1996.

Faccioli, Emilio, ed., *L'Arte della Cucina in Italia*, Turin 1992.

Field, Carol, *Celebrating Italy*, New York 1990.

Forbes, W.A., *De Oudhollandse Keuken*, Bussum n.d.

Frati, Ludovico, ed., *Libro di Cucina del Secolo XIV*, Livorno 1899. Facsimile, Sala Bolognese 1979.

Geddes, Olive M., *The Laird's Kitchen*, Edinburgh 1994.

Graham, Peter, *Classic Cheese Cookery*, London 1988.

Hollandse Keuken-Meid, Amsterdam 1746.

Holt, Geraldene, *French Country Kitchen*, London 1987.

La Natura Morta al Tempo di Caravaggio, exhibition catalogue, Rome, Musei Capitolini, Naples 1995.

La Varenne, *Le Cuisinier François*, Paris 1652.

Langmuir, Erika, *The National Gallery Companion Guide*, London 1994.

Laurioux, Bruno, *Le Moyen Age à Table*, Paris 1989.

Llopis, M. Martínez, *Historia de la Gastronomía Española*, Madrid 1989.

Marchese, Pasquale, *L'Invenzione della Forchetta*, Soveria Mannelli 1989.

Martinez Montiño, Francisco, *Arte de Cocina, Pastelería, Viscochería y Conservería*, Barcelona 1678.

Massialot, *Le Cuisinier Royal et Bourgeois*, Paris 1691.

Mata, Juan de la, *Arte de Repostería*, Madrid 1791.

McGee, Harold, *On Food and Cooking*, London 1986.

Menon, *La Cuisinière Bourgeoise*, Paris 1746.

Messisbugo, Christofaro, *Libro Novo nel qual s'insegna a far d'ogni sorte di vivanda*, Venice 1557.

Metz, Vittorio, *La Cucina di G. Gioachino Belli*, Rome 1972.

Montagné, Prosper, ed., *Le Trésor de la Cuisine du Bassin Méditerranéen*, 1930.

Moor, Janny de, *Tafelen in Nederland*, Amsterdam 1996.

Nyland, Petrus, *De Verstandige Koch, of Sorgh-vuldige Huyshoudster*. Reprint with introduction by Joop Witteveen, Amsterdam 1993.

Platina, Bartolomeo, *Il Piacere Onesto e la Buona Salute*, ed. Emilio Faccioli, Turin 1985.

Reboul, J.-B., *La Cuisinière Provençale*, Marseille 1895.

Riley, G., 'Taintede meat', *Spicing up the Palate*, Proceedings of the Oxford Symposium on Food and Cookery, Totnes 1993.

—, 'The Gastronomic Michelangelo', *Food, Culture & History*, London 1993.

—, *The Dutch Table*, San Francisco 1994.

Ríos, Alicia, and March, Lourdes, *El Arte de la Cocina Español*, Barcelona 1993.

Salvatori de Zuliani, Mariú, *A Tola co i Nostri Veci*, Milan 1978.

Schino, June di, *The Splendour of the Table*, Rome 1992.

Scully, Terence, *The Art of Cookery in the Middle Ages*, Woodbridge 1995.

Smith, Eliza, *The Compleat Housewife*, London 1758.

Spanish Still Life from Velázquez to Goya, William B. Jordan and Peter Cherry, exhibition catalogue, National Gallery, London 1995.

Taruschio, Ann and Franco, *Leaves from the Walnut Tree*, London 1993.

Tolkowsky, S., *Hesperides, a History of the Culture and Use of Citrus Fruits*, London 1938.

Van't Veer, Annie, *Oud-Hollands Kookboek*, Utrecht 1966.

Zannini de Vita, Oretta, *The Food of Rome and Lazio*, Rome 1994.

List of Artists
& Paintings

Index

PICTURE CREDITS